SURVIVING
MEXICO'S DIRTY WAR

In the series

Voices of Latin American Life

edited by Arthur Schmidt

SURVIVING
MEXICO'S DIRTY WAR

A Political Prisoner's Memoir

ALBERTO ULLOA BORNEMANN

Edited and Translated by
ARTHUR SCHMIDT AND
AURORA CAMACHO DE SCHMIDT

TEMPLE UNIVERSITY PRESS
Philadelphia

Temple University Press
1601 North Broad Street
Philadelphia PA 19122
www.temple.edu/tempress

⊗

The paper used in this publication meets the requirements
of the American National Standard for Information Sciences—
Permanence of Paper for Printed Library Materials, ANSI Z39.48-1992

Library of Congress Cataloging-in-Publication Data

Ulloa Bornemann, Alberto, 1941–
[Sendero en tinieblas. English]
Surviving Mexico's dirty war : a political prisoner's memoir /
Alberto Ulloa Bornemann ; edited and translated by
Arthur Schmidt and Aurora Camacho de Schmidt.
p.   cm.   —   (Voices of Latin American life)
Includes bibliographical references and index.
ISBN 13: 978-1-59213-422-9   ISBN 10: 1-59213-422-X (cloth : alk. paper)
ISNB 13: 978-1-59213-423-6   ISBN 10: 1-59213-423-8 (pbk. :alk. paper)
1. Ulloa Bornemann, Alberto, 1941– .   2. Political prisoners—Mexico—
Biography.   3. Lecumberri (Prison).   I. Schmidt, Arthur, 1943– .
II. Schmidt, Aurora Camacho de.   III. Title.   IV. Series.
HV9512.5.U44A3 2006
365'.45092—dc22   2006012479
[B]

2   4   6   8   9   7   5   3   1

CONTENTS

SURVIVING
MEXICO'S DIRTY WAR

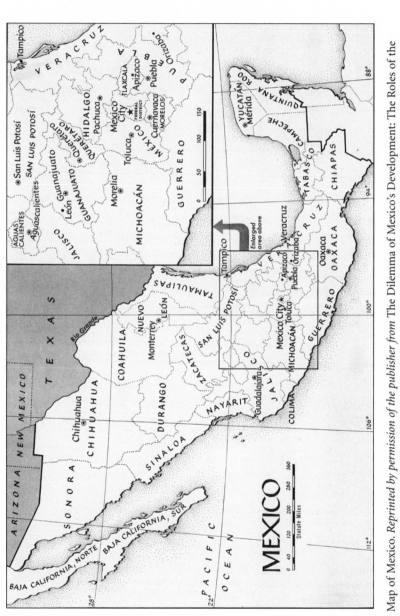

Map of Mexico. Reprinted by permission of the publisher from The Dilemma of Mexico's Development: The Roles of the Private and Public Sectors by Raymond Vernon, Cambridge, Mass.: Harvard University Press, Copyright © 1963 by the President and Fellows of the Harvard College.

Introduction

Translating Fear

A Mexican Narrative of Militancy, Horror, and Redemption

AURORA CAMACHO DE SCHMIDT AND ARTHUR SCHMIDT

> *The writer's role is not free from difficult duties.*
> *By definition he cannot put himself today in the service of those*
> *who make history; he is at the service of those who suffer it.*
> —Albert Camus[1]

I N *Surviving Mexico's Dirty War: A Political Prisoner's Memoir*, Alberto Ulloa Bornemann gives readers a text of uncommon critical power. Thirty years after he was captured by the Mexican authorities because of his political involvement with southern armed rebels, he rescues a key moment in Mexican history through a difficult act of memory and literary imagination. Literature here does not mean fiction, but narrated fact, an account of lived experience where words vibrate with a life of their own.

The literary canon is rich in prison literature: Ricardo Flores Magón, Oscar Wilde, Emma Goldman, Victor Serge, Rubin "Hurricane" Carter, Antonio Gramsci, Eldridge Cleaver, Aleksandr Solzhenitsyn, Václav Havel, Nelson Mandela, and so many more. But whereas Ulloa Bornemann's narrative deals profoundly with the harsh realities of life in prison in Mexico City, it goes beyond it. First, it was not written at the time of his incarceration. It has appeared a generation later as part of a widespread Latin American set of reflections on the era of tumultuous revolutionary and counter-revolutionary struggles that followed the triumph of the Cuban Revolution in 1959. As one analyst of Latin America's "dirty wars" has noted, for a region "populated by 'recovering authoritarians,' . . . recovery begins with memory."[2] In Mexico, where the issues of holding officials accountable for the deeds of state terror still remain unresolved, memory and justice are often said to go hand in hand. The editors of the magazine *Nexos* recently remarked that "Saying 'never again' to the systematic and unpunished violation of human rights means saying today—yes to memory and yes to justice."[3] Second, Ulloa Bornemann's story encompasses the author's initiation into the militant left of the late sixties and early seventies. Whereas some former guerrillas in Mexico have published short accounts of their personal experiences, studies of armed movements, and even fiction, *Surviving Mexico's Dirty War* stands out for its descriptive power and its depth of self-criticism.[4] It is the product of Ulloa Bornemann's painful awakening to the fact that he had been wrong, that the answers to Mexico's deep-seated political, social, and economic problems did not lie in armed struggle.[5]

TESTIMONIAL TEXTS

In the last third of the twentieth century, Latin American literature saw the development of a special kind of chronicle: the testimony. Subjects, especially women who never before had access to authorship, spoke about their lives as representative of the lives of many others, in a denunciation meant for readers beyond their nations. Often written in collaboration with an educated editor, testimonial texts reconstructed the microhistories of a former slave, a slum dweller, peasants, miners, indigenous communities, and guerrilla fighters.[6] *Surviving Mexico's Dirty War* is a testimonial text because it too bears witness and illuminates a reality that had been hidden from view. Like other testimonial authors such as Esteban Montejo, Elvia Alvarado, Domitila Barrios de Chúngara, or Rigoberta Menchú, Ulloa Bornemann imbues his narrative with a moral force. His story contains a tacit accusation, directed not at people, but at an entrenched power structure that allows unspeakable horror to be unleashed when the state exercises its repressive apparatus. Still, there are many differences between most testimonial texts and the narrative of Ulloa Bornemann. He comes from an upper middle class family and is well educated.[7] He is the sole author of his text. And while denunciation is part of his account, it is not its purpose. Readers soon realize that they have been allowed into a deep personal reflection, an act of remembering that yields an unforgiving evaluation of what once looked like a heroic stance—the wager of one young and promising life to revolutionary change in Mexico.

For readers of Mexican literature, some parts of *Surviving Mexico's Dirty War* could hark back to *La sombra del caudillo* (*The Shadow of the Strongman,* 1929) by Martín Luis Guzmán (1887–1976), especially the scene in which Axkaná González is abducted and blindfolded in a fast-moving car. Both

Axkaná and Alberto Ulloa Bornemann reconstruct the city in their minds at every turn the car takes before reaching a final destination where each will be tortured. More than a simple coincidence, the kinship of these two texts created seventy-five years apart resides in the depiction of a murderous regime in which innocence or change are almost impossible, and in the representation of Mexico City as a space equated with violence.[8]

Surviving Mexico's Dirty War appropriately belongs in the company of other literature on the Latin American dirty wars of the Cold War era that took place in parts of Central America and the Andes, and in the Southern Cone countries of Argentina, Brazil, Chile, and Uruguay. Films, texts, and truth commission reports have portrayed the horrors of political violence, in particular the abuses of counter-insurgency regimes that arose between the mid-1950s and the early 1990s. Today citizens who suffered under those regimes continue their efforts to prevent their official crimes from passing into oblivion, most notably the Chileans pursuing legal measures against General Augusto Pinochet Ugarte and the Argentine Mothers of the Plaza de Mayo whose children and grandchildren were disappeared during the purges of the military.[9] One internationally famous text is Jacobo Timerman's *Prisoner without a Name, Cell without a Number*, a gripping story of thirty months of prison, isolation, and torture. Timerman was the Argentinean-Jewish editor of *La Opinión*, and like Ulloa Bornemann, an intellectual and an expert in communications. He argued in vain that legal public trials constituted the best method for combating subversive political violence. For Timerman, it remained essential for regimes to offer channels for diverse political expression. "No one is immune to episodes of violence and terrorism," he wrote, "yet it should be possible at least to avoid a situation in which terrorism and violence are the sole creative potential, the sole imaginative, emotional, erotic expression of a nation."[10]

MEXICO'S ONE-PARTY SYSTEM

Some readers in the United States may be surprised to discover that Mexico had a smaller dirty war of its own, one certainly lesser in scale than those of the Southern Cone, but one that nonetheless resulted in the terrible cruelties that Ulloa Bornemann depicts in his narrative. How did Mexico slip into the "episode of terrorism and violence" that forms the context for *Surviving Mexico's Dirty War*? What were the motivations, as one of Ulloa Bornemann's interrogators demanded to know, of a young man "educated in a Catholic private university, who had set aside the opportunities that his family background and education offered him in life and had decided instead to join a big, messy upheaval in which he had nothing to gain and much to lose?" Mexico's legal system, its politics, and its cultural life all find themselves engaged with these questions today.

It is clear that Mexico's guerrilla movements and its dirty war were the products of a collision between a restive society and an increasingly anachronistic and repressive ruling system, hostile to independent forms of political expression. Since 1929, a single party, known during its heyday after 1946 as the Partido Revolucionario Institucional (PRI—Institutional Revolutionary Party), had monopolized political power in Mexico. During the "peace of the PRI," the official party won all the electoral contests for important offices. State and party remained virtually inseparable. An authoritarian presidency stood at the center of the system. Chief executives served six-year terms, each playing the determining role in the selection of his successor. Designed as a solution to the threats of further civil strife that followed the Mexican Revolution (1910–1917), the system of one-party rule provided a long period of stability combined with significant economic growth and an expanding system of government benefits. For a generation, the regime managed to imbue the official tradition of the Mexican Revolution with the atmosphere of "continuous and ceaseless renovation."[11] Between 1940 and 1970, the Mexican economy expanded more than six-fold, sustaining one of the highest and most consistent growth rates in the Third World. The PRI embraced a variety of political currents within its ranks, permitted an open if ineffectual set of opposition parties, and demonstrated a remarkable capacity to buy off dissidents, co-opting them into the world of officialdom.[12] For those operating outside its limited range of tolerance, the government employed an apparatus of selective force and intimidation, including a national intelligence service—the political police to which Ulloa Bornemann refers—responsible to the president and his closest officials.[13]

Eventually, however, the "eternal future" of the one-party system fell victim to the social changes that its policies had done so much to engender. By the time that Ulloa Bornemann attended the Universidad Iberoamericana in the 1960s, Mexico had become a younger, more urban, and more unequal society, ill suited for the constraints of an authoritarian political system derived from an earlier, more traditional, and more rural world. Twice as many Mexicans existed than in 1940; over half were under twenty years of age. More than 40 percent lived in communities larger than 15,000 in population; nearly one in every five Mexicans resided in the Mexico City metropolitan area alone. As the economy grew, so did inequality. The personal income of the top 20 percent of society had risen to sixteen times that of the bottom 20 percent, an increase over the ten to one ratio that had prevailed after World War II.[14] The government reacted to change by becoming more closed and authoritarian, particularly under the presidency of Gustavo Díaz Ordaz (1964–70), dubbed "a soldier of the system" by one Mexican historian.[15] Early in his presidency, Díaz Ordaz clashed with intellectuals, with politicians seeking reforms in the official party, and with a doctors' movement in government hospitals. In 1968, a landmark breach opened between state and society when the government repressed a popular student movement in Mexico City. With their élan and with their agenda of moral and political reform, the students held a good deal of public sympathy. They sought an end to corruption, freedom for political prisoners, the liberalization of political life, and the abolition of sections of the penal code that the government arbitrarily used to jail political dissidents. Shortly before the 1968 Olympic games were due to begin in Mexico City, the government attacked a rally attended by thousands in the Tlatelolco plaza, killing between three and four hundred, and detaining over two thousand.[16] The massacre abruptly and traumatically brought the student movement to an end, opening a new and often painful chapter of political and social struggle in Mexico.

BEYOND TLATELOLCO

For many young activists, Tlatelolco proved a defining moment. "After 1968, it seemed armed struggle was the only alternative," commented Gustavo Hirales, an expert on Mexican armed groups and former member of the 23 of September League, a prominent guerrilla movement of the 1970s.[17] Yet not all those inspired by 1968 picked up arms. Many engaged in political and civic struggles that eventually helped to bring about a greater liberalization to Mexican political life.[18] Some of Mexico's most prominent urban popular movements were organized by activists from Política Popular and Organización Regional Compañero, both founded in the wake of "lo de '68." Often operating clandestinely, both organizations shared the influence of Maoism and the desire to live and work among the "masses," getting involved in their daily struggles for housing, services, and other basic needs.[19] Surviving Mexico's Dirty War reflects these same idealistic impulses at work in Ulloa Bornemann. He abandoned work and family in order to dedicate himself full-time to the revolutionary struggle. He attempted to live for a while with a poor peasant family. He gave of his time and possessions, driving dissidents to various parts of the republic, donating his car to the cause, and offering shelter in his apartment to those on the run from the political police.

Yet, as towering as the impact of 1968 was upon Mexico, one must not regard "every major development of the following three decades as flowing inexorably from the student-popular movement and its bloody repression."[20] As Ulloa Bornemann's story shows, other factors, both before and after 1968, also exercised powerful influences. The tumultuous events of 1968 scarcely appear in *Surviving Mexico's Dirty War*. (As a member of the Liga Comunista Espartaco, Ulloa Bornemann followed its line and stayed away from the student movement because it lacked roots in the peasantry and the working class.) Before 1968, like so many others of his generation, he found himself captivated by the Cuban Revolution, in particular by the mystique of the heroic guerrilla fighter Ernesto Che Guevara, who embodied "the social utopias and dreams of an entire generation." Despite the failure of his naive trip to Cuba in October, 1967, Ulloa Bornemann continued to demonstrate "the exaltation of will" that so characterized El Che, the notion that "there was no obstacle too great for willpower."[21] As was true with Guevara, Ulloa Bornemann's enduring obstinacy obliged family members to undergo great suffering, especially his wife Tere. Like Guevara, Ulloa Bornemann's willfulness exposed him to repeated dangers that at the time appeared more heroic than mistaken. Unlike Guevara, however, his misjudgments did not prove fatal. "Today," he remarks in *Surviving Mexico's Dirty War*, "I am very conscious of the good fortune I had."

As recent historical scholarship has increasingly emphasized, the "peace of the PRI," really constituted a political myth. Mexico was not a quiescent society that suddenly awoke in 1968 with the advent of the student movement. Even in the midst of Mexico's "Golden Age" of political stability and rapid economic growth after 1940, diverse and substantial resistance movements, both rural and urban, punctuated public life.[22] Among the most notable were the strikes and protests of teachers, railway workers, and others in 1958 and 1959. The government responded to these serious challenges with a combination of minor concessions and major force, including long-term jail sentences for some of the railway leaders. But authorities could not prevent generational change and the impact of the Cuban Revolution from percolating through left-wing politics in Mexico throughout the 1960s.[23] The experiences of Ulloa Bornemann demonstrate an element of continuity in resistance movements that links the post-World War II years with the generation of the 1960s and 1970s. *Surviving Mexico's Dirty War* expresses Ulloa Bornemann's high regard for Mónico Rodríguez Gómez, former member of the Mexican Communist Party, and inveterate participant in many rural and urban popular struggles for over thirty years. Rodríguez Gómez was exactly the sort of dedicated figure that Ulloa Bornemann and his *compañeros* admired in their search for authenticity in revolutionary struggle. The Organization, the loosely constructed clandestine movement to which Ulloa Bornemann belonged, identified with other radical tendencies noted for their freedom from rigid left-wing orthodoxies. Three movements, all of which originated before 1968, appear prominently in his narrative.

LEFT-WING RESISTANCE MOVEMENTS IN MEXICO

Ulloa Bornemann joined the Liga Comunista Espartaco after his return to Mexico following his "naive and stupid trip" to revolutionary Cuba in 1967. The Liga originated as the Liga Leninista Espartaco after the departure of the well known writer José Revueltas from the Mexican Communist Party in 1959. Over time, the Liga merged with other dissident groups, distanced itself from Revueltas, and changed its name and views. Its new perspectives identified "popular masses" as revolutionary protagonists more than the traditional proletariat. The Ho Chi Minh Section constituted the most active element within the Liga Comunista Espartaco in establishing ties with workers, peasants, and teachers in central and southern Mexico. When the 1968 student movement arose, the Liga Comunista Espartaco doubted its significance, stayed out of the events of that year, and ultimately dissolved. The Ho Chi Minh Section went its own way. Dionisio and Isauro, two of Ulloa Bornemann's closest compañeros, helped produce a devastating critique of the behavior of the Liga leadership in 1968. Some from the Ho Chi Minh Section participated in urban popular movements during the 1970s, while others created the Organization, described by Ulloa Bornemann as a "remnant" of the Ho Chi Min Section.

In some places, *Surviving Mexico's Dirty War* describes members of the Organization as "Espartaquistas Jaramillistas," referring to the political influence of a second radical tendency, that of the long-time revolutionary activist from Morelos, Rubén Jaramillo. For an entire generation, from the cane workers struggle in the early 1940s until his assassination by the military and police in May, 1962, Jaramillo devoted himself to peasant and worker causes in his home state. He took up arms against the government on several occasions, organized strikes and protests, and established his own political party, the Partido Agrario Obrero Morelense (PAOM). He claimed to have won his two races for the governorship of Morelos in 1946 and 1952.[24] Jaramillo's personal and intellectual influences upon the Organization were extensive. Many members of the Ho Chi Minh Section came out of the PAOM. Younger activists particularly admired his courage, rectitude, and independence. Like Mónico Rodríguez Gómez with whom he collaborated at times, Jaramillo gave his entire life to local social issues. Although he cooperated with the Communist Party on occasion, Jaramillo preferred his own autonomy to party orthodoxy. On more than one occasion, he survived assassination attempts and refused payoffs from the government and private interests. The political platform of the PAOM stressed land reform, autonomy for peasant communities, the unity of workers and peasants, and women's participation, all measures that appealed to the participants in the Organization.

More problematic but certainly even more influential in the life of the Organization—and in the experience of Ulloa Bornemann—was its relationship with a third radical movement, the insurrection in the state of Guerrero of the Partido de los Pobres under the direction of Lucio Cabañas Barrientos. Guerrero offered stark contrasts between the opulence of international tourism associated with the postwar development of Acapulco and the enduring poverty of much of its citizenry. For generations, as Ulloa Bornemann notes, the state had been a region of harsh social conditions, local governmental despotism, and movements of popular resistance.[25] In the traditions of "Guerrero bronco," public school teachers had often taken on instrumental roles in community life, furthering local improvements, intervening in relations with government, and, in the generation after World War II, organizing movements for greater democracy and accountability in state and municipal politics. Teacher training institutes in both Guerrero and Mexico City became centers of civic organizing. Guerrero teacher activists were influenced by a dissident teachers movement— the Movimiento Revolucionario del Magistrado (MRM) that emerged in Mexico City in the late 1950s and would be an important precursor to nationwide popular movements in the late 1970s and 1980s.[26] Both Genaro Vázquez Rojas, another Guerrerense teacher-activist turned guerrilla leader, and Cabañas belonged to the MRM. Each undertook armed campaigns in the mountains of Guerrero when repression from the state and federal governments made peaceful civic action impossible. Genaro Vázquez Rojas found himself forced into hiding after an army attack on a peaceful protest in Chilpancingo, the capital of Guerrero, resulted in the deaths of eighteen people in December, 1960. Jailed in 1966 and subsequently liberated in 1968 by an armed commando of his followers, Vázquez Rojas operated an independent guerrilla campaign until his death in an automobile accident in February, 1972.[27]

Cabañas' guerrilla uprising proved the more significant of the two, lasting until his death in battle in December, 1974. He originally took to the hills in May, 1967 after police in Atoyac attacked a demonstration and killed seven people including his brother. Two years earlier politically powerful local figures opposed to Cabañas' social activism had forced his transfer to a teaching post in the distant north-central state of Durango. Cabañas emerges in *Surviving*

Mexico's Dirty War as a courageous, but provincial and quixotic figure. While undoubtedly influenced by the Cuban Revolution, his outlook clearly was more homespun, reflecting the inspiration not only of Marx, Lenin, and Guevara, but also of the Mexican anarchist Ricardo Flores Magón and, above all, the Guerrerense environment in which he had been raised and educated. He deeply felt the injustices that the common folk of Guerrero experienced at the hands of local *caciques* (political bosses) and well-off property owners. He joined the Mexican Communist Party, leaving it after a short time because of what he considered its lethargy and opportunism. The armed contingents of his Partido de los Pobres drew recruits from the highly impoverished zone of the Costa Grande in Guerrero, long an area of rural unrest and conflict between *ejidatarios* (communal farmers) and the merchants and private landowners who controlled water resources and the distribution of coffee and other principal cash crops.[28]

As readers of *Surviving Mexico's Dirty War* will readily note, the strategy of the Partido de los Pobres was eclectic and depended highly upon Cabañas and the force of his personality. The Brigada de Ajusticiamiento undertook to execute local "exploiters" and abusive officials, and the Partido de los Pobres never transcended its regional origins to become a national political movement. For all of the travels Lucio (or Miguel, as Ulloa Bornemann often calls him, using his *nom de guerre*) undertook to various parts of Mexico, he failed to establish a solid partnership with any of the other armed movements operating in Mexico at the time. As was the case with these other movements, by 1971 the Partido de los Pobres came to rely upon bank robberies and kidnappings as the principal means of financing itself. Ulloa Bornemann narrates his great discomfort with these tactics, particularly the assault upon a Mexico City branch of the Banco Comercial Mexicano and the 1974 kidnapping of senator Rubén Figueroa Figueroa, the wealthy patriarch of a well-entrenched Guerrerense political dynasty and the PRI candidate for governor at the time. As Ulloa Bornemann feared, robberies and kidnappings proved self-defeating, alienating revolutionary resistance movements from society while at the same time corrupting them internally.

THE DIRTY WAR AND IMPUNITY

Ulloa Bornemann mentions many of the armed radical movements that proliferated in Mexico in the early 1970s—Movimiento de Acción Revolucionaria, Comandos Lacandones, Procesos, Guajiros, Liga Comunista 23 de Septiembre, and Frente Urbano Zapatista. This militant, but highly splintered Mexican left flared up only briefly and was largely gone by 1976, extinguished both by government repression and the suicidal futility of its own tactics. The impulse to extreme radicalism accelerated after the Corpus Christi Massacre of June 10, 1971, a landmark event that Ulloa Bornemann mentions in *Surviving Mexico's Dirty War* in which twenty-five students died, and many more suffered injuries when armed Halcones attacked their peaceful demonstration in Mexico City. Government responsibility for the massacre went right to the top. "It is well established that the Halcones are an officially financed, organized, trained and armed repressive group . . . ," wrote the Deputy Chief of Mission at the U.S. Embassy shortly after June 10. "It stretches the imagination," he added, "to believe that [President Luis] Echeverría could not have forced the disbandment of the Halcones had he so desired or that he was not aware of plans to severely repress the June 10 demonstration . . . ."[29] Echeverría, president from 1970 to 1976, was engaged in a double game, the full dimensions of which are still not known. On the one hand, socially generous, populist policies characterized his regime. Echeverría reached out to the country's youth, expanded higher educational opportunities, initiated a mild political opening, fired some of the major officials associated with the Corpus Christi massacre, and officially disbanded the Halcones (although, many continued working for the government. Ulloa Bornemann labeled many of his jailers in the Campo Militar Número Uno as ex-Halcones). On the other hand, as Secretary of Gobernación in 1968, Echeverría bore a major responsibility for the student killings at Tlatelolco. During his presidency, the Mexican government engaged in a concerted dirty war of unprecedented scale throughout the country that employed beatings, armed violence, torture, and disappearances.

Since Mexico has not yet established an official "truth commission" of the sort created in other countries victimized by state terrorism, many aspects of the government's dirty war of the 1970s remain shrouded in secrecy. U.S. government documents make it clear that American diplomatic officials knew of these events, but they chose to downplay them and thus avoid any publicity that might create difficulties for U.S.–Mexican diplomatic relations. During these years Amnesty International reported on government human rights violations in Mexico, but the full extent of these abuses remains to be clarified. The National Human Rights Commission, established by the Mexican government in 1990, reported documenting 350 cases of persons "disappeared" at government hands between 1974 and 1978, but many in human rights organizations consider the number to be higher. Officials killed at least 143 captives on military bases and arranged to have their bodies jettisoned into the sea from government helicopters.[30]

Despite the breaking of the PRI's monopoly hold on the presidency in 2000, the National Human Rights Commission and a Special Prosecutor for

Social and Political Movements of the Past have remained notably unsuccessful in bringing criminal or civil charges against officials guilty of human rights abuses. Human Rights Watch has labeled the work of the Special Prosecutor's office "deeply disappointing." Mexican courts have repeatedly ruled against its poorly presented charges of genocide against former president Echeverría for the Tlatelolco and Corpus Christi massacres, most recently in July, 2006. In February, 2006, disgruntled employees of the Special Prosecutor leaked a confidential draft report detailing the crimes of the dirty war. In late November, 2006, just before leaving office, the Fox administration issued an 800-page report from the Special Prosecutor that constituted the first unequivocal government admission of past official responsibility for the crimes of the dirty war. Nevertheless, impunity and prosecutorial ineptitude have constituted, in the words of an editorial in the daily *La Jornada*, "a devastating blow for a country that has for over three decades clamored for justice in the crimes of presidential power." Although the dirty war has long since ended, serious human rights abuses and patterns of official impunity have not. It would be hard to argue with the editorial's view that Mexico cannot "aspire to a civilized, peaceful, and legal order of conviviality" unless it establishes the full historical truth and responsibility for the abuses of the past.[31] Major massacres have taken place in recent years—at Aguas Blancas in Guerrero in June, 1995 and at Acteal in Chiapas in December, 1997—while over four hundred women have been slain or disappeared over an eleven-year period in the cities of Ciudad Juárez and Chihuahua. "Arbitrary detention, torture and ill-treatment by police [have] remained widespread, particularly at state level," according to Amnesty International. "The authorities [have] failed to combat these practices effectively or to ensure judicial remedy to victims."[32]

HORROR AND FEAR

Ulloa Bornemann knows the world of official impunity quite well. It is a world of fear and helplessness. Only by luck did he move from his two months of secret detention in the Campo Militar Número Uno into the judicial system. Had he not been tortured into revealing the name of Dr. Ignacio Madrazo Navarro—Luis in his *nom de guerre*—and had Dr. Navarro's family not had powerful social and political connections, Ulloa Bornemann might well never have made that transition. His fate, in all likelihood a clandestine death, the normal mode of departure from the Campo Militar Número Uno, would have remained a secret buried by the weight of time. When officials came to remove Ulloa Bornemann from his cell (in order to transfer him into the hands of civilian law enforcement authorities in downtown Mexico City), one of the

Halcones confiscated his sandals, so certain was he that Ulloa Bornemann would no longer need them. In his experience no prisoner ever left the clandestine military prison alive.

Ulloa Bornemann escaped an almost certain death when he left the clandestine Campo Militar Número Uno, but he remained far from safety until his amnesty in 1978. Although prison constituted a fearful world of confinement and violence for both the political prisoners of 1968 and for Ulloa Bornemann, many of the former also regarded their cells as an extension of the university. "The time spent behind the walls of Lecumberri provided [student movement] leaders a physical space to do what they longed to: devote themselves to study."[33] This was not the case for Ulloa Bornemann. Like the leaders of 1968, he was a university-trained intellectual, but *Surviving Mexico's Dirty War* depicts no element of "intellectual liberation" in his prison experience. His days editing the inmate newspaper *Oriente* provided a momentary escape from the daily oppression of his incarceration, but this respite proved to be only a short-lived hiatus that promptly ceased when the government removed prison reformers from their administrative control of the Reclusorio Oriente.

The stories told in Ulloa Bornemann's narrative, in other prison literature, and in the testimonial writings from other Latin American dirty wars have one element in common: they portray horror. Prison is a closed space where violence defines everyday reality. Violence can be organized vertically, through a chain of command as Ulloa Bornemann discovered behind the walls of Lecumberri and Santa Martha Acatitla; but violence can also result from the interaction among inmates, as *Surviving Mexico's Dirty War* reveals in its tales of the drug-addicted, down and out convicts like Guillermo Zúñiga and the prison "capos" such as Alberto Sicilia Falcón or David Noriega. Other than the moments of family visits, no human transaction is possible without the likely presence of violence. Indeed, a prisoner must be constantly aware of the possibility of losing his life, as Ulloa Bornemann said in a recent television documentary:

> Being in prison presents a very delicate situation. One has to be very alert. All of your senses must be in a state of alert at all times because many things can happen, right? It may be that someone wants to cause trouble for you, and he will place a marihuana cigarette among your belongings, and then accuse you. And the guard comes and discovers it, and a new legal case is opened against you, for example. Or maybe you rubbed someone the wrong way, or he feels that you have done him wrong, that you

have injured him. So at your slightest moment of distraction he comes and sticks a shiv in you. And you can die, just like that! [34]

As readers of _Surviving Mexico's Dirty War_, we soon become aware of the superfluity of the prison population, the low value of anybody's life. Studying prison narratives, Ioan Davies writes:

> Prison writing is centrally about violence. The beginning of a sense of violence is the awareness of death. Prison writing, more than most, is contemplation of death, our own deaths, the deaths we impose on others, the deaths imposed on us by others, the great gamble between our deaths and theirs.[35]

That great gamble with life is framed in fear. In this book readers will find over seventy expressions of fear, fright, dread, terror, despair, anguish, anxiety, affliction, pain, uncertainty, tension, panic and other variations on the theme of horror. It will be neither a simple repetition nor a monotonous framework of events. Each occurrence expresses the state of mind of the protagonist, who experiences it from the standpoint of subjugation. Early on after his apprehension, Ulloa Bornemann was reduced to outward passivity at the hands of an all-powerful authority for whom his life was useless and his death bore no cost. When we asked the author whether his arrival at the clandestine jail at Campo Militar, where he was first detained, had produced repugnance—at the absolute lack of sanitary facilities, awful food, and the presence of rats and vermin—he answered: "No. When you feel terror you cannot feel anything else."[36]

"Terror" is not the same as a great fear of something clearly defined, a well known enemy whose strength can be sized up. The famous study of Bulgarian-French theoretician Julia Kristeva on horror and abjection remarks on this quality:

> There looms, within abjection, one of those violent, dark revolts of being, directed against a threat that seems to emanate from an exorbitant outside or inside, ejected beyond the scope of the possible, the tolerable, the thinkable. . . . A massive and sudden emergence of uncanniness, which, familiar as it might have been in an opaque and forgotten life, now harries me as radically separate, loathsome. Not me. Not that. But not nothing, either. A "something" that I do not recognize as a thing. A weight of meaninglessness, about which there is nothing insignificant, and which crushes me.[37]

This is the terror of the tortured body or the body about to be tortured. It implies isolation, separation from those one loves. It cancels meaning, and therefore, language, as Elaine Scarry wrote in *The Body in Pain*. It can only be apprehended from the outside, in memory and the imaginative act. In a society in which state terror is a systematic practice all institutions are in jeopardy, as the experience of Argentina and Chile in the 1980s has shown. Moreover, the "culture of fear" is difficult to eradicate.[38]

The publication of Ulloa Bornemann's story in English is not intended to feed a U.S. thirst for what Mexican writer Juan Villoro calls "literature of the open wound...monochrome, distorting, sentimental, and written for ideological children."[39] Ulloa Bornemann does not indulge in his past suffering. He does not profit emotionally from his experience: he lays it bare for us to know. He does the opposite of simplifying the reality of his involvement in a guerrilla movement that failed. At every turn there is surprise, nuance, introspection, judgment. His is a literary memory because only literature can bring us into the experience of one man's survival and transformation as if they were our own.[40] An unusual degree of honesty in self-criticism makes this book unique.[41]

CONTRADICTIONS AND COMPLEXITIES

Surviving Mexico's Dirty War: A Political Prisoner's Memoir brings the illegal and corrupt actions of the Mexican judicial system and prison authorities out in the open.[42] It also discloses the workings of armed rebels in a clandestine world. We are amazed at the ignorance, brutality, and senseless cruelty of those in power, and appalled at the naïveté, lack of discipline, and criminal actions of guerrillas and inmates. In this way, the narrative is an important contribution to the slow work of democratization, as it produces a consciousness of those ills and their dire results. Those evils do not always have the last word. One also learns about enlightened officials—Dr. Sergio García Ramírez, for example—who were working to change the system, and sees human solidarity at work, sometimes heroically.

The world depicted in this narrative is a masculine world. Soldiers, guards, the jailers and most of the jailed are men. With few exceptions, women are not revolutionaries, but men's *compañeras*. In Latin America the fantasy of the hero, fed by the legendary life of Che Guevara, requires a masculinist social arrangement. Despite the book's critical deconstruction of power, male prerogatives are largely unquestioned.[43] Here Ulloa Bornemann's story parallels the narrative of the student movement in which males have "come to dominate public discourse about '68, almost as spokesmen of a generation."[44] The book's relegation of women to the background provides an accurate reflection of the male attitudes that dominated leadership roles in the 1960s–70s, not only in the Mexican student movement, but more broadly throughout Latin American revolutionary organizations in the generation after the Cuban Revolution. For those detained in 1968 and for Ulloa Bornemann as well, the salience of the prison experience has provided a predominantly masculine cast to the narrative.

Social status also shapes facets of Ulloa Bornemann's narrative. Readers of *Surviving Mexico's Dirty War* may notice an emphasis on racial markers as the narrator describes people's physical appearance. Perceived good looks or the degree of pigmentation in somebody's skin correlates most of the times to that person's place in the social scale. The text makes assumptions about white supremacy subliminally. This is not surprising, since Ulloa Bornemann's revolutionary involvement and his incarceration switched him from one social class setting, where lighter skin tones prevailed and certain comforts and privileges were taken for granted, to rural and urban lower class environments, where darker skins were the norm. As a postcolonial people (the child of imperial Spain), Mexican society remains acutely aware of an individual's location in the hierarchical continuum from Indian or African to European.[45] Colonial legacies are usually rife with ambiguities. Racial features in Mexico often serve as markers for class status and even signifiers for moral qualities. While incarcerated at the Campo Militar Número Uno or at the civilian jails of Lecumberri, Reclusorio Oriente, and Santa Martha Acatitla, Ulloa Bornemann found himself in the hands of individuals—often racially different from him—for whom work for the government as a soldier or prison guard constituted economic security and possible social mobility. They lacked education and training, and they occupied subordinate positions within hierarchical organizations imbued with cultures of authoritarian behavior and corruption. Having a "subversivo" of a higher social status in their hands brought an inversion of power relationships that both sides—jailer and prisoner—reflexively registered in racial terms.

Surviving Mexico's Dirty War contains some silences, but not only because no account can ever be complete. A few times the author seems to stop at a threshold and decides not to enter. This is part of his narrative strategy, and probably his wish to protect somebody's privacy. His ordeal is also the ordeal of his family. Especially moving is the role of his wife, María Teresa Alvarez Malo de Ulloa, a woman of tremendous intelligence, strength, and fidelity. She demonstrates these qualities in Arturo Ripstein's recent release of *Los héroes y el tiempo (Heroes and Time)*, presented at the Cannes Festival in May, 2005. This documentary interviews once more the four men, including Ulloa Bornemann, that Ripstein filmed thirty years ago in his earlier work, *Lecumberri*, giving voice this time to family members who relate what the incarceration of a husband or a father meant to their lives.

Since the time of Ulloa Bornemann's amnesty in 1978, Mexicans have taken great strides to overcome the traumatic era of the dirty war and to assert themselves. Civil society stood up to government incompetence in 1985 when two earthquakes devastated sections of Mexico City. Major electoral opposition to the regime in 1988 shook the political system to its foundations. A flourishing of popular movements and civic organizing has characterized the last twenty years. The 1994 Zapatista revolt in Chiapas generated a widespread domestic and international response. The Mexican left has become a major participant in the country's more open political system, one no longer dominated by one official party.[46] The major news media offer a greater variety of opinion and journalistic independence.[47] Yet as with the question of accountability for the abuses of the dirty war, the country remains far from having resolved its most pressing issues. As the 2006 elections demonstrated, widespread skepticism prevails in Mexico about the capacity of the political system to produce good candidates and effective policies. The country's historically unequal income distribution has continued to become more inequitable. Economic growth has been too anemic to generate an adequate amount of jobs and opportunities. Serious overcrowding still characterizes prison conditions. While armed radical groups no longer disrupt cities, narcotrafficking, street crime, and kidnappings do cast the specter of violence over urban life.[48]

We asked the author how he would describe his book to young men and women who want to change these pressing circumstances:

> This is the memoir of a young middle class man who lived in an undeveloped country full of economic, political, and social injustice. This man believed that revolutionary activity would provide a way out of marginality for many people in his country. He thought he would also find himself, and a sort of happiness in self-fulfillment in that process. But he suffered from a great ignorance of the history and the social and political structures of Mexico. No young person should attempt to act politically without preparation and study. A moral impulse is at the basis of their desire to address injustice, but that is not enough. Young people must avoid the easy trap of believing that there are only good and bad people, and that their wishes and hopes put them on the side of the good. They should know that reality is always more complex than they think, and far more difficult to face.[49]

Albert Camus, whose life was marked by strife, said that writers do not write for the makers of history, but for its sufferers ("ceux qui la subissent"). In the same Nobel banquet speech he said that writers aim at "stirring the greatest number of people by offering them a privileged picture of common joys and sufferings." This Alberto Ulloa Bornemann has done superbly well.

ONE

A Sad and Cruel Underground

MY CAPTURE

THEY WERE SPIRITING me away. I sat wedged between two men in the backseat of a Volkswagen, my eyes taped shut and a blindfold over half my face. Wide strips of duct tape painfully bound my hands together over my waist. A military overcoat had been thrown over me to conceal me. Although it reeked of cheap tobacco, in my forsaken state I welcomed the warmth that its thick wool gave my freezing body. The car engine faltered, but I didn't want it to fail. That was the greatest absurdity of all, as if I were in a hurry to arrive at our destination! There they would surely treat me worse than they already had! But I didn't want to be left with these men on the shoulder of the Cuernavaca–Mexico City toll road, half a kilometer from the pear-shaped curve known as *la pera*. The emptiness of the highway in the middle of the night made me shiver as I imagined the most terrible scenarios awaiting me at the hands of these unknown men transporting me in complete silence.

Only fifteen to twenty minutes had elapsed since we had left the last place where they'd held me for several hours until dark. Despite the blindfold, I could still see something if I looked downward with my right eye, pressing my chin on my chest. Through a very narrow gap, I could clearly spot the boots and the lower edge of the olive green pants of the soldier who had taken custody of me in the Cuernavaca Military Zone. He'd helped me from the car of the judicial police and led me to a dingy room. There I lay on a thick quilt waiting for them to haul me off at any moment for further interrogation. Prostrate, I tried to remain calm and fend off the fear that threatened to overpower my stomach, heart, and mind. Meanwhile, I could hear a basketball bouncing off a backboard and floor, the voices of some invisible players mixing with the sound of their rapid steps, dribbling, and sudden stops. On the other side of my door, a guard marched back and forth, the same man who moments earlier had brought me an egg sandwich with some cola with which to wash it down. I'd felt the hard bread as it pressed my closed lips against my teeth. At first, I didn't know what it was, but then I realized: "If they're feeding me, they're not planning to torture me right away." I had to swallow fast, mouthful after mouthful forced down by the imperious will of the guard. With both anxiety and relief, I slurped the liquid that he offered in complete silence. Once I had finished eating and drinking, my own audacity stunned me. I heard myself asking the guard for a cigarette. Wordlessly, this invisible soldier strengthened my belief in human solidarity, answering my request by sticking a lighted cigarette between my lips before departing. I was left to enjoy the smoke, surprised to receive considerate treatment in such a place, maybe even a gesture of solidarity from a supposed "class enemy."

All that had happened just a few hours before. Now, as the hum of the car had become normal, it allowed me to think. If I was lucky, I would be in prison a minimum of ten years. "But it's idiotic to think in those terms," I said to myself with a shudder. "Most likely they'll disappear me in the Campo Militar Número Uno." I didn't know what had befallen "Jacobo," the *compañero* from Movimiento de Acción Revolucionaria (MAR). (I later learned that his real name was Javier Gaitán Saldívar). Jacobo and I had been detained together in front of the Las Estacas spa, a few hundred meters from Colonia Alejandra in the municipality of the Tlaltizapán in the state of Morelos. At the time, I was driving Isauro's Volkswagen on our way back from swimming in the river. Nor did I know anything about the fate of any of the other compañeros who had been harvesting beans that day. The "Organization" (that's what we called the projected new type of revolutionary group we were trying to construct, but had not yet named) had sown beans among the corn stocks on a plot of land we'd rented for that purpose. I remember the moment when the state judicial police of Morelos cut us off with their car. Jacobo and I were listening to the beginning of the "24 Horas de la Tarde" news show on the radio. Zabludovsky, the program's host, was saying something about the father-in-law of President Luis Echeverría Alvarez, kidnapped by a guerrilla group from Jalisco. For half an hour, we'd swum in the green transparent waters of a beautiful stream flanked by tall walls of bamboo that paralleled the highway. We felt fresh, clean, and satisfied, without a worry in the world.

Only an hour and a half before, the heat had been killing me. Feeling an impulse to plunge into the river, I used the presence of Jacobo as a pretext to go swimming. Since he was from northern Mexico, I suggested that we take him to see the lovely tropical waters under the bridge where the compañeros and I swam frequently. It had also been my idea to invite him to participate in the meeting with "Dionisio," Isauro, and the others, especially those from Playa Vicente, Veracruz. Jacobo came from Chihuahua. It was his responsibility to transfer some money through a contact of ours to the political prisoners from the MAR currently held in Lecumberri. He and I had been in touch for a month. I'd helped him return home in a Volkswagen loaned to us by "Héctor," a sympathizer of the Organization. The three of us drove to the city of Chihuahua, where we left Jacobo along with a 30 mm M1 carbine, two magazines of fifteen rounds each, and an extra supply of cartridges. We had traveled with this arms cache strapped to the springs of the rear seat together with a cardboard box of mountain boots.

We'd left the Federal District quite early in the morning and had driven along the Pan American Highway virtually non-stop, reaching Chihuahua shortly after midnight. By itself, the trip would have been tiring but tranquil, had we not encountered a Federal Judicial Police roadblock at the state border between Chihuahua and Durango. Staring ahead along a straight stretch of the road, we could see a judicial policeman waving to us to stop. He held his right arm high, a submachine gun in his hand. All three of us felt as if we'd reached the end of our revolutionary adventure.

Just in front of us, we could see that the feds had stopped a car with gringo plates and were rummaging through all its suitcases. One of the agents approached the left side of our Volkswagen. He leaned forward for a better view of us and the inside of the car. Right off, he asked me to open the glove compartment. After inspecting it rapidly, he ordered us out of the car. He then proceeded to ask us who we were, where we were going, and what the purpose of our trip was. Jacobo identified himself with his driver's license, I think, telling the agent that he was a shoe salesman taking his friends to visit his relatives in Chihuahua. Héctor presented a university ID, saying that he taught film studies. I used my card from the Rural Program of the National Productivity Center, where I had worked for three years before leaving the job six months earlier. The agent opened the trunk of the car and began to sort through the tote bags containing our changes of clothing. I was positive that there was nothing incriminating in Héctor's or mine, but I had no idea what Jacobo had brought along. When the agent had finished looking through the bags, he approached me for a cigarette and a light. I complied, realizing that he wanted to see if my hand would tremble. I truly don't know why, but my hand held steady as I lit his cigarette. I remained acutely alert, but at the edge of my nerves. Again the agent approached the car. He squatted, extended his right arm, and searched with his hand under the front seats. Meanwhile Jacobo and I gave each other the look of men condemned to a firing squad. Héctor mumbled something unintelligible and pretended that he needed to pee. I almost had a heart attack when the agent reached under the back seat through an opening that we had carelessly left. Half an hour later, we still couldn't get over it! Incredible as it seemed, somehow the agent did not turn his hand upward to see if there was anything hidden within the springs of the back seat. Probably tedium and the minute inspection just given the gringo car had saved us.

The heavy-set soldier on my right kept leaning over, suffocating me. He couldn't sit still in the inadequate rear space of a VW. Its engine had steadied, and the car proceeded onward with a continuous hum that invited sleep. I figured that we were near Tres Marías. Soon we would end our climb, and the car would descend faster toward Mexico City. My thoughts were racing, both imagining virtual future scenarios and recalling events of the recent past. Some of these memories connected directly with what had happened since noon of the day before, others didn't. A deep anguish and rampant anxiety seized me as I thought of my wife Tere and my little daughter Teresita. I had imposed my full-time commitment to the Organization on them. My frequent absences and the abandonment of my job in order to "serve the people" had left them to provide for themselves. Stunned by fear during the first night of our detention in Cuernavaca in the offices of the Judicial Police of Morelos, I had stupidly revealed my marital status, my fatherhood, and my family's address. Immediately a policeman had threatened to seize both my wife and daughter and to bring them to be tortured and raped right before my eyes. I had spent the whole night in a small concrete room with my heart in my throat, tormented by innumerable bedbugs that constantly bit my arms and legs. Minute by minute I cursed my own stupidity and cowardice. I was gripped by anguish as I understood my predicament. Should my wife and daughter actually be brought to the detention center, I would have to confess everything that I knew in order to save them from harm. Only then did I accept for the first time how foolish I had been to imagine that I was brave enough not to reveal secrets even under torture. But that was not my only crass mistake. Another error tormented me. I had left cassettes in the car containing recordings made in the Sierra de Atoyac de Alvarez by none other than Lucio Cabañas Barrientos himself, known among us by his pseudonym "Miguel." He'd used a small tape recorder that I had purchased at his request and taught him how to use. I also chastised myself for bringing along in the car some illustrated Chinese Spanish-language brochures on tunnel warfare and the prolonged popular war. I wasn't normally so careless. On the contrary,

I always had made sure to carry nothing damaging either in the car or on my person. Usually we never bore arms nor carried them in our automobiles, even though I knew we'd collected a few, surely zealously hidden away somewhere by peasant compañeros of the Organization.

The first time I'd served as Lucio's chauffeur, I asked him whether he and his buddy "Gorgonio" would be armed during a trip we were about to take to the city of Durango. In case they were, I would also carry a gun. But Lucio said no, that he never traveled with weapons. It was better to follow this policy, he said, since the government didn't possess any recent photographs of him. With no weapons around, the police wouldn't have any reason to detain him. He related that just a few days earlier the Preventive Police of the Federal District had stopped him as he drove on Ignacio Zaragoza Avenue, the eastern gate to the city. As Gorgonio was his witness, Lucio said, he'd solved the problem by giving the patrolmen a few pesos. What I am trying to say is that we were very careful: we knew that it was important not to attract attention to ourselves and our activities. Almost everyday, we journeyed from the Federal District to Morelos or to the south of Puebla either in pairs, in groups, or by ourselves. We generally returned to Mexico City late at night, although it was not unusual for us to spend a night or two with our peasant compañeros in their homes or in the open air. During the years 1973–74, it was quite easy to encounter military or police roadblocks on highways near the capital.

It was my good fortune that they never seized Tere and our child. Months later, I knew that my loyal compañero Isauro, in spite of the risk, had made the valiant effort to reach Tere that very night, advising her to clear out of the house we'd been renting in Contreras on the outskirts of Mexico City. She should never return. Good old Isauro. He'd lost his VW when Jacobo and I were detained. Now he'd been obliged to travel all night by a series of bus connections—first, from the bean field to his own apartment in the eastern part of the Federal District, taking his wife (a teacher like himself) and his two-and-a-half year-old daughter to safety, and then crossing the city long after midnight, from east to west, to Contreras on the remote southwest edge of the huge urban sprawl.

The coat hid my identity and protected me from the cold, but its penetrating odor of cheap tobacco provoked an irresistible desire to smoke. Only now I didn't dare ask those silent soldiers for a cigarette. I couldn't have guessed how difficult getting a smoke would be for months and months thereafter.

The engine hummed softly and steadily. Soon we would reach the expressway toll booth at the southern end of Mexico City. At that point it wouldn't be difficult to know whether or not we'd be heading on the beltway toward the Campo Militar Número Uno. I'd driven around that part of the city so often that I knew precisely every light, every speed bump, ever curve, and every entrance and exit of the beltway. Needless to say, I could never mistake the sweet and sour stink (like sauerkraut, my mother used to say) of the Loreto y Peña Pobre paper factory near Copilco. I focused my attention on all those clues. When the soldier in the front passenger seat announced that they were taking me toward the Indios Verdes, I already knew that we were going instead toward Lomas de Sotelo. (Only now as I write do I realize that they were driving me in one of the two cars that the Morelos judicial police had "taken for safekeeping" from us.)

THE CAMPO MILITAR NÚMERO UNO

When the car finally stopped, I heard the driver inform someone at his window that we were expected inside. (I had registered the intricacies of our arrival in my mind. We'd taken the side road, made a broad turn to the left as if around a traffic circle, then gone straight again, after which we executed a U-turn to the left, going back along what must have been a broad avenue with a traffic island, until we made another right turn and stopped after some speed bumps.) The VW jolted as it started up again. It moved ahead slowly as if searching for something, halting a bit later. The copilot said, "I'm going to ask where it is." He opened the door and left the vehicle. I heard his rapid, nervous steps move away from us. I had the clear impression that he was walking on a stone pathway covered with sand. Nobody had to confirm for me where we were. We'd entered the Campo Militar Número Uno. Nor could anyone ever say that I hadn't made a great effort to reach that site!

The soldier returned with someone who led us to our destination. Nobody spoke. The guide must have directed the driver with hand signals. A few turns later, the VW came to a standstill once more. As I was freed from the weight that had oppressed the right side of my body, I felt a pair of hands forcefully remove me from the vehicle. At the same time, I became aware of some loud tropical tune that assaulted my ears. Somebody searched my pockets rapidly, finding—lucky guy—a fifty peso bill in my sport shirt. He also made off with Dioniso's denim jacket that had rested over my arms. Very rapidly I was lifted by the elbows and borne downstairs amid the murmur of different voices. The strident music brought to my scared memory scenes from Gillo Pontecorvo's film, *The Battle of Algiers*, in which Algerian pro-independence fighters were tortured while a portable turntable played a record at peak volume. The singing voice of Rigo Tovar took possession of my ears:

For some time sorrow overwhelms me,
and the memory of her love makes me cry.
Suffering follows me everywhere;
I cannot live without her warmth.
Woman, where have you gone?

The murmuring voices subsided. I was escorted into what appeared to be a cell, judging by the metallic sound of the lock and of the door's opening and closing on a track. I crouched against the wall, feeling my way around and trying to peek through the tiny gap allowed my right eye. It was indeed a very narrow cell, with no more furnishings than an uncovered toilet. Suddenly I felt extremely tired. I sat on the floor and removed the sandals I was wearing. Placing them under my head as a pillow, I lay down. My body had not yet relaxed when they had already returned, opening the cell door and ordering me up in loud, insulting voices. Again they lifted me up, this time without my footwear. Climbing up some steps, they deposited me on a school desk chair. Somebody ordered my blindfold to be removed along with the patches of duct tape that covered my eyes. A good part of my eyebrows and eyelashes pulled off with the tape. When I could focus my eyes finally, I saw two men sitting before me at a table. The older one was dressed in a gray turtleneck sweater and somewhat darker woolen slacks. He was a light-skinned, distinguished looking man with short gray hair. The other man was younger, and appeared as if he were Israeli or gringo; he wore a khaki trench coat. I couldn't help seeing him as a CIA agent, the typical suspicion of those days. A third man was present, the one who had ripped off my blindfold and patches.

As soon as he'd stood in front of me, I was sure that I'd seen this third fellow before. Unlike the other two, he was brown-skinned. He had a regular straight nose and a medium-sized mouth with thick lips. His abundant, black, and slightly curly hair hung just a bit over his forehead. I spent a long time trying to remember why he looked familiar. One day—chance or destiny?—an old issue of a magazine I'd seen before fell into my hands again. Was it *Por Esto* or *Siempre*? I can't remember. It featured a commemorative article on the June 10, 1971 government assault on student protesters. One of its pages contained a photograph depicting several Halcones armed with M1 carbines barricaded behind an automobile parked on the Mexico-Tacuba Avenue in front of the Normal School. This man appeared in the picture, standing behind the others, leaning forward a bit, and turning toward the camera with a disapproving anger on his face. His right hand gripped a .45 caliber automatic. He looked about thirty-five or forty years old. Until this magazine issue, nobody had seen this photo—two similar pictures published in the newspapers the day after the terrible event only showed two very young men, one with an M1 and the other with a semi-automatic.

The man in the sweater began the interrogation by asking me what I knew about the group that kidnapped José Guadalupe Zuno, President Echeverría's father-in-law. In the face of such a provocative, unexpected question, I thought how ironic it would be to incur torture over something I was ignorant about. I answered that I was aware of only what the papers, radio, and TV had told us—that the Frente Revolucionario Armado del Pueblo had taken responsibility for the action. He didn't ask any more questions, instead requesting that the dark man measure me. Unhappy with the results, he took charge himself. This disconcerted me. Were they measuring me for my coffin? Once this operation concluded, they returned me to my cell where they finally unbound my wrists. After a while, a young blond guard, short and stocky, opened the door about eight inches wide. He passed me a red plastic plate with rice, beans, and two thin, brittle tortillas. "Here God punishes but lets you feed," he told me abruptly. The ominous character of the only decorative element of the interrogation room weighed on my mind: to my left on one of the blood-splattered white walls hung a calendar reproduction illustrating a hunting scene in which a terrified deer, already lying on the ground next to a tree, was fiercely attacked by four mastiffs egged on by two horsemen with spears at the ready.

> I am afraid that you may fly from my hand like a bird.
> I am afraid that all I do may be in vain.
> I am afraid to live, but I am also afraid of death.

While I was trying to eat with difficulty—I had neither fork nor spoon—the radio broadcast a song by "Los Bríos" that seemed made to order. Music blasted at full volume most of the time, overwhelming my ears. The radio sat by the stairs, always set to stations like La Charrita del Cuadrante or the super hot, ticklish, fun-loving Radio A-I, Canal Tropical! The strident noise started at six in the morning, ending only at ten at night; the sole moments of silence occurred during the few minutes that the radio stations devoted to news. Then our young guardians would cut off the electric current to save themselves the task of going downstairs to the level of the cells to change the station. Those were the only moments we ever had in the dark, and we enjoyed them very much, wishing they would last longer. We understood this methodic behavior. The custodians were instructed to make it impossible for us to hear the news, thereby insuring our disconnection from the external world. The shrill sound of the radio readily served to undermine our mental health, weakening day by day the few psychological defenses we might still possess. The constant sound prevented us from identifying the noises coming from the surface and the area surrounding the clandestine jail, making it harder for us ever to determine our location in the remote chance that any of us detained in that basement ever faced a legal sentencing process or returned to society in freedom.

The young guardians that fed us also bore the responsibility of conducting us to the interrogation room. There they assisted the agents of the Federal Security Office and the officers of the Military Police in their techniques of torture: they dunked us to the point of asphyxiation in the water basin or in the steel drum under the stairs; they beat us; and they applied electricity to our naked, wet bodies. In their custodial role, the guardians removed us from the cells on Saturday to allow us to bathe with bucketfuls of freezing water from the basin. They performed regular watches in the corridors in front of the cells. Not surprisingly, the guardians were also human beings who put the least possible effort into their work. Thus they tried to avoid as much as possible having to go downstairs to the level of the cells and be exposed to the blasting sound of the radio.

A short while after having arrived in the basement, I became convinced that these young men were Halcones. I want to be precise about this. None of the men who interrogated me, subjected me to torture, or watched me during my time at this location was ever in uniform. I think that only once did one of them, who behaved as if he was in authority, come with someone else in uniform. Even that time, they remained without caps, ties, or any insignia on the collars of their shirts. They covered their bodies with thick gray nylon jackets that dangled open hoods over their backs.

It didn't take long before I realized that Jacobo was a fellow prisoner here. I got a glimpse of him when they took him to the interrogation room. Seeing him pass by the corridor in front of my cell, flanked by two Halcones, caused me considerable anguish. I feared that he might mention Dionisio or any of the other compañeros he'd just met at the bean field meeting in Morelos. This would have forced me to face questions and pressures I wasn't sure that I could resist. I still remained quite unsettled on his return from the interrogation room. Even when I knew that I was taking a stupid risk, I stuck my arm out between the cell bars. Stretching as far as I could, I caught the attention of the occupant of the next cell, whom I could not see. I asked him to pass a message all the way down the line to Jacobo—he was not to mention either Dionisio or Isauro. I never found out whether he did or not, but during those early days, nobody grilled me about them.

The basement cells lay along two parallel corridors connected by a third where the interrogation and torture room, the water basin, and the stairway were located. At the time of my arrival, the cells of both corridors appeared to be occupied. I was housed in the second cell of the corridor to the left of the bottom of the stairs. The first section of the corridor contained a room with a disguised window in the far wall, used to observe the person undergoing interrogation next door. A young woman with a coastal accent was imprisoned in that room; I could hear her in conversation with one of the custodians who visited her often, seemingly in some sort of courtship. From a cell adjacent to mine came another young voice with the same accent, apparently that of her brother. Between the cells hung bulbs that illuminated the corridors in a yellow-tinged light. From inside the cells—six in the first corridor, five in the second—all we could see was a monotonous white wall crowned by three narrow grated vents. When the news broadcasts were due on the radio, the guards regularly cut off the electricity. If it was daytime, for a few minutes we could view three beams of light radiating downward through the vents. The spectacle of thousands of dust particles floating in the sunlight entertained us as we stuck our hands out between the ochre colored cell bars in order to enjoy—alone and together—the silence, the relative darkness, and the caress of the sun.

I don't remember the details of the first night that I spent in the basement. It's possible that I slept well, since I hadn't slept the night before. I'm sure that I woke up in a start at the violent sound of the radio, turned on every day at six A.M. with fastidious military punctuality. Invariably, the Halcones would interrupt our sleep by tuning to a request show that featured the famous songs of Pedro Infante. The one Halcón on duty would make his rounds along the cells, after which he would sweep and mop the three corridors. At that early hour, the partner of the person cleaning the floors (they would alternate tasks every other day) would bring us breakfast from a kitchen apparently not too far away. They never failed to bring us our food precisely on time. They must have been keeping a military schedule. But meals were skimpy, good for making us lose any possible extra pounds. To drink, we received a small plastic cup with lemonade. Any additional water to quench our thirst had to come from the toilet tank. They also gave me a used toothbrush—used by who knows how many before me! Sometimes after meals, a guard would come by with toothpaste, squeezing some on the bristles so that we could brush properly. This prophylactic measure was, I suppose, a way of preventing dental crises among the detained, given the physical distress that dental problems would cause us, not to mention the practical complications for our jailers who would be obliged to do something to alleviate the situation.

INTERROGATION

Around ten in the morning of the day after my arrival, two men came for me. One of them was an Halcón who watched us, a man of light brown complexion, somewhat fastidious in dress and appearance, with a very thin mustache and a prominent tuft of hair above his forehead. From then on, he would assume a very negative attitude toward me while appearing to be very interested in Jacobo and almost complacent toward him. The other one, of lighter skin, light brown eyes, and taller stature, called the shots. His right hand and forearm were covered by a plaster cast.

Wordlessly, they opened my cell and took me to the room in front of the water basin. They made me undress. Tying my hands together behind my waist, they covered my eyes with a dirty blindfold. As I stood, they wet my torso and applied electricity to my nipples with a simple wire with the insulation stripped off at the end. Insulting me at the same time, they demanded that I confess to the assaults and kidnappings in which I had participated. In pain, I started to babble a negative answer, bringing a formidable blow to my left side, which knocked me like a bolt to the floor. I couldn't breathe. My arms and legs refused to obey me.

"Stand up, you son of a whore!" I heard them yelling, while I literally saw stars.

"Wait a second!" I moaned motionlessly.

"Who do you think you're talking to, you son of a whore?" the man with the cast answered as he began to kick me forcefully.

I don't know how I managed to rise, but I understood that the thug had hit me with his cast. He was going to destroy my ribs with it. So I decided to admit to something—transporting a few old weapons all by myself to a deserted location in the state of Guerrero that lay along the highway between Acapulco and Pinotepa Nacional on the Costa Chica.

My admission saved me momentarily from greater punishment. The military officer sent me back to my cell, very happy at having obliged me so quickly to confirm my involvement in subversive activities. Locked up once more, I saw the same Halcón haul Jacobo away.

"Now it's his turn!" I said to myself, fearing for us both. I carefully explored my aching and probably broken left rib cage. Maybe I hadn't done so badly after all. Everything had happened so fast that I really agonized more over what could happen later. They didn't take long at all with Jacobo. I soon saw him return. He didn't look badly hurt. Whenever someone was removed from a cell, the occupants of all the others felt their hearts race, their mouths go dry, and their breathing shrink to a minimum. One could cut the thick silence with a knife. During interrogations, the Halcones turned off the radio so that the rest of us prisoners could hear the screams of the wretch whose turn had come. I don't remember exactly when, although I know it happened during the first few days of my arrival, they brought a young educated man—as his speech revealed—from somewhere else to the basement. I never saw him, but I do know that they submerged his head several times in a steel drum full of water until they drowned him. How can I be so sure since I never saw it? I can only say that I couldn't hear the voice of the victim any more, and that one of the torturers said, "This prick has had it." Later trying to contain my fear and rage, I listened to them ascend the stairs, carrying the body in silence as if they were burdened in their souls for what they had just done.

When the Halcones turned on the radio again, Roberto Carlos was singing:

> When I was a child, what joy
> To play soldier day and night . . .
> The cat that is in our sky
> Will not go home if you're not there . . .
> You have no idea, my love, how beautiful the night is
> I feel that you are in that star . . .
> The cat that is sad and blue
> Never forgets that you were mine . . .

I don't know whether I have clearly described the atmosphere of the basement during the first period of my detention. The house was practically full. The Halcones would take one prisoner out to help them distribute meals. The task consisted in holding the tray while the Halcón passed the meals into the cells after opening the doors several inches so that the inmates could grasp the plate. I seem to remember that during the first few days they always chose the same person to help. This partner in misfortune, I learned later, was Professor Inocencio Castro. Castro had set up the arrangements for Rubén Figueroa Figueroa to come talk to Lucio Cabañas at a previously designated location in the Sierra in Guerrero. There the guerrilla leader held the advantage, and his forces surprised the *cacique* by taking him captive.

At certain moments, the basement could generate noise of its own. One could hear the murmurs of conversations, in spite of the radio's merciless supply of cumbias, boleros, and the ballad of the moment. On the second day after my arrival, when I was trying to take a nap by stuffing my ears with little balls of bread to dull the noise, I was surprised by the racket of people galloping down the stairs and moving rapidly through the corridor. While the first few men organized a roll call of the prisoners, two others joined the stocky blond guy, stopping in front of my cell. They ordered him to release the lock and slide the door open.

Five or six agents seated me in the school chair in the interrogation room. Their boss looked like a stereotype, with big dark glasses, a finely trimmed mustache, an enormous gold bracelet on his right wrist, a Rolex on the left, and two rings, a gold one with a diamond on the left ring finger, and a platinum one with ruby on the right. The commander said to me: "You are in the hands of the federal executive power. For you, anonymity and clandestinity are finished. Remember, according to your own rules you had the obligation to keep silent during the first seventy-two hours after your detention. Those are now over. Understand that between you and us lies an unbridgeable abyss. You can only cross it by cooperating with the government. I'm all ears—tell us your story."

Since I had nothing prepared in advance, I began to weave a story as I spoke. I invented that I had gotten involved after my reencounter with "Rubén," a former high school classmate named José Luis Díaz González. I had run into him at a conference on the Vietnam War. We both were interested in the subject. At the end of the lecture and the ensuing debate, we decided to go for a cup of coffee to the Sanborn's in San Angel in order to reminisce about our old times in the Mexico City School, located at Campos Elíseos and Lamartine in Polanco. After that meeting, we had many others. He invited me to join the Liga Comunista Espartaco, and so the two of us became more and more imbued with the revolutionary themes of the moment: Cuba, Fidel Castro, Che Guevara, Mao Tse-tung, the Cultural Revolution in China, etc. After a short while, José Luis invited me to participate actively in transforming Mexico by committing myself to the true Mexican revolutionary movement. He spoke to me about the Partido de los Pobres, whose leader Lucio Cabañas Barrientos conducted its struggle from the mountains of Guerrero.

The truth was very different. I had joined the Liga Comunista Espartaco after a naive and stupid trip to Cuba in 1967. My first contact—and later group leader, "Luis" —would receive many years later the National Award for Medicine. But I told the federal agents that I accepted the invitation of José Luis Díaz González. After that, I had to fulfill different tasks for the Partido de los Pobres. Some of them were simple and easy, others like conveying weapons (once) or compañeros (several times) to Guerrero were full of risks. While I spoke, one of the agents took notes. I couldn't check to see whether they also had a tape recorder. When I came to a halt in the narrative, the commander said, in a tone of condemnation:

"Very good. We've already heard what you wanted to tell us. Now we're going to see what you haven't wanted to say."

In a gruff voice he ordered: "Get on with it! Strip him! You two, tie his hands behind him and blindfold him!"

I wanted to protest, but I could only babble incoherently while they ripped off my clothing, secured my hands behind my back, and tied a stinking blindfold around my head.

The commander again ordered harshly: "To the water basin! Let's see how much this stupid bastard hasn't told."

They lifted me up, and before I could invent another story, several agents submerged my head backwards in the cold and dirty water of the basin. I remembered then how I needed to act: finding strength in my despair, I twisted and lifted my body as much as I could, trying to stay out of the liquid. A compañero who had already suffered the experience of the "well" had instructed me to resist vigorously as soon as I was dunked. That way my torturers would not be able to determine when asphyxiation might really set in. I eagerly searched through my brain for a creditable story to tell without having to identify anyone. In and out of the water I came, each time more anxiously. My heart was pounding inside my breast. My lungs, about to burst, imperiously demanded their quota of air. Severe coughing spells contorted my body. As best I could, I spoke, promising to talk. The commander grabbed me forcefully by the hair and threateningly burped in my face: "If you come out with some horseshit story, I'll bust your ass, you prick."

I decided to describe my participation, as a member of the Jaramillista Delegation of the Liga Comunista Espartaco in the second meeting of the Partido de los Pobres high in the Sierra of Atoyac, during the month of May of the previous year, 1973. I described in broad brushstrokes the ideological trends and politics expressed at this meeting; and the different invited organizations present: PCM, Unión del Pueblo, MAR, Liga Comunista 23 de Septiembre, and the Espartaquistas Jaramillistas. I revealed the approximate number of those gathered, close to two hundred, half of whom had been invited. But I denied knowing the personal identity and individual trajectories of those attending, since we all used pseudonyms, and since we had ascended the Sierra via different routes guided by unknown persons. Even if I had been forced to say more, I couldn't have. I had depended on a contact in Acapulco who could only be located by compañero "Isaías," part of the top leadership of the Brigada de Ajusticiamiento del Partido de los Pobres. I knew Isaías since on several occasions I had transported him from the Federal District to the port city of Acapulco in Guerrero and back. I also described the debate that took place between Lucio and a small group of Liga Comunista 23 de Septiembre members: "Joel" and "Sylvia," "Renato," "Roque," and "Julián." The five were initially invited to spend a minimum of three months with the Cabañas group. The debate centered around whether or not the five should have written provocative, pointless, and incendiary flyers to distribute among the rural highway construction crews. Their pamphlets urged the workers to arm themselves, descend upon Atoyac de Alvarez, and expropriate food, medicine, and clothing for themselves and their families. This initiative took place behind the back of the leadership of the Brigade, in open contradiction to its political directives. Inciting heckling against Lucio, the five invitees accused him of being a populist and reactionary *caudillo*. To many, their divisiveness seemed like sabotage.

More than anything else I sought to qualify my own political position in the context of these guerrilla organizations. I tried hard to describe what our group—a remnant of the Ho Chi Minh peasant section of the Liga Comunista Espartaco—thought that the line of the popular movement should be. Whether it was armed or not, we believed that the movement should build upon close contact with workers and peasants. We should rely on their experience and wisdom, taking into account the context prevailing in our country and the world. We knew not to impose our own ideological conceptions or to force them to do things that they were not yet ready to undertake. I vehemently explained to my interrogators that our Organization coincided with Lucio in many of our analyses and practices, but that we disagreed with him on many other points. Some of our differences were pretty basic, such as the matter of *foquista* guerrilla warfare, a tactic that Lucio adopted frequently, forgetting his own origins. All of this was rigorously true, but I made sure that I didn't tell the feds that the friendly collaboration of our Organization with the Partido de los Pobres and its Brigada de Ajusticiamiento had begun earlier when Lucio decided to undertake armed struggle in the mountains. Our collaboration based itself upon reciprocal knowledge and trust generated by the fulfillment of many mutual agreements among the leading ranks of both organizations. Some of the leadership of both groups shared a common origin in the state of Guerrero, having studied as Cabañas did in the Normal Rural School of Ayotzinapa. During the interrogation, I simply continued the story I had invented at the beginning of that day's session, so I kept firm in the conviction that José Luis Díaz González was the one who invited me to the meeting of the Partido de los Pobres in the mountains.

The commander expressed special interest in the contents of the tapes that Lucio had recorded. He wanted to know more about the plans to divide the Brigade into three relatively autonomous groups. At that time there were about one hundred guerrillas in all, who would be split up to operate in three distinct regions. I answered that I only knew what Lucio said in the recording. The commander then asked how the tapes happened to be in my possession, and what had I been ordered to do with them. I said that José Luis had asked me to make copies, since I had expertise in the matter—which was true—and that we were going to distribute the copies among the different groups whom we had connections with. We aimed to influence their revolutionary practice away from the type of voluntaristic *foquismo* to which Lucio so easily fell prey.

THE REAL STORY

The real story was different. Gorgonio was the one to put the tapes in my hands as Lucio had asked him to. This took place in the town of Santa Clara in the house of don "Jesús," a worker-compañero whose family sympathized with the Organization. Lucio had sent Gorgonio to suggest to us that we receive Rubén Figueroa's ransom money. The large majority of the Organization had completely disavowed Figueroa's kidnapping by the Brigada de Ajusticiamiento. We thought that revolutionaries should not behave as the bourgeoisie did. Our deals should always be totally trustworthy. Even with somebody like Figueroa, we revolutionaries should keep our word of honor. In general, Lucio's demands for freeing the governor were altogether excessive. Particularly mistaken was the requirement that all ordinary prisoners be freed. Early on I'd become familiar with the list of demands that Lucio had created for some future "netting of a big fish." When the US Consul in Guadalajara, Terrence George Leonhardy, was kidnapped by the Frente Revolucionario Armado del Pueblo (FRAP), Lucio had learned the news while a guest in my house. In exchange for Leonhardy's life, the FRAP demanded the freedom of a large group of political prisoners from various affiliations along with their transport to Cuba. I remember that we were watching TV in the dining room of the house that I rented during those days in Colonia Jardín Balbuena, Retorno #4, at the corner of Iglesias and Calderón. When Jacobo Zabludovsky disclosed the news over the tube, Lucio commented that he'd ask for more if he were ever in the FRAP's position. I recall having replied that I believed the moment would come when the government would simply refuse to grant any concessions to any group in exchange for anyone's life. That had already been the case in Brazil and Uruguay. Lucio dissented, assuring me that he would know how to extract his demands from the government.

With regard to Lucio's request, I told Gorgonio that I would never participate in such an operation. The Organization should stay out of it. Speaking against Lucio's invitation provoked fear, anguish, and sorrow all at once for me. It was the first time that I opposed participation in an action openly and forcefully, but I saw clearly that we should not get involved. In addition to the ideological and political disagreement that I had with the kidnapping, I knew that if we participated, we'd undoubtedly get screwed. The logic and maybe the instinct underpinning my speech helped Dionisio, Isauro, and the others, I gather, to reject the proposal. Gorgonio appeared to understand; he humbly told us not to worry, that there were other options.

Later Gorgonio told us briefly how "the old motherfucker" Figueroa had escaped his guards two or three times when they were overcome by sleep. Scared and angry, they later recaptured him downhill. He also informed us that most of the members of the Brigada de Ajusticiamiento wanted to shoot Figueroa after receiving the fifty million peso ransom. This confidential revelation disgusted me even more. It was the logical follow-up of the trap deployed for the cacique. The political cost to the credibility of all segments of the popular movement, armed or not, could have easily been foreseen.

No less surprising was the story that Gorgonio told about marijuana smoking among several members of the Brigade. He recounted how Lucio— realizing that some of the group would go into the forest to smoke—had given them permission to light up in camp. As a consequence, those boys carried so much weed in their backpack that they lacked room for provisions essential to survival in the mountains. Gorgonio presented all of this in a spirit of disapproval of Lucio's decisions, adding that many of those young men had been recruited in parts of the Sierra where people grew and trafficked in marijuana and poppy flowers. Perhaps, I think now as I reflect on these developments, these situations were only natural, a product of the economic, social, and political milieu, of local history, of a limited popular culture that had been conditioned by excessive poverty, by the brutality of oppression in the cacique system, and by the absence of formal education. Tyranny by local caciques went back at least one hundred years, but it had reached new heights in the hands of the Partido Revolucionario Institucional (PRI) over the last few decades. The Brigada de Ajusticiamiento del Partido de los Pobres couldn't be immune from the social virtues and defects of the region and Guerrero at large, since most of its members came from that state. The practice of the Brigade of allowing peasants to come in and out of the armed group every three months as long as they showed disposition, curiosity, or personal interest—even a utilitarian interest—possessed some logic, although it was criticized by the expelled group from the 23 de Septiembre. On the other hand, that logic was limited since Lucio's idea derived from historical experiences long past—the wars of Independence and Reform, the anti-interventionist wars against France and the United States, and the 1910 Revolution (Emiliano Zapata and his Liberating Army of the South fundamentally).

For some actions Lucio would deploy peasants; for others, trained combatants. As a tactical strategy for prolonged popular warfare, Lucio's approach would seem to make sense. But in terms of real human capital, conditioned by precarious and politically-repressed social structures, it didn't. Necessity, always opportunistic, would push men to desertion, and from desertion to denunciation. I now think that this contradiction accounted in part for the failure of Lucio Cabañas Barrientos and the Brigada Campesina de Ajusticiamiento del Partido de los Pobres. These were the contradictions among the people—Mao *dixit*—which the enemy knew how to exploit efficaciously. In addition, the movement underestimated its enemy and overestimated the objective and subjective conditions prevailing among the peasantry in Guerrero and in the rest of the country.

Digressions aside, the commander was intrigued. He wanted to understand the motivation of someone like me, educated in a Catholic private university, who had set aside the opportunities that his family background and education offered him in life and had decided instead to join a big, messy upheaval in which he had nothing to gain and much to lose.

The interrogation lasted some three hours. As the agents tired, the tension slacked off until they offered me a soda and cigarettes. In the end, the commander ordered that I be given a pack of filter Raleighs. "Let him have the whole thing, the poor bastard is not going to smoke for a very long time," he said in a tone of false commiseration that perturbed me no end. I shared those cigarettes with Jacobo and someone else, I have forgotten whom. Before he left, the commander said that he would be back the next day with the Ministerio Público in order to bind me over to a penal judge. Once back in the cell, I vacillated between my heartfelt hope that that would be true and a great skepticism deriving from the cold logic of reason.

I can't remember what happened at that time to Jacobo. Memory fails me as I try to recall whether he was taken from his cell for interrogation as would have been the normal practice. It seems strange that I don't remember any kind of violence in the place after my return to the cell. This in no way intends to suggest something negative about Jacobo's behavior—only that if he was interrogated, his session was faster than mine and without the kind of violence that I could have registered from my cell.

DISAPPEARED

Nothing happened the next day after or the third, fourth, or fifth, so I soon realized that the commander had lied to me about announcing my consignation before the authorities. The idea of my disappearance without a trace or mortal remains for my wife, daughter, and parents began to cause me serious torment. I spent hours and hours thinking of how to notify them of my detention. I wondered how each one of the Halcones would respond to the promise of reward money from my father in exchange for taking him a message indicating that I was alive and where I was detained. But I was afraid of making a mistake and hesitated about incurring this risk with any of them. I couldn't stop fantasizing all the time about what Tere or my father would have to do, and from whom they would have to seek help. In my mind I would go over every one of my father's friends and acquaintances. He had been a publicist for many years and knew many people in the country's most important newspapers. I would try to communicate mentally with Tere, naturally without any success, to let her know that I was alive, that she should wait for me, that she shouldn't forget me. I imagined tragic situations with vivid anguish and dread, such as returning years later to our last address in Contreras, immensely grief-stricken that my two Teres no longer lived there. Or I would imagine Tere living with someone else, after having waited in vain for my return. Or Tere convinced that I had abandoned her. On the radio, Rigo Tovar poured forth pain and nostalgia:

> For some time sorrow overwhelms me,
> and the memory of her love makes me cry . . .
> . . . At night I ask the stars
> to tell me if she remembers my love . . .
> . . . But I can't find more solution
> than a languid light in the dark . . .

In all, the long dead hours of confinement could not stay empty. It was imperative to spend the time in some activity or fantasy, exercising my muscles by repeated squats and pushups, learning to play chess with "Noé," a young guy in the next cell whose name I can't recall, but who said that he'd been detained in the state of Hidalgo seven months earlier. Since I was only beginning to learn the game, I proved indecisive and quite clumsy as I moved the minutely carved pieces made from bread crumb on a piece of cardboard with black and white squares drawn on its surface. According to Noé, this flimsy chessboard had been created by Ignacio Salas Obregón, "Oseas," leader of the Liga Comunista 23 de Septiembre who had been wounded when he was captured after a shootout in Tlalnepantla. The first week of September 1974 marked almost five months in the Campo Militar Número Uno for him.

As I recall this last fact, I also remember something else that happened that day. The commander that interrogated me (and also Jacobo, I'm more sure of that now) walked by the cells after having returned my compañero to his. He reached the end of the corridor and remained some twenty or thirty minutes by the cell belonging to Ignacio Salas Obregón according to Noé. It seemed to me that his stay lasted an eternity. Nobody moved in any of the cells or the corridor; nobody even dared to clear their throat. The quiet low voice of the commander could be heard like a continual murmur. I couldn't hear whether Oseas said anything to him at all. I figured that the commander was either threatening him or offering him something in exchange for information. Noé, by now one of those who had been there the longest, later told me that Salas Obregón remained firm and strong, even brightening up when he recounted how his compañeros executed the industrialist Fernando Aranguren in Guadalajara, whom they had kidnapped and for whom they had demanded a sizeable ransom. Only a few days later they came at night for Salas Obregón and several other prisoners, apparently all from Guerrero. If memory serves, among them was Professor Inocencio Castro. Some days earlier he had exclaimed, "Now I'm fucked! They're going to kill me!" when he learned from the radio that Rubén Figueroa had been liberated by the army. The radio had remained on due to a lapse on the part of the Halcones. They removed all these prisoners, blindfolded and hooded, one by one, single file, their hands bound. During this operation, those in charge yelled at the remainder of us in the basement, threatening us so that we'd keep our eyes glued to the rear wall of our cells with our backs to the corridor. As the ruckus, the shouts, and the movement of people subsided, we returned to normal, to the radio, and to its "super hot and ticklish" music. Thus we recovered our cardiac and respiratory rhythm, realizing that only three of us were left. They'd almost emptied the place. The cells of the corridor behind us lay vacant.

For a day or two, Jacobo, Noé, and I found ourselves locked up in the consecutive central cells of the first corridor. During the regimented silences of the radio, we could talk a little bit. At night, especially during those nights when the second pair of Halcones was in charge, we could tell each other jokes, coming apart at the seams with nervous laughter for hours and hours until dawn. Every now and then, one of these two Halcones, a dark man with Indian features, straight hair, and agile mind and body, would give us hard, salted tortillas that had been toasted, a feast for us. This Halcón used to remark that he would sit on the top step of the stairs after providing the tortillas just to hear us chew them with delight. This same man demonstrated an interest in my sturdy Otomí *huaraches*. Each time he encountered me, he would look at them covetously. Besides the tortillas, he would also hand us a cigarette or a match to light a cigarette butt discarded by one of the other Halcones. For Jacobo and me, smoking became an obsession. From the moment we opened our eyes in the morning, our struggle began to secure a butt or a full cigarette. We devised all sorts of stratagems. The worst of it was that we even went as far as rolling tobacco strands in newspaper or toilet paper, something that produced throat irritation, cough, and nausea.

About a month after we had been locked up in the basement, they detained a young man who identified himself to us as soldier. It appeared to be a case of desertion, but just in case he was a spy, we kept a very prudent distance from him. He spent several days locked up in a cell near ours. When they were about to remove him, he managed to pass me a twenty-peso bill. We were intrigued by his behavior, without being able to determine with certainty why he had done that. Jacobo proposed that we ask one of the custodians to buy us cigarettes and matches. I was doubtful about this, but the overwhelming desire to smoke got the best of me, so I asked the man who gave us the toasted tortillas. He in turn inquired where the money had come from. I simply told him that I'd had the money from the beginning. Hours later we were smoking contentedly; he'd given a pack of Faros, but no matches, saying that he would provide the light.

I now begin to recall another Halcón taller than the others. He was light-skinned, a blondie from the boondocks. He spoke with a singsong accent from Sinaloa. His colleagues said that he was afraid to descend to the cells—several times the spirit of those who'd died there had scared him. They made fun of him and constantly challenged him to come down to keep us company. At the beginning, I thought that he was putting us on, trying to scare us with his acting, but later I became convinced that the man was truly afraid. A short while after my arrival in the basement he disappeared, never to be seen again.

Luck favored me on the day of my arrival. Instead of the blanket that others received, I got a thin quilt. It was very dirty and worn. At the beginning that revolted me, but in time I came to appreciate the quilt as true treasure. It served both as bed and blanket; it isolated me from the cold floor of the cell and the frigid air that blew in at night through the corridor vents. Each time I had to change cells, the quilt stayed on the floor, since I was never warned that they were moving me. Each time it required litigation with one of the Halcones to regain my treasure. Once, on a Saturday about a month after my arrival, I had to spend more than twenty-four hours rolled up in the quilt. In order to discourage lice and mites, I'd decided to wash all my clothing. It took an entire day for everything hanging from the bars to dry off. During the first few weeks of my tenure at the camp, we would leave our cells one by one on Saturdays for bucket baths to one side of the water basin and the steel drum under the stairs. But later the Halcones brought a hose to each cell so that we could bathe with Fab detergent; we also had to wash the floor and to sanitize the edges of the very reduced space of our cell with creolene, a powerful disinfectant. Two months later I gave up my quilt in a gesture of impulsive solidarity, not without guilt, but that's a story to be told later.

As I was saying, I suffered from knowing that I had disappeared without being able to communicate with my loved ones to let them know why they had not heard from me. My distress grew day by day, leading me inexorably to the limits of despair. I came very close to the edge one night when a new group of prisoners arrived in the Camp, hooded and blindfolded with their hands tied. Their speech indicated that they were indigenous men from somewhere in the Huasteca in the state of Hidalgo. I asked one of them locked up in the cell next to mine where they were from. He sounded like he was about seventy years old. The old man answered that he had been detained two years ago in the Sierra of Hidalgo, two long years separated from his family. They had last been locked up in a barracks whose iron grated windows allowed them to see the countryside. The military had transferred them here to the basement in an army truck covered with a canvas top. Listening to him, I couldn't prevent a deep sob. I wept abundantly, opening the floodgates of my sorrow. In my mind and heart, my wife, my daughter, and my parents became painfully present. I had never been so forsaken in my life. On the radio Los Bríos went on singing:

> *I'm afraid of leaving and regretting my departure*
> *I'm afraid of gambling and regretting to have lost*
> *I'm afraid of looking for you some day and knowing that you left*
> *I'm afraid of knowing that eternity doesn't exist*

It was true. I didn't know much about physical or moral suffering. My parents had given me a comfortable material life that I hadn't known how to appreciate at the time or express gratitude for. During those years, my problems were of another character. Communication with my parents, particularly with my father, had been awkward. It's not that he was especially arbitrary or despotic; for him, my adolescent problems were simply remote. The things that seemed to bug him were a door we'd left open or a change in the location of his favorite ashtray or his round pipe holder (he possessed over ten pipes, all

of which he smoked in an order whose rationale he never explained to us) or
we'd distracted him from reading the afternoon newspaper at dinnertime.
Nervous, irritable, uncommunicative in these years, my father would raise his
voice frequently, although I never heard him swear at home. Only once, when
I was fifteen, did he give me a thorough spanking and then with considerable
justification. I had just flunked eight subjects in the first semester of my second year of junior high, a year that I was already repeating. I had played hooky
to go to Chapultepec Park with Ramiro Gamboa, Jr., Juan Luis Alvarez Gayou,
and other classmates.

Since my mother also had a strong character and will, as a couple they neu-
tralized each other during their daily disagreements. Mother's hands were
prompt to punish, and if I managed to grab her arms, she would kick me on
the shins. She possessed not an ounce of patience. Doing homework every
afternoon under her supervision could easily turn into a torture session. On
my father's side, I don't remember that he ever played with me during my
childhood or gave me a kiss or a spontaneous caress. I do remember that I
was afraid of him, and that if I needed to ask him for something, I would ask
Tesa, three years younger than I. She would have to do it for me. At that point,
Dad would tell my sister that I should ask him personally. Since I had then no
recourse, I would approach him trembling and state my request, which naturally he denied me immediately, as a matter of course, I think. Consequently,
my fear grew stronger each time, leaving me less ready to ask him the next
time. Years later our communication improved a bit. He used to pick me up
midmorning on Saturdays at the Instituto Luis Vives where I was in my last
year of high school, taking me with him to practice shooting with a rifle or a
shotgun at a club to which he belonged. We also shared times—both good and
bad—hunting together two or three weekends a year in the states of Mexico,
San Luis Potosí, Tamaulipas, and Guerrero. White-tailed deer, wild turkeys,
boar, pigeons, or ducks constituted our game. Every Sunday, I had to help him
clean the weapons, all of them duly registered with the Ministry of National
Defense, and to reload both the rifle and shotgun cartridges. I didn't mind
doing it. I only regretted not being able to get out of it now and then.

On one hunting trip when I was seventeen, I asked him for permission to
smoke, and he answered yes. Thereafter, I smoked openly. One day he
announced that I would fulfill my obligatory military service a year ahead of
schedule in the ranks of the Navy Infantry, starting the following Sunday. The
news didn't bother me entirely, because in some way it confirmed for me that
I was no longer an adolescent. What I hated was missing every party for almost
a year. I had to be up early ever Sunday morning and arrive at the Riviera
rotary in Colonia Navarte by seven ready to march until one in the afternoon.

The indigenous men from Hidalgo were taken away the following day just as they had arrived, blindfolded and hooded, with their hands tied to one single rope. None of them had faced interrogation. The case of two men from Guerrero who arrived one or two weeks later proved quite different. They came escorted by a swarm of agents, who immediately tortured them for several hours. By then I was the sole occupant of any of the cells in the back corridor. I didn't understand my relocation, unless they simply wanted someone that otherwise unoccupied wing. The new arrivals were placed in two cells at a distance from one another in my new corridor. The older one, who seemed to be the uncle of the younger, was housed next to me. The man continued to groan softly but painfully. He said that the soldiers had beaten him hard in the vehicle on the way to the Campo Militar Número Uno. He had been removed from his home violently, and during the transfer they had fractured several of his ribs. The younger, the main object of that investigation, was captured in the same home. Through the screaming, swearing, and painful groaning from their interrogation, I found out a few things. The first question for the boy concerned the location of Carmelo Cortés, a former Brigade member that Lucio Cabañas had expelled for a year. The expulsion served as punishment for Cortés' political and ideological deviations as well for the multiple mistakes of his leadership during the months Lucio had spent in Mexico City seeking a cure for the tremendous migraine headaches that assailed him. By the time the men from Guerrero arrived, Carmelo had broken off his ties with Lucio, and he was heading his own guerrilla mini-group, Las Fuerzas Armadas Revolucionarias.

I was terrified, trembling from head to toe as these two were tortured. The officer in charge was the same one that had beaten me with his plaster cast. He now participated personally in their barbarous punishment, roaming back and forth between the interrogation room and the cell of my new neighbor. His questions received monosyllabic responses in a low voice. Through beatings and electric shocks, the officer sought to confirm what the younger man had testified by escalating the pressure on him.

All of a sudden I spotted the officer heading toward me, his plaster cast gone. Bathed in sweat, an electric cattle prod in his right hand, he swayed as he walked. His entire manner spoke of giving orders and being obeyed. He'd been trained to punish anyone who disobeyed his commands without a second thought. Before he'd uttered anything, I'd guessed his intentions: he was going to try out the cattle prod on me. He leaned over to where I was sitting on the cell floor, exclaiming: "You! Test the power of this fucker!" Referring to the younger of the two men, he went on: "Either this bastard can take a whole fuck of a lot or this fucking thing has gone dead." He placed the points of the instrument on my shirt sleeve and turned it on. The truth was that I didn't feel a thing, but I let out a very convincing "Ow!" as I jerked my right arm back. The creep's face lit up. "Ah, so it works!" Satisfied, he made an about-face and swaggered off, relishing in advance the pain he was going to inflict on the boy.

Before long they hauled the young man from the torture chamber in order to force him to give in by dunking him in the water basin. This time they used the water board technique, tying him naked to a wooden board. This prevented him from moving and enabled them to submerge him at will. Since they carried this out in the corridor near my cell, I got to watch the whole operation. From where I was I could observe them, but they could not see me. They dunked him several times for increasingly long periods. When he began to loose consciousness, they revived him by shocking his wet body with an electrical wire with the insulation peeled off at the end. The boy begged them not to dunk him again, saying that he couldn't take it anymore. But they continued until he looked so bad that they quit. They untied him and placed him half-dressed in one of the cells of my corridor. Later, around dawn, his uncle and I could hear him struggling to open the padlock of his cell door. In his frenetic, desperate movements, he remained impervious to the din he was making or to what might befall him. Together, his uncle and I tried to calm him. I explained that even if he managed to open the padlock and get out into the corridor, he wouldn't be able to get past the locked door at the head of the stairs. On the other side would be armed soldiers with enormous guard dogs, or so I'd been told when I first arrived. He continued at it for a while longer, but eventually gave up, exhausted. A few hours later they came for both men. Shirtless and shoeless, the young man asked for his garments back. One of the soldiers replied: "Don't worry, you're not going to need them anymore." The young man was a brave one. He'd withstood a tremendous punishment without informing on Carmelo or on anyone else. I marveled at his fortitude and integrity, really envying him. Nevertheless, I've got to say that I wasn't sure then, nor am I now, that his suffering and probable death were worth it.

WITH THE CLANDESTINE RESISTANCE

When Lucio Cabañas ended his convalescence in Mexico City and returned to the Sierra de Atoyac, he resumed leadership of the Brigada Campesina de Ajusticiamiento and faced a host of internal and external problems. Through his authoritarian and sectarian ways, Carmelo Cortés had lost the confidence of many people among the villages of the Sierra. The fashion in which he carried out his tasks and his disciplinary measures against several compañeros had generated considerable discontent within the Brigade. For example, he ordered that nobody could get married in the church within the zone of influence of the Brigade. Instead, revolutionary authority—that is, he himself—would perform marriages. He sowed discord within the Brigade, taking advantage of his position to steal away the girl friend of another compañero. He set up a dogmatic, voluntaristic, petty-bourgeois disciplinary system that he applied by the book to peasants. For them, this had nothing remotely to do with fighting against the bad government. Lucio punished Carmelo by removing him from the Brigade and shipping him off to us in the Federal District. We were to get him settled among the people where he could live with his compañera and learn from the humble. In addition, we had to find him a trustworthy dentist for his dental problems.

We fulfilled these tasks diligently. We set Carmelo up in a rented room in the Santa Clara neighborhood in the state of Mexico where our compañeros among the inhabitants helped him every day. We ferried him to the dentist as often as necessary, each trip putting ourselves at considerable risk since Carmelo (along with Carlos Ceballos) was an escapee from the Chilpancingo jail. The army as well as both state and federal police forces were looking for him. The Organization took good care of him, even catering to his whim to have white gold fillings in his front teeth: a rather extravagant wish for a proletarian revolutionary, I thought; the habits of someone from the southeastern coast, explained the understanding Dionisio. Some of these tasks fell to me, in particular stopping in often to see how Carmelo was doing, scheduling his dental appointments, and taking him to and from the dentist.

During one of these occasions, Carmelo related to me how he and Carlos Ceballos ("Julián") managed to escape from the Chilpancingo jail by boring a hole in the wall of their cell. They were under arrest for having robbed a bank in the port of Acapulco. Every day the two covered the noise made by their rudimentary tools by playing records of popular songs from the Mexican Revolution. They hid the deepening hole in the wall behind a poster of Emiliano Zapata. Finally they managed to flee one night in the midst of a fierce thunderstorm, but not without a moment of tragicomedy. Following Carmelo out through the hole, the somewhat more robust Carlos Ceballos got stuck. Carmelo Cortés recounted to me how he took advantage of the moment to give Carlos a hard time, teasing him that he'd have to leave him trapped there since he couldn't risk being discovered and jailed anew. In the end, Carmelo pulled and pulled Carlos by his arms, placing his own feet against the wall of the jail. At last Carlos squeezed through the hole, and both men took right off for the mountains that surround the city of Chilpancingo. Two or three days later they made contact with some members of the Partido de los Pobres, who helped them rejoin the Brigada de Ajusticiamiento in the Sierra of Atoyac.

Another time I brought Carmelo a document from the Ho Chi Minh peasant section of the Liga Comunista Espartaco for the purpose of initiating a revolutionary critique of its political and ideological errors along the lines of the Chinese Cultural Revolution. The document also criticized the mistaken leadership of the Political Commission of the Central Committee and the actions of the rest of the Espartaquista militants during the popular student movement of 1968. I was convinced that the document was good and naively thought that it would appeal to Carmelo, helping him understand better both his situation and the nature of the tasks facing the revolutionary movement in the future. Instead, I received from Carmelo a demonstration of arrogance, sectarian disdain, hostility, and disrespect. He brought us to the brink of telling each other to fuck off. I restrained myself, not wanting to put this all on my head alone. Besides, Carmelo was packing a powerful Colt .38 Special, and I had nothing. I simply urged respect for me and the organization that was sheltering him.

I had to deal with Carmelo on two other occasions. One day he announced his desire to return to Guerrero and requested help getting back to Acapulco. In vain, I reminded him that Lucio had sent him to us as a punishment that had not yet been lifted. Since we could not hold him against his will and were unable to communicate with Lucio right away, Dionisio and Isauro decided that it was best that we help Carmelo get back. So early one morning I went to pick him up along with his compañera. Carmelo appeared dressed from head to toe in white. He really looked good, even elegant, although a bit flamboyant. He hadn't missed a detail—even his moccasins and his socks were white as was as his belt. Every stitch of clothing was new. I thought that if he wanted to attract attention, this was certainly the way to do it. His compañera was more naturally dressed in informal clothing appropriate for Acapulco.

Carmelo's partner was light-skinned, with blond hair and refined manners. I had gotten to know her before when the compañeros of Santa Clara under the direction of "Juan" had organized some meetings with the people of Octavio Márquez Vázquez, known as "César" and head of the MAR during this period. At these meetings, we learned some of the rudiments of Korean martial arts, exchanged experiences, and undertook excursions into the hills surrounding Xalostoc and Santa Clara. Our hikes served as tactical explorations that furthered our physical, ideological, and political preparation. The young woman was agreeable, somewhat naive, but not significantly more so than many of the rest of us attending these meetings of afternoon revolutionary conspiracy. I sort of remember that she spoke about problems at home. It was evident that she came from an upper-middle class family. She behaved normally with me during her time in Santa Clara and even on the trip to

Acapulco. But months later, when Isauro and I kept an appointment with Carmelo in Acapulco, she treated us with cold disdain. She was simply another person. Carmelo let us know that he didn't want anything more to do with us—in truth, much to Isauro's relief and mine—and we broke off connections with him. Assuming a radical, voluntaristic, and sectarian stance, he was engaged in setting up the FAR, a group of his own in opposition to the Partido de los Pobres. In a public document Lucio issued a call to all those in Acapulco, the Costa Grande, and the Costa Chica who wanted to create their own insignificant groups at the expense of militancy in the Partido de los Pobres. The true struggle had not yet begun, yet these tiny groups split over and over. Denunciations and proclamations flew over who was more revolutionary than the others. We never saw Carmelo again. Sometime later rumors circulated that his group had kidnapped a wealthy Lebanese woman from Acapulco named Margarita Saad, whom they ended up atrociously strangling to death. One version had it that the strangler was none other than Carmelo's compañera, the young woman of delicate features and educated manners from the meetings with the MAR on the outskirts of Santa Clara. But years later I found out that José Arturo Gallegos Nájera assumed responsibility for having strangled Saad with an electric cord.

In the end, the government killed Carmelo Cortés in Mexico City. According to the police and army versions that appeared in the newspapers, he died during a confrontation in the parking area of the Sears store on Ejército Nacional Avenue. Carmelo had stopped by to pick up some glasses, and apparently the optometrist had recognized him and informed authorities. Nevertheless, others maintained that he'd died under torture, and that his body had been dumped at this location. The eyeglass version of the story doesn't strike me as ridiculous if we remember just how vain Carmelo was.

I had an interview with Isauro for the first time because of my problems with "El Indio" and his compañera "Leticia" in the town of Atlatongo in the state of Mexico near San Martín de las Pirámides. He listened to my complaints and made the decision to bring me into the work that he and Dionisio had undertaken in the state of Morelos and in the south of the state of Puebla. Both were in charge of the Ho Chi Minh peasant section of the Liga Comunista Espartaco, composed in particular of former members of the Partido Agrario Obrero Morelense of Rubén Jaramillo in the uplands of Morelos and in southern Puebla in the region of the Atencingo sugar mill. Both were the principal figures behind the document that had demolished the political leadership of the LCE that I referred to earlier in my discussion of Carmelo Cortés. The sectarianism of El Indio had made me the victim of his hostility. According to him, everything that I did or said was bourgeois. No matter that I had put my time and automobile to the service of the Organization. For example, I traveled to Atlatongo very early in the morning on weekdays, putting my own job at risk in order to take a nephew of "Felipe," our principal contact in the area, to an emergency hospital in La Villa after he severely fractured his leg. Following his medical treatment, I returned him back home. I then had to race my Opel at high speed to my job as a radio producer in the offices of the Rural Productivity Program at the street corner of Río Nazas and Río Rhin in Colonia Cuauhtémoc in Mexico City. I would get there around 12:30, my heart beating wildly at arriving so late. During the several weeks this went on, El Indio never once condescended to accompany me, the supposed bourgeois, even though he had enough free time to do so.

A former political prisoner of the popular student movement of 1968, El Indio had studied philosophy at the UNAM. He was committed to securing a job as a rail worker for the Ferrocarriles Nacionales de México where the LCE had a sectional cell. El Indio wanted to keep faith with the Maoist slogans of "serving the people" and "be like the people, uniting with them." It didn't seem to me a bad idea. In fact, the example of El Indio attracted me a great deal, and I wanted to engage in something similar. Nevertheless, from the start he prejudged me and always demonstrated a negative attitude toward me, perhaps because of my social origins, my ownership of an automobile, or my ways of interpreting socialism. For example, I remember one incident when we went to harvest corn with Felipe on his plot of land. The operation obliged us to cut the stocks and to carry them to a site where they were being piled up. Obviously, this was a task that none of us had ever undertaken before, a tough and tiring job under the heavy rays of the sun. We helped out until lunch, when we took advantage of the hour to excuse ourselves and to say goodbye, our faces reddened from the sun. I made a comment about how good it would be to live in a socialist society where everything would be fully mechanized, and there would be no need to suffer the physical burden of manual labor. I never should have said it. El Indio accused me of being bourgeois. He launched into an immediate justification of manual labor and personal suffering as the only route to human happiness and the only means of undoing human alienation. I replied that Marx and Engels conceived of socialism and communism as the culmination of a technologically advanced capitalist society. Because they had skipped stages of development, Russian and Chinese socialism had consequently, I argued, not been able to attain the civilizational stage envisioned by the two German thinkers.

Another time El Indio informed me that compañero Felipe was engaged in dubious activities, having done some business with the rich man of the town, a man that El Indio characterized as a cacique. This news surprised me in my naïveté. Felipe was a worker who had participated in a reform labor union movement in Sanitarios El Aguila, under the direction of Armando Castillejos, the labor lawyer. Over the years he'd been in contact with militants of left-wing organizations like us, listening to ideological raps and receiving all sorts of printed propaganda. I had brought Chinese picture magazines to his house, an action that El Indio, of course, disapproved of. For some reason I inspired some sympathy in Felipe, perhaps even respect. I took it upon myself to scold him for his attitude toward the rich man of the town. I was astonished when a very annoyed Felipe rejected the accusation: "It's not true; I've always been in the opposition. I've always been for the PAN."

Felipe's departure confirmed my suspicion that we were committing ideological and political mistakes with these good people; what's more, we were wasting time. The economic, political, and social condition of Felipe and his family was far from being that of a poor peasant or a proletarian. Our Felipe owned two or three cows and sold most of their milk, about eight to ten liters per animal each day. He also cultivated alfalfa on the two hectares he was entitled to use as an *ejidatario*, using some for his cows and selling the rest. He harvested fruit from the family orchard (I recall some wonderfully sweet *capulines*). Felipe also raised sheep, turkeys, hens, and some pigeons; in addition, he was a salaried worker at a foundry. Obviously he had problems and lacked many things as did millions of Mexicans! But, all in all, he had it pretty good.

At a personal level, Felipe and his relatives were fine people, very straightforward, hardworking, and loyal in their friendship. However, we had other purposes, not quite those of cultivating close personal relationships. We were there in order to organize cells for both open and subversive forms of political action. We took advantage of the needs of people in order to influence their thinking and to move them toward organized actions already decided upon by the heads of the Organization. Our unacknowledged goals required that we gain their confidence. So we provided them with doctors and medicines, used clothing, rides, books, pamphlets, and magazines. We gave classes in knitting and embroidering. We even brought unskilled labor—our own—to some of the tasks of the peasantry, etc. El Indio followed the tactic of blending into the background as much as possible, toning down political and ideological content in our dealings with folks. His only goal was to win their confidence without revealing what was really going on. Paradoxically, the behavior of El Indio was that of a *ladino*.

While I may run the risk of being misunderstood, I want to contrast this style of working with another that I came to know during these years, one that took place in Huetamo, Michoacán, deep in the hot country. I traveled there to get to know a radio show run by Sister Gabriela, a nun in the Servants of the

Immaculate Conception involved in producing and broadcasting programs with a social and religious bent in this region. She'd sought me out for some technical assistance, a mutual friend having told her about a show I produced for the Rural Program of the National Productivity Center that was broadcast throughout the Bajío. There on the outskirts of town where it was forty degrees centigrade in the shade, I got to witness these nuns in action among the peasants. I then understood the attitude of "solicitude" that Mao Tse-tung said we should demonstrate among the people. These nuns dedicated themselves entirely to the people, without any hidden agenda, without trying to blend into the background, with sincerity, and with a passion for assistance "without any thought for themselves," even putting their lives at risk. This ought to be our style of work, I enthusiastically told myself as I drove a Volkswagen from my office around the outskirts of Ciudad Altamirano after I'd returned to the Federal District. With me was Manlio Tirado, the star and sole reporter of the radio program that we produced. Manlio was the brother of the famous *comandante mexicano* of the Sandinista National Liberation Front in Nicaragua.

If we're considering styles of work, we ought to describe "Rafael." Like El Indio, he was a former political prisoner, not from 1968, but from 1969, who had been a primary school teacher and was, like his brother Dionisio, from Guerrero. Once released from Lecumberri, he joined the Atlatongo group despite the displeasure of El Indio and his compañera Leticia. Along with Rafael came Marcela, also a teacher and somewhat older, her two children from a previous relationship—a boy and a girl—and their own baby. Rafael possessed a direct and expressive personality, outgoing and outspoken. He always exercised leadership, proving both persuasive and attentive to detail. Rafael brought with him the super-Maoist attitude characteristic of the *Red Book*, the newspaper *Pekín Informa*, and the magazines *China Illustrated* and *China Reconstructs*. He possessed a certain petulance that he'd acquired in Argentina, a country that he'd visited under a teaching scholarship. There he'd also become fond of compañera Evita, whom he admired for her popularity and continued presence in the hearts of Argentine working people. Rafael could not satisfy his desire for leadership with El Indio and Leticia, both of whom he'd known, dealt with, and confronted in Lecumberri. So instead he exercised his passion for being in charge with me and with my wife Tere, who during this time yielded to my insistence that she accompany me. We accepted this for a while. Not wasting a minute, Rafael began to establish new contacts in Atlatongo and surrounding areas, something positive that expanded our radius of operation. However, the conflict of personalities, dogmatic behavior, exclusive work styles, vanity, and political jealousies soon created great friction among us, notwithstanding our frequent reading of Mao's *On the Correct Handling of Contradictions among the People.*

El Indio, Leticia, and the rest of their companions refused to go out to the town or to return to the city in my car. We usually journeyed to Atlatongo on Sunday afternoons. Things always took a while, and we often made our trip back to the Federal District at night. So when El Indio and his compañera ostensibly decided to return by bus, this formed a clear line of division with those of us who came and went by car, not to mention making it unlikely that they'd get home before midnight even if they could get a bus right away. I ought to add that Leticia traveled with her newborn son in her arms wrapped in a *rebozo*, a badge of her popular outlook. This whole situation unfolded before the astonished eyes of our compañero Felipe and his family. They couldn't understand what was going on among us. They had certainly seen how useful having an automobile at your disposition could be for the rapid and timely movement of anyone sick. They also realized the convenience of not risking yourself on the roads at night. The reaction of El Indio was irrational and sectarian, lacking in comradeship and solidarity. Most likely one of El Indio's motivations derived from the fact that both Marcela and Tere, simply and naturally, had known how to awaken sympathy among the women of Felipe's family by finding points of contact and conversation. For example, they knitted or embroidered with them, activities that Leticia was not good at. In spite of the determination with which she approached her relationship with the community, Leticia's bearing was more that of someone of university background.

To tell the truth, we had our failings at times as well. One morning Rafael suggested that we visit a *ranchería* near Atlatongo. I can't remember if he had set up a contact with someone or whether we were just going to get to know the place and strike up a relationship with anyone around who seemed willing. In any case, on our way back we had a flat tire. I had to change it and naturally ended up rather dirty with the dust of the road all over my hands and face. We hadn't been back on the road before long when we came upon a stream. With great relief, I pulled the car over to wash my face and hands. Rafael went nuts, going on and on about how I should not clean up and should avoid all such "bourgeois impulses." I ignored him, getting out of the car and washing up. But this episode brought a break between his dogmatic authoritarianism and my unwillingness to submit to him. Our relationship could no longer be the same.

Of course, I was not exempt from this sort of foolishness. I recognized no truth other than my own views. I didn't even try to convince Tere; I just imposed my will in everything. I used the slightest opportunity even to indoctrinate my little daughter Teresita. I read to her all sorts of bad Chinese or Russian literature that happened to fall into my hands. I scolded her every time she appeared to ask something of the maid who performed the domestic chores in our house or of those working in the homes of our relatives. I repeated to the point of exhaustion—her exhaustion, naturally—how important it was not to leave any morsels of food on her plate. She ought to think of the millions of boys and girls who had nothing to eat. For a long time, I refused to have a TV in the house, even though all her cousins and schoolmates had one. In short, I felt myself imbued with the truth, with an historic mission; those who thought otherwise were simply mistaken or inferior.

Paradoxically, it fell to Rafael to make me realize one aspect of my irrationality. One day I invited him home, and it occurred to me to show him the wall of my bedroom where I'd hung a gallery of portraits of Mao Tse-tung cut out of Chinese magazines—Mao the young student, Mao heading the Long March, Mao in Yenan constructing the Red Army, Mao on the stand in Tiananmen Square reviewing the Red Guards—in all, a display of the cult of personality. Poking fun of me, Rafael genuflected in front of the wall and made the sign of the cross. Red with embarrassment, I realized my mistake. Nevertheless, I didn't remove the pictures right away. In truth, I liked looking at them and found it hard to imagine the bare wall without the presence of the Great Helmsman, the Red Sun of our hearts, there to lead us in waves of successive masses of people to the triumph of socialism and communism in Mexico and the rest of the world, as in the very beautiful painting by Augusto Ramírez, the quite famous *Zum*.

AN ETERNAL THREE DAYS IN THE CELLS

I had just begun an early afternoon nap when the Halcón who disliked me spoke. He told me to get up, leave the cell, and take my quilt with me. I complied immediately and abandoned the cell for the corridor where I stood looking forward toward the stairs. At the head of the hall sat a person in one of the school desk-chairs. He wore pistachio-colored pajamas and seemed quite pale. I had no difficulty in recognizing him despite having seen him only once briefly when I went with Juan, my new connection with Dionisio and Isauro, when he interviewed this person outside the Xola metro station in Mexico City. The thin young man was a member of the Organización Partidaria (Liga Comunista 23 de Septiembre) who asked Juan to provide a place for the night for a pair of his compañeros who had been urgently obliged to flee their safe house. My presence proved fortuitous. Right off Juan asked me for my help with the two. Once I accepted, the young man walked off in search of his compañeros. He and Juan left them with me. I put them in my car, asking them to keep their eyes closed until I said it was okay to open them. We went to my house in the Colonia Jardín Balbuena, where I introduced them to my wife, and we ate supper.

The male was a thin man, about thirty-five years of age with intellectual airs. He insisted in discussing the political issues that seemed paramount at that time in his organization with Tere and me. The couple must have assumed that we belonged to the same group. I opted to let them know that we intended only that they spent a safe and secure night in my house. Pretending that I had to get up early to go to work, I suggested that we get some sleep; we gave them one of the three bedrooms of the house for their use. Very early the next morning, I heard them in the kitchen washing the dishes from the night before. I invited them to stay for breakfast, but they claimed to have an appointment that could not be put off and asked if I wouldn't take them to the nearest Metro station. As we said goodbye at the subway, they left me with a document that the man had written entitled *In the Light of This History of Battles*. Years later, when reading through and getting to know the first-hand testimonies of members of these groups written in their own words, a suspicion entered my mind. Without having the faintest idea who he was, I had given shelter in my house to none other than the famous *Viejo*, Rodolfo Gómez García of the Liga Comunista 23 de Septiembre.

To return for a moment to the arrival of Wenceslao José García ("Chilo" or "Sam") in the basement of the Campo Militar Número Uno, the annoying Halcón placed me in the cell closest to the beginning of the hallway and lodged the new arrival way at the opposite end. They wanted to keep Wenceslao well away from any of the rest of us. The newcomer evidently was recuperating from some sort of surgery. He walked slowly, with short steps and expressions of pain on his barely bearded face. A short time later they brought him a mattress too large for his cell. The Halcones appeared tense and worried, making constant trips up and down the corridor and stopping for a while in front of Wenceslao's cell to ask him one thing or another. Shortly thereafter a paramedic uniformed in white arrived with a medical bag in his right hand. He spent a time treating Wenceslao, and from his comments it seemed as if he had administered several injections. I began to wonder if Wenceslao's conditions didn't have something to do with a news report that I'd managed to hear on the radio a few days before due to sloppiness on the part of our custodians. The item concerned a shootout and police chase in the area of the Parque Hundido near the Liverpool department store at Insurgentes Sur and Félix Cuevas. Under the cover of night, we tried to find out who the new prisoner was, and what had happened, but Wenceslao remained quite reserved.

He did confirm that he'd been involved in the Parque Hundido incident. A burst of machine gun fire had brought him down, wounding him several times in the abdomen. He'd received treatment at the Central Military Hospital, a facility that was quite nearby, he said. Apparently they had removed a few centimeters of his intestines. Wenceslao spent the night complaining of the pain from his wounds, while Jacobo, Noé, and I remained awake, worried about his delicate condition.

The next day the feds came to look for him, producing a great racket as they descended the stairs. I lay on the floor, wrapped in my quilt with my head toward the door of the cell. When all the noise awakened me, I raised my head, and I thought I saw Miguel Nazar Haro pass by at the head of a group invading the place. Amid insults and shouts, they ordered us to place our backs to the hallway. Uncontrollably, my body shook from head to foot. They had turned off the radio, and it wasn't long before we heard first muffled moaning and then genuine howls emanating from the depths of our tortured compañero. This savage session lasted around two hours. My mouth was dry and bitter tasting. I broke out in a cold sweat, and a great angst gripped my stomach. We could hardly breathe. Nothing sounded in the corridor or in the cells. Even the two Halcones on guard were tense and uncomfortable. At one moment, Wenceslao's cries became especially terrible, and then an ominous silence followed. A few of the agents emerged from the interrogation room, and I overheard them ask the Halcones for soap to wash their hands. I imagined them covered with blood, and Wenceslao destroyed as a result of the barbarities that these wretches had inflicted upon him. One agent ascended the stairs and returned a moment later with a doctor who continued to protest the prisoner's transfer and torture when his condition was so delicate. I imagine that one of them brought a stretcher because I heard another remark about "positioning him carefully." Soon I listened to their efforts to get up the stairs. Wenceslao's cries had been so intensely strong during his interrogation that his subsequent absolute silence convinced me that the feds were faking it, and that in reality they had gone overboard and killed him.

In the hours and days that followed, we were jolted into one shudder after another. The soldiers and the federal security agents constantly brought young people for interrogation in the habitual manner. I was able to exchange a few words with one of them because they put him in the cell adjacent to mine. The kid was very scared, but he still confirmed for my benefit that all of them had been connected with Wenceslao and the shootout in Parque Hundido. He also confirmed that they were from the state of Oaxaca. The episodes lasted only three days, but they seemed eternal. Then these detainees were taken just as they had been brought in, and I never knew anything more about them again.

TRAINING AS A MILITANT

Juan, the compañero who had put me briefly in touch with Wenceslao the first time, was my second contact with the members of the tendency headed by Dionisio and Isauro. He was a youth of twenty-three who proudly referred to himself as a worker, although in reality he was a service employee of a governmental unit. Tall and somewhat brawny, dark-skinned and round faced, he expressed much with his somewhat round, middle-sized eyes. In his speech one could detect the strong influence that Dionisio's personality and mode of expression exerted upon him. Just the same, he had his own touch. When he spoke, an oblique half smile inched over his face, party uncovering his strong set of teeth. The smile could mistakenly give the impression of irony, but in reality it could express contentment, surprise, or anger. Usually he had a mysterious, conspiratorial air about him, and he always seemed to be in a hurry, claiming the fulfillment of obligations all over the city. However, I didn't mind acting under his orders since I sought to guide my participation by the Maoist slogan of "to learn from the working class," and thus I tended to see him in idealized terms, a rather frequent weakness with me.

Juan was the one who took me to Santa Clara to link up with don Jesús and "Filomeno" and the rest of the proletarian compañeros of that area. Rather rapidly I got involved in their tasks and problems, gaining their acceptance, or so I think, soon after my arrival. Don Jesús and Filomeno were workers who had participated in union reform movements. Like Felipe from Atlatongo, they had taken part in the labor struggles at the El Anfora factory. Afterwards, they had remained in touch with some left-wing militants whom they had gotten to know during the preparations for the strike. Dionisio knew how to take advantage of these old *Espartaquista* ties conscientiously, developing effective political work with these men. As a result of his activities in Santa Clara, everyone loved and respected him; even more importantly, they paid attention to him. Juan was the person in charge of the day-to-day political work in the area. He too had gained the confidence of young and old alike. A short while after I began to get involved with them, they invited me to participate in some mysterious meetings with people from another organization. Lowering his voice and opening his eyes wide, Juan informed me that "they are much more advanced than we are and are serious." He said that the meetings took place during the afternoon on some plots of land on the outskirts of Santa Clara, a spot relatively well hidden from the indiscreet gaze of others who might chance by.

They proved to be militants of the MAR who had received instruction in combat tactics and techniques in North Korea. They were teaching the compañeros the rudiments of Korean karate. I joined in these practice sessions and began to learn the basic movements of attack and defense. The chief instructor was a young man of twenty-five, certainly an expert in what he taught, who moved with extraordinary agility and skill. Apparently he was one of the best leadership elements in the MAR and an individual very much sought after by the army and political police. I suspect that he was the person known as "El Marino."

In order to make these practice sessions, I had to skip out from work before the office closed, take at the corner a bus from the Juárez-Loreto line that left me at Insurgentes Centro and Sullivan, in front of the Mothers' Monument. There I jumped aboard a Bellas Artes-Lindavista bus which carried me to a spot north of the city about the same level as the Basilica of Guadalupe. I would then board a third bus heading to Xalostoc and Santa Clara in the state of Mexico. I had to cross Santa Clara completely and head out into the countryside, walking rapidly toward the place of our training. All of these complications for my quick arrival—forty-five minutes—stemmed from a guilty eagerness to proletarianize myself and to provide an unsolicited demonstration of revolutionary political decisiveness in the face of El Indio's accusations of my petty-bourgeois behavior. I placed my car at the service of the group for its eventual use by Dionisio in carrying out his assigned tasks in the states of Morelos and Puebla.

I'd done the same thing shortly before with my 125 cubic centimeter Yamaha motorcycle. I lent it first for the scouting out phase of a job undertaken by the people of MAR at the request of compañero "Benito," a Yalatecan Indian from Oaxaca and leader of his community who was famous within the *Espartaquista* ranks for his radicalism and toughness. When they returned the motorcycle to me some days later, I gave it to the Organization to be sold as a precautionary measure since I had no idea what the *marinos* had been up to with it. The family of a teacher compañero known as "El Hippie" was charged with its sale, but some fake buyers ended up robbing the bike by pretending that they wanted to try it out on the street.

One afternoon El Indio showed up at the training location. Our surprise and disgust at bumping into one another was mutual. Nevertheless, neither of us said anything. But it wasn't long before El Indio took the initiative against me by asking for a meeting with César and all of the participants. During the gathering, he discredited the poor quality instruction in personal defense that we had been given, comparing it with the education given by members of the Mexican Pentathlon at the Monument to the Revolution. They practiced falling on asphalt, not on grass as we did. In his view, everything we were up to was a waste of time. Then he lit into my presence there and accused me in particular of having abandoned the work in Atlatongo. El Indio then told César that the North Korean training had been an error, an insulting mistake on his part that couldn't go without a response. César replied to El Indio that he was off base and even came to my defense. I also spoke and made it clear that I had left Atlatongo on Isauro's instructions and because of El Indio's sectarian attitude. El Indio withdrew and never showed his face there again. Wherever he went, he instigated these sorts of difficulties. Many in the Organization considered him closed off and unapproachable.

Besides the personal defense practice, the Santa Clara compañeros organized excursions to the Sierra of Guadalupe surrounding the town, as part of preliminary training for future, more serious climbing. We hiked to the peaks of the tallest mountains, Tlalayote and Madroño, where *tejocote* trees grew abundantly. They produced the most fragrant and delicious fruit, similar in color and size to small apples. We would gather them and eat them with delight. As we climbed, we would also cut the tenderest leaves of the *nopal* cactus and later in the day grill them inside *maguey* stalks on the embers of a campfire. The Santa Clara compañeros always had enough tortillas, chiles, and avocados with them, so that when everything was put together we had a true country feast. From the heights we could look down at the Sosa Texcoco Company's spiral-shaped plant, a producer of spirulina algae, as it reflected the solar brightness of the day. At the end of one such afternoon, full of crimson clouds to the west, I remember looking over the valley, suddenly and feverishly engrossed in myself. I stood at the summit of the Ehécatl Mountain, so named for the Aztec god of the wind, with my back to the Picacho and Santa Cruz peaks. In my vivid fantasy, I saw an army of young guerrilla fighters, like a swarm of bees, attacking the armed forces of reaction and imperialism at strategic points of the periphery of the great Mexican city, a military offensive similar to the Vietnamese Tet. All of this, I am sure, was a great excess.

Another time we decided to come down from the hills by a different pathway, a longer one known only to the Santa Clara guys, which led directly into the town of San Cristóbal Ecatepec. As we came down a slope that terminated in pastures covering the broad foothills, much to our surprise we discovered that our leaders had placed us smack in the middle of a herd of ferocious cattle. The bulls stared at us with apprehension, raising the powerful armor of their heads to follow our every move as we hurried downward. In the group led by César was "Angela," apparently his partner. Later I learned she was the daughter of one of the most important members of the group of Professor Arturo Gámiz García. Both Angela's father and the professor had been killed in the September 23, 1965 attack on the military headquarters at Ciudad

Madera in Chihuahua. Also with us was "Yolanda," the young woman later to become Carmelo Cortés' partner after he snatched her away from "Eduardo" from the MAR. Eduardo spent a while in the Brigada Campesina de Ajusticiamiento learning and teaching. In one of our excursions, Yolanda proudly announced that she would no longer be coming to the meetings since she planned to join Eduardo up in the mountains. I never met Eduardo. He'd been with the Santa Clara group, but he'd headed up into the Sierra of Guerrero before my arrival.

In addition to the excursions, we also shared another activity with the people from MAR, a weekly Saturday afternoon meeting with a group of young Yalalteca textile workers from Oaxaca, whom we had met through compañero Benito. Economic necessity along with social and political pressures had expelled them from their communities. They had migrated to the Federal District in search of a future, finding employment in the textile industry. As one might guess, they lacked any formal education or political training and had only a rudimentary industrial experience. Most likely they only agreed to meet with us because Benito had asked them to. As a rural teacher, he had the personal attributes and political and social prestige in their eyes required for his authority to have weight. Since these fellows from Oaxaca were mere apprentices in their trade, complete understanding between them and our group proved difficult. Angela always participated in these meetings as a representative of the *marineros*. She was short, shapely, and fairly attractive. It was pleasant to hear her speak with her *norteño* accent. She always projected a sense of warmth and camaraderie. In one of our uphill hikes, we were surprised by a forceful sudden shower. Her wet white blouse revealed a brassiere hardly able to contain her big, firm breasts. César was with us on that occasion, and I remember feeling envious when in jest he leered at Angela as she removed her blouse and put on the pullover that had been tied to her waist.

Tere came with me to our last meeting with the Yalaltecas during the time when I was trying to incorporate her in my political activity. At the end of the meeting, Angela asked me for a ride so that she could keep a nearby appointment. She also said she needed to talk to me confidentially. The request placed me in an awkward position with Tere, but I decided to take the risk and to ask my wife to wait with the Yalaltecas while I drove Angela to her destination. On the way, Angela told me that this would be the last time we would see each other. She was being sent elsewhere, implying that she would be up in the mountains, but not in the state of Guerrero. When we came to the place of her appointment, I had the distinct impression that she wanted to make this farewell something very personal and expected the same reaction from me. Truly, she was so warm and seductive that I was tempted to initiate some kind of physical contact. But I remained conscious of Tere waiting for me. I didn't want to betray her and look for difficulties in our marriage. Nor did I want any trouble with César, something that could unleash political problems along with real personal danger for me.

LIFE WITH LUCIO

In the summer of 1973, when I was host to Lucio Cabañas, I took him to one of the customary meetings with the Yalaltecas, without letting them know his identity. I remember that Lucio remained silent during the discussions we had. The workers described their problems in the factory and their difficult relationship with the leadership of their sweetheart union. Near the close of the meeting, Lucio asked for permission to talk and then gave a speech about the need for poor people to organize in order to create a just and humane society. He encouraged the workers to persevere in their efforts to remain united and to keep their fighting spirit alive. As he spoke, I realized how difficult it was for him not to reveal his identity. He talked about the struggle in the Mexican countryside and in the southern mountains, depicting the living conditions of many poor Mexicans like them and their reasons for armed rebellion against the bad government. The Yalalteca compañeros listened very carefully, sitting stiffly. I never found out what they thought about Lucio's comments or what they understood from his words. On the way back home in the car, Lucio confessed he didn't know what to make of the industrial workers' problems. From the perspective of the Brigade and the armed guerrilla struggle in the fields, he wasn't sure how to approach them or their battle.

The first time I drove a car for Lucio Cabañas we journeyed to the city of Durango. I had joined Dionisio, who had gone to meet him somewhere near Nuevo Atzacoalco. Dionisio had told me only that they needed a car and a driver to take a member of the Partido de los Pobres somewhere in the Republic. I must confess I suspected who needed transportation, since Juan had revealed to me that Miguel—Lucio's pseudonym—was around, lowering his voice and looking even more conspiratorial than usual. We met Lucio and his buddy Gorgonio at a corner near the house where he was lodging. Once I had been introduced, Dionisio left me with them to make our arrangements for the trip. Lucio said then that he needed to go to Durango and recommended that we leave the next day. I said that was fine with me, but that I needed to know whether they would be armed, so that I could be prepared. I didn't want to be in the midst of a shoot-out without having at least some means of defending myself. But as I have already said, Lucio indicated that they would not carry arms. I breathed a sigh of relief. The next morning I picked them up at a location close to where they had spent the night. I drove a Volkswagen lent to me by a couple of anthropologists. The car was fairly new, and we made the trip to Durango very quickly without any trouble. I don't remember anything on the way north other than my own sense of pride and complacency at the good fortune of being able to help Lucio Cabañas and to know him closely.

As is widely known, Lucio Cabañas was transferred by the Ministry of Public Education from Atoyac de Alvarez, in Guerrero, to Nombre de Dios, in Durango. The transfer constituted a reprisal by the state governor Raimundo Abarca Alarcón for Lucio's leadership of the parents' association in its struggle against the principal of the Modesto Alarcón Federal School, Genara Reséndiz de Serafín, and the coffee growing caciques who supported her. The months he spent in Durango allowed Lucio to make contact with some of the reformist and revolutionary activists of the state. As soon as we arrived in the city, we went directly to the house of a local veteran of past social campaigns. A professional educator, this man was now getting on in years. Along with his wife and other relatives, he received Lucio and his unknown companions with enthusiastic and generous hospitality. They immediately shared their food with us and gave us a bedroom for the night with a double bed and a cot. Gorgonio did not take more than three seconds to announce that he would sleep on the cot. Already he was sitting on it. His rapid reaction left Lucio and me visibly uncomfortable.

Lucio would not let anyone best him again, so he quickly chose the free side of the bed. I had to lie down on my belly, with my head against the wall, clinging to it despite my fear of the notorious Durango scorpions. Near dawn, I was awakened by several blows on my legs. I half rose, wondering what the matter was. I realized that I was still curled up in my corner. It would have been impossible for me to have hit Lucio unwittingly, provoking a violent retaliation on his part against my legs. Only then did I observe that Lucio remained profoundly asleep, moving his arms in the midst of a nightmare. As I dropped back asleep, I wondered whether Gorgonio had grabbed the cot so fast because he knew what would come later.

Very early the next morning our host left the house, looking for a person with whom Lucio needed to talk. A while later in the middle of a very good breakfast that the lady of the house had kindly prepared for us, her husband returned with the man. He was thin, light-skinned, with light colored eyes and brown-grayish hair; he must have been about thirty-five years old. He sported a big handlebar mustache and had the air of being an intellectual. Lucio and this "Alejandro" greeted each other effusively and talked separately for a long time. Later, close to noon, Lucio asked Alejandro to come along with us in the car and guide us to some locations in Nombre de Dios. On the way Lucio told us about his experiences in the struggle and his life in that small town. That was how I found out that he had been romantically involved with a woman here, and that one of the purposes of our journey included stopping by the house where she had lived. The trip took only two hours. Once we got back to the professor's house, Lucio and Alejandro spoke together for another half an hour, and then our visitor left hurriedly.

Lucio now conversed with the professor again while Gorgonio and I remained near the entrance of the house by the carport. After a short while the bell rang. Situated practically by the door, I foolishly opened it without thinking. While Gorgonio and I stood there startled, a half dozen unknown youth, with bright eyes and nervous breathing, rushed into the house. I was about to alert Lucio when I saw that Alejandro entered with them. He greeted me and offered a calming gesture. Far from accepting it, I complained to Gorgonio: "What the heck! Why is this guy bringing all of those people in here?"

Lucio welcomed them all in the bedroom that had been assigned to us. Once everyone was seated, he sent Gorgonio to let me know that he wanted me present there too. I complied, but in truth I was quite upset and worried about the extremely loose way that Lucio dealt with his own security—and also with ours and that of the host family. The six or seven young men belonged to the Frente Popular Independiente, involved in organizing the *precaristas* or squatters of the city of Durango and sustaining their readiness to fight, particularly over their housing demands. Alejandro appeared to be a teacher like Lucio, perhaps because he was from Guerrero and a member or former member of the Movimiento Revolucionario del Magisterio (PCM). During the meeting Lucio spoke about the Partido de los Pobres, the Brigada de Ajusticiamiento, and the struggle of the poor of Guerrero in the Sierra and along the coast. He indicated that from the mountains of the South they remained attentive to the struggles underway in Durango. They were convinced that soon it would be possible to coordinate everyone's efforts in order to launch a new revolution that would benefit the very poorest. Miguel did not reveal his identity as Lucio Cabañas, but it was evident that the young men knew or had a feeling of who he was. Their attitudes, a mixture of curiosity and rapture, made this clear. I thought that this circumstance rendered our presence there more dangerous. We'd have to hustle out of the city as soon as the meeting ended. To make things even worse, Lucio suddenly pointed me out as a representative of the Jaramillista movement that was growing and becoming more organized in the states of Morelos and Puebla as well as in the Federal District.

The meeting finished in a little while, and at last the group of young men left. Instantly I threw myself into convincing Gorgonio of the necessity of our departure without delay. Fortunately, he agreed, and we both let Lucio know what we thought. Our arguments were reasonable; both Lucio and the professor thought it wise for us to abandon Durango promptly. We got ready in an instant, offering our thanks for the family's hospitality and care. Once in the VW, we headed as fast as possible toward Mexico City. As I drove I kept my eyes on the rearview mirror in case a vehicle might be following us. I was concerned that the young men from the FPI had seen our automobile parked in the centrally-located carport of the house. During the early hours of the return trip I felt as if the police or the army were going to intercept us at any moment. Luckily I was mistaken. Nothing happened, but my fears were not groundless. Not long thereafter, we learned that only a couple of days after our precipitous departure, a powerful rumor about the presence of Lucio Cabañas circulated in Nombre de Dios and in the low income neighborhoods on the outskirts of the city of Durango.

A FLEETING HOPE

Days and days went by. The time since my arrival in the Campo Militar Número Uno weighed heavily on my spirit. I registered the despair that overwhelmed me in the hard to see spots of the various cells I occupied—vertical lines for days crossed by a horizontal line for each week. Right beside this marker of time I wrote my name and date of detention. My state of anguish caused me to imagine, whether awake or asleep, magical solutions to my confinement. More and more frequently as the weeks passed, I experienced strange and intense dreams when I napped after breakfast or after the mid-day dinner. These constituted a vital resource that enabled me to escape the tedium and the ever-present infernal sound of the radio. I dreamed of people who had previously been important in my life. One was Professor Vicente Carreón, sub-director and subsequently director of the Mexico City Secondary School and an English teacher for those beginning the language. I spent three years, from 1954 through 1956, at that school, which was located at the intersection of Campos Elíseos and Lamartine in the Polanco section of the capital. In my dream, a pack of military and Federal Security police tirelessly pursued me. I took refuge in the school, hiding from them in the director's office. There in a state of great agitation I asked Vicente Carreón for help, all the while explaining to him how I had gotten into this awful mess. It was the sort of vivid dream that makes it hard to determine whether or not it reflected actual events. I recall waking up in astonishment at having dreamed about Professor Carreón. He had long since disappeared from my memory. The passage of time and all my activities had caused this part of my adolescence to fade away.

Little by little as the hours went by, I brought back my recollection of a magnificent teacher, jovial and fun, who taught English quite well with his own personal method. Professor Carreón was a serious, brave, fair, and understanding man. Maybe that's why he returned to my memory at a time of great danger for me. His large, straight, well-formed nose and nearly perfect elliptical nostrils stood out in my mind.

My dreams suggested a search for an ideal father to aid me in this time of tribulation. Many times in these days I cried out to a God in whom I did not formally believe. I had surreptitiously picked up a sharp pebble from the floor near the water basin. In the moments in which desperation turned into prophetic ire, I used it to scratch, more than to write, distinct slogans on the painted walls of the cell foretelling the future historical punishment of my jailers and eventual executioners. I wrote sentences such as "Working people will unfailingly punish their hangmen" or "The interests of the people are certainly worth dying for." In truth, these words provided me with little consolation, and they failed to strengthen any confidence that at some point I'd be liberated from this clandestine prison.

In the midst of these moods, I recalled a very intense experience during my trip to Chihuahua with Jacobo and Héctor. As I drove the car along the interminable straight line northward, an extraordinarily strong desire to procreate a son with Tere came over me. This surprised me. For several years, in the name of my dedication to revolutionary duties, I had imposed my wish to limit ourselves to our daughter Teresita. The emotion of the idea of once again being a father ran through my entire body, producing a degree of happiness that was virtually euphoric. I promised myself that as soon as possible I would create the conditions to fulfill the call of being. I kept my state of internal exaltation to myself, saying nothing to my compañeros. I continued driving the Volkswagen at a good clip while intimately caressing my premonition of happiness at the side of this son who had begun to speak to me from an uncertain future. But all of this acted as nothing more than material for my memory and my dreams. The bars of the cell, the merciless volume of the radio, and the constant and tireless fear—those were the elements that defined my reality.

I heard two new prisoners speaking to each other, virtually yelling, in the first cells of the back corridor. At this point, I was locked up in the rear cell of this same hallway. I had heard the noise of their arrival, but I still had not seen them. They sounded strange, like nothing before that I'd heard in that place. One afternoon, one of the Halcones let me out to help him carry around the food tray. This offered me the chance to see them. They were two badly beaten, half-dressed individuals, with tattoos over their arms, chests, and shoulders and their heads shaven bald. At first I thought that they were soldiers, but once I heard them speak, I realized that they were lumpen, members of the urban underclass. Their presence seemed totally anomalous to me. What were these unfortunates doing in a clandestine military prison? Who had brought them here and why? What had they done? It didn't take me long to find out. Later at night I was able to ask them from my cell. They told me that they had broken into an automobile containing several boxes of explosives. The vehicle turned out to belong to an army officer. They'd been picked up at their cardboard and tin shacks on the outskirts of Chalco and brought to some barracks that contained stables. There the grunts had shaved them, beaten them as they hung from a beam, and dunked them nearly to the point of drowning in the troughs that the horses drank from. They inquired about where we were, who I was, and why I was held in detention. I explained things the best I could, but they couldn't understand the idea of a political prisoner or of a jail for guerrilla enemies of the government, although they did listen somewhat attentively as I explained the latter. They lasted only a couple of days. Early in the morning of their third day, a short officer with educated manners and an air of authority turned up. He wore a thick green military jacket with a hood, and his uniform bore neither tie nor insignia. He seemed alarmed at the presence of the two prisoners and ordered that they be removed immediately. The older of the two, who acted as the boss, reacted strongly when he heard several individuals coming to remove them from the cell and take them who knows where. He began to shout to his friend that younger one ought to take the blame for everything, and that he would later visit him in "the big house" to make things easier for him and to get him out fast. The unfortunate thieves believed that they would be taken before a judge. They had no comprehension of the dimensions of the mess they had gotten themselves into. Nor did they understand what these men who bound their hands and blindfolded their eyes could do to them.

Another episode in which civilians with no apparent connection to guerrilla activities were involved took place about a month, I think, after my detention. This time I didn't know how many people were placed in the cells along both hallways. I did manage to talk a bit at night to the one in the cell next to mine. He informed me that they had been detained for no reason at all while aboard a cattle truck traveling through a pass in the Ajusco. They had been searching for cattle for a *charreada* that they'd organized. That's what he told me. Obviously, I thought that he'd hidden from me what they'd really been up to, and why they were taken to a clandestine prison. But then he added that everything was under investigation, and that if the military police verified the truth of what they had said, they'd be able to go free. The conversation revealed that this guy and his companions were engaged in the sport of *charrería*. When I heard this, my heart skipped a beat. Various close relatives of my wife were also *charrería* enthusiasts. I took the leap of asking if he had heard of any of them. He replied that he knew one of my wife's uncles. I risked asking him, should they be set free, to make contact with this man so that he could inform Tere and my father that I was held in the Campo Militar Número Uno. It was a desperate and surely hopeless move on my part. It seemed highly unlikely that he'd want to look for more problems with the military. Awhile later they removed these prisoners from their cells and took them away. I begged the God I didn't believe in to make sure that this young man kept his promise to give word of my location. For at least a week I remained in a state of uncertainty. Then inadvertently I switched to another form of self-deception or distraction—the improbable idea of my formal processing before a judge.

LUCIO'S MISADVENTURES

I recall now that she seemed really lovely, her fluffed-up and free mane floating around her beautiful face. Her sensual, brilliant, and sweet eyes caressed the onlooker. She was radiant and delighted in her beauty and attractiveness, freely communicating the happiness of being pretty and admired. Lucio seem hypnotized in front of the television screen. The truth was that he really liked Verónica Castro. He watched her over and over without tiring of it, as if he was talking to her sweetly and softly with his eyes, perhaps caressing her with the half smile hinted on his lips, barely restraining the impulse of the hand in its desire to touch the screen as if it were really her face and not a new electronic image. The advertisement for Splendor shampoo repeated over and over during the commercial breaks of the afternoon soap operas. It also appeared in the evening prime time line-up of US TV shows dubbed in Spanish and the "24 Hours" news program of Jacobo Zabludovsky. Lucio looked at me unperturbed while I ranted and raved against the programming on Televisa and Channel 13, including the commercials, even the one with Vero that he liked so much. Once he turned the tables on me, saying that back in the Sierra there weren't any "such pretty" things as appeared on television. Months afterwards, when Lucio was back with the Brigade, Dionisio let me know that he'd complained about me, accusing me of having criticized him many times and of having constantly badmouthed the things he liked so much to watch on television. He was right. I spent time letting him know all about the very elementary violations of security that he frequently committed. I would declare that I was talking about his safety, but it was my safety and that of my family as well, of course.

As to the rest, Lucio was absolutely right in saying that "such pretty things" didn't exist in the Sierra to entertain the members of the Brigade during their long periods of inaction and boredom. It so happened that our cultural references were extremely different. Nothing puzzled me more than spotting a book on Lucio's night table with the title *How to Build Character?*, whose author indicated his status as a Jesuit with the letters S.J. after his name. The other book that Miguel read at this time was *The Bandits of Río Frío*, by Manuel Payno, a classic that seemed to me less alien to his background and struggle.

After Durango, I drove Lucio to the city of Zitácuaro in Michoacán. We left my house in Colonia Jardín Balbuena one morning quite early. We again traveled in the Volkswagen belonging to the married couple of anthropologists. This seemed to me a rather risky decision since anyone who had visited Miguel in Durango could well have given information about the car to the political police or to the army. But we couldn't get another auto soon enough to satisfy Lucio's rush to be on time for an appointment that he'd made some time earlier. On the road Lucio said that he was worried about our not bringing any medicine with us. He wanted to stop off and visit a poor peasant family that he'd known on a previous visit. He had given them some medicines that they were very grateful for, and he wanted to bring some more that he'd promised. Lucio suggested that we stop off at a pharmacy somewhere along the way and load up a good supply of medicines. This idea struck me as both extravagant and dangerous. I couldn't see myself standing at the pharmacy counter asking for several boxes of various antibiotics, antiallergenics, eye drops and ointments, and medicines to combat rheumatic ailments or diarrhea without being able to specify any of their commercial or technical names. This would certainly seem strange and raise suspicion. I discussed the matter with Lucio, convincing him that on another occasion we'd be able to provide both medicines and a visit from one of the doctors who were friends of the Organization. In any case, we did drop in to see this family.

The peasants received us with notable distrust and barely appeared to remember Lucio. They invited us to eat with them, as is the custom of villagers in Mexico. Lucio spoke to them about the poor and about the harsh conditions under which most Mexicans had to survive and work, especially peasants. The members of the household listened attentively, but it was obvious that they were asking themselves who we were and what we were after. I imagined that we could not simply arrive driving a nearly new automobile, dressed in clothes that, while not luxurious, were certainly better than theirs, and then talk to them about poverty. I had the impression that they must be thinking that surely we were members of some protestant religious sect. They appeared to me more and more uncomfortable as Lucio insisted in the necessity that we poor people organize in order to improve the conditions in which we all lived. Yes, he included me as well as himself within the ranks of the poor. It was a disaster, but the worst was yet to come. As he noticed that his words had not chipped away at these people's distrust, Lucio acted impulsively without thinking carefully about what he was doing. He quickly stuck his hand into the interior pocket of his jacket and pulled out a thick wad of 100, 500, and 1000 peso bills, urging them to accept it, something of course that they would not do. Several times he insisted that they take the money in order to buy the medicines that they needed, but the more he insisted, the more closed off the people of the household became. We had to get out of there tail between our legs.

The principal purpose of the trip was to visit a young woman teacher who lived in Zitácuaro in whose house we lodged for a day and a half. I don't remember now clearly whether Lucio talked with other people in town. I seem to have walked around the area with both of them. Maybe another person or two went with us. At night, Lucio slept in the room belonging to the teacher. I had the impression that theirs was an old personal relationship mixed with political interests.

During this trip, we visited a young, recently married couple in one of the new low-income residential zones on the edge of Zitácuaro. I don't know how Lucio got in touch with the young teacher since neither knew the other. What I do recall is that when we visited the couple in their modest home, I was impressed by its order and cleanliness, the typical petty-bourgeois "good taste" in decorating and arranging the details of a little house. The two radiated warmth, harmony, and simple happiness. Lucio spoke with the husband and revealed his identity to him. Most likely he did this under the impact of the young man's freshness, sincerity, and openness of spirit. The truth was, however, that they had just met, and it seemed hardly prudent to me to have made such a confession. These types of situations repeated themselves with worrisome frequency during the trips that I made with Lucio. Several times I told him that it didn't seem right for him to personalize the struggle so much. The correct course was for us to construct a political organization rooted in the people, based upon agreements and a consensus on a collective political direction. (Not for nothing was I an *espartaquista* militant, a quite modest and rather late heir of José Revueltas). Lucio could have spoken of the Partido de los Pobres and the Brigada de Ajusticiamiento and mentioned that he was a member of the leadership, but he didn't have to tell everyone he'd just been introduced to who he was, not just for reasons of security, but above all as a matter of principle: we had to establish political relationships with people, not engender *caudillaje*. When we said goodbye to the young couple in their fragile, well ordered happiness, I couldn't repress a thought about the immense danger to which they were exposed, and about which they surely were not fully conscious.

Back again in Mexico City Lucio continued to feel ill, so Dionisio and Isauro decided that he ought to be examined by a specialist who had been a militant in the LCE since its founding. At first, we didn't tell Luis the identity of his patient. He reviewed the records of the examinations by previous doctors, including x-rays and an encephalogram. Lucio suffered periodically from extremely strong headaches accompanied by nausea and a loss of balance, a combination that left him prostrate in a hammock in the guerrilla camp for a week or two at a time. There had been fears of a tumor or parasites, but the x-rays had not revealed any. Neither had the encephalogram indicated anything definite. In light of all this, Luis decided on an angiogram, consisting of an intravenous injection of a contrasting substance that would circulate with the blood and illuminate the arteries and brain vessels in an x-ray of the head. Lucio gave his okay, so I took him to Luis's house from where we proceeded on to a nearby laboratory for the exam. Before we left his home, Luis pulled me aside to advise me that this test was dangerous. If the patient proved allergic to the injected substance, he could die on the spot, and there was no way to tell in advance how his organism would react. I shivered at the thought! What an enormous responsibility! I could not put this on my shoulders alone, so I revealed to Luis who his patient was. My medical compañero looked me in the eye and with great seriousness said: "Let's do it." Despite his serenity, I could not stop envisioning and fearing disastrous consequences. I said to myself: "Imagine Lucio Cabañas dying during the test! I'd suffer the blame, of course!"

I sat outside the x-ray room, a bundle of nerves for more than an hour and a half. The longer the wait, the better I felt. If Lucio had proven allergic, Luis would have let me know immediately of the fatal outcome. At last, my medical compañero emerged and invited me in to a dark room to view the x-rays mounted on a panel of florescent light. As I looked on, he examined them in detail, unable to find anything abnormal except what seemed like a lightly inflamed cerebral cortex. As treatment, Luis prescribed a delicate drug that Lucio would have to take in progressively larger doses at fixed hours over ten days; it would produce secondary side effects, some of them bothersome, he added. He warned that under no circumstances should Lucio suspend taking the medicine over its indicated period. To do so might have fatal consequences. Just to make things more complicated, Luis informed me that he'd be out of town in the days ahead on his annual vacation.

Every day Lucio swallowed a larger number of pills than the day before. At first, all went well, and he experienced no secondary effects, but on the fifth day he fell victim to an uncontrollable diarrhea. That very day we had to drive to Morelos to one of the villages located up in the mountains above Oaxtepec. There we attended a meeting with Dionisio, Isauro, and the rest of the Jaramillista members of the leadership of the Organization that we were out to build by ourselves in this part of the country. The meeting concerned a variety of matters that were the responsibility of both the Organization and the Partido de los Pobres. After an exchange of reports and opinions, we ate lunch. About six in the evening, Lucio and I commenced our return to the Federal District via the Cuautla–Amecameca–Chalco route. Lucio had not ceased having to go to the bathroom all morning and afternoon. He opposed taking the prescribed medicine any more. In the face of his resistance to continuing treatment, and with great anxiety over the possible consequences of this, I felt obliged to inform him of what our medical compañero had told me about suspending the pills. Lucio agreed to continue with his required doses.

Between Cuautla and Chalco, I had to stop several times so that he could urgently get out of the car and go behind the bushes. The situation seemed to get worse. Even though I knew I would not find him, I looked for a public telephone from which to call Luis. Nobody answered. So Lucio proposed we look for another doctor that he knew. He called and fortunately reached him in his office. I drove to his address, following Lucio's instructions. The doctor ushered us in, examined the medicine, and listened to my explanation of the situation. He immediately told us to suspend the medicine that Luis had prescribed, casting aside the latter's warnings with great assurance. At that point, I didn't know what to think, but I felt relieved at being freed from responsibility by a doctor that Lucio had confidence in. As time passed, I learned to weigh the opinions that doctors gave. To all appearances, nothing happened to Lucio from the suspension of the treatment except that the diarrhea ceased.

TWO

The Long March

FURTHER EPISODES WITH LUCIO

ON THE THIRD TRIP that I undertook with Lucio Cabañas, we journeyed to the port of Veracruz. This time Isauro lent us his vermillion-colored Volkswagen, a bit of an older model, but with a motor in good shape. The lack of a radio was an inconvenience, particularly since the cold outside air poured through the hole in the dashboard. We left on a Friday night. I'd had to work all day at the Rural Productivity Program. The chilly, humid air at that hour hit us directly in the face and chest. The dull and monotonous noise of the motor plunged Lucio into a deep sleep. Meanwhile, I attempted to anticipate the curves of the road in time while watching out for the intense nighttime traffic of the trailer trucks—heavy, long, and dangerous—that looked as if they were trying to force us off the road. I drove on like this for about two hours before I began to succumb to sleep. My eyes must have closed for a few fractions of a second. I opened them just before the car would have plunged us into the gorge. I turned the wheel instantly, straightening the car back to the road. Lucio was shaken forcefully by the jolt of the VW. He grunted, but did not wake up. We'd had a close brush with death on that difficult highway! I did not hesitate—as soon as I saw a flat area next to the shoulder, I stopped and went to sleep until the sun came out.

The noise of uninterrupted traffic, the high beams of trucks and buses coming and going, and the narrow space of the driver's seat prevented me from resting properly. As soon as I saw the first light of dawn, I started the car again.

At this, Lucio woke up and settled himself on the seat. We exchanged a few words and headed straight to the sea at a good speed.

Many years had gone by since I'd stepped on the sand of the beach at Mocambo. Long ago, I took a spectacular tumble on the stone breakwater, badly hitting my head. I'd been walking carelessly at night, moving against the hefty northern wind along the slippery surface near the massive harbor lighthouse. At the time, I was a boy of eleven, thin as spaghetti, with a "brush" haircut and a tiny strand of hair hanging over my freckled forehead. My mother called that style "a la Boston" with a pride worthy of a better cause. I had been invited by my aunt Adela, my mother's youngest sister, her husband Santiago, and my cousin Manolo, several years younger than I. We were spending a few days in the house of my uncle's parents. He was a *jarocho*, a man from Veracruz, loved by everyone. An electrical engineer by profession, he possessed a degree from ESIME, the Superior School for Electrical and Mechanical Engineering, and was also an enthusiastic ball player. In his parents house I slept in a hammock for the first time. I also saw—surreptitiously and with previously unknown sexual excitement—an issue of *Vea* magazine, an avant-garde pornographic publication of those days, left on the armoire of our host. On that trip, for the first time, I also heard the famous *alvaradeño* popular speech, thanks to two ladies who lived nearby and uninhibitedly exchanged the most amazing series of unsavory words, passionately insulting each other in my presence. That was my second visit to Veracruz. The first time I had traveled with my parents, and we had stayed at Hotel Mocambo, right on the ocean. At night, the beach was full of giant crabs and deep holes at low tide. I almost drowned in one of those.

Two and a half hours later, we arrived at the edge of the port city. Lucio proposed that we head to Boca del Río for something to eat, taking the short cut to the right of the intersection. We had free time, since the people we were supposed to meet were at work. We did that, and soon we were sitting on comfortable canvas chairs under a *palapa* in one of the restaurants on the beach. We ordered fried sea bream and something to drink from an attentive girl, while we listened to the music played by a *jarocha* band. For about ninety minutes, we rested from the wear and tear of the trip.

Somewhat refreshed, we decided to return to the port city. It was still too early to contact the people Lucio was after, so when we arrived at the main intersection, instead of going directly to town, we proceeded straight ahead to the coastal highway. Lucio was interested in observing the terrain surrounding the eastern slope of the Sierra Madre. Once there, we stopped at Antigua, near the Villa Rica de la Vera Cruz, in order to see the ruins of the several hundred year-old city council building founded by the Spanish conqueror Hernán Cortés. Later we visited the Totonaca archaeological zone of Cempoala by the banks of the Actopan River, where Cortés met with the Fat Cacique and later engaged in a fierce battle with Pánfilo de Narváez. We climbed up the Main Temple and saw the great square and the fields and peasant houses that surround it. As we were leaving, Lucio stopped to write something in the guest book. Unfortunately, I did not have the curiosity to read what he had written and learn how he had signed his name. But if the 1973 book is still kept somewhere, any interested person will be able to read the message of the leader of the Partido de los Pobres.

Around five o'clock we went back to town, getting there just after dark, when the blue-black sky was filled with stars. I don't remember in which direction we traveled through the city or which neighborhood we visited. What I do recall clearly is the presence of a young woman and two young men, all three school teachers like Lucio. We spent several hours in their company. Although I don't recollect much about the house, I can still visualize a closed corridor without windows, a stairway that led us there, and the five of us sitting on the white tiled floor. Lucio spoke with them for a long time. Defeated by fatigue, I fell asleep right then and there until morning. The delicious smell of coffee that the *profesora* had just prepared made me open my eyes and get up. She served us a cup of the aromatic beverage and brought us sweet rolls, all in haste because Lucio had things to do that morning. We bid our farewell to the kind professors and left the city bound for the northeast on the highway to Nautla and Tecolutla. We went by each spot that Lucio thought of potential strategic importance in the event of a *foquista* opportunity. In my eyes, this was senseless and absurd, contradicting even the origin and development of Lucio's own experience. Before we knew it, it was dark again.

Close to nine o'clock in the evening, we went back on the same highway to Alvarado, and from there to the town of Carlos A. Carrillo, in search of someone else Lucio needed to see. That person turned out to be the town's parish priest, Carlos Bonilla Machorro, who had caught the attention of the national press a few months earlier, at the beginning of the administration of Luis Echeverría Alvarez. In December, 1972, and January, 1973, he supported the sugar cane workers' movement at the San Cristóbal Sugar Mill, the biggest in the country. When we got there, Lucio asked me to remain in the car while he walked to a house. The area looked poor and was dark; there were hardly any pedestrians around. Some music was audible, but most of all I could hear dogs barking back and forth endlessly. I waited for Lucio for more than two hours. Boredom and apprehension were making me despair when I saw him coming back, accompanied by a man. They stopped in the dark, near the car, and they said good-bye, patting each other in the back and then sharing a vigorous hug.

Leaving Carlos A. Carrillo, we started our return to the Federal District. As had been the case on the way there, Lucio soon fell asleep. I felt very tired, but I was anxious to get home. The night turned colder as we ascended to the high plateau. A sharp jet of frigid air came in through the hole in the dashboard, making the trip more uncomfortable. Every once in a while I stopped on the shoulder of the desolate road to keep myself awake and empty my full bladder.

I was enjoying the thought of being home and embracing my wife and daughter as I came close to Colonia Jardín Balbuena. But my joy turned to worry and distress. In the parking area near Retorno 4, I spotted the green minivan of Margarita Dalton, the writer, and her North American friend Katia Sheehan. Since it was only 6:15 A.M., I guessed that they were guests in our house, invited by Tere. It so happened that Tere did not know the true identity of Miguel, because I had not considered it prudent to inform her. But the presence of Margarita and Katia in our house complicated the situation. To make matters worse, Tere had given them the room where Lucio had previously stayed. I had to inflict on Tere my decision that her guests clear out that very morning. I could not expose either Lucio or them to the danger of state reprisals based on any lack of discretion or excess of liberality. My dear wife had to cover for me once more, all because of my ideology and political plans that she scarcely shared. At that time I could justify almost anything in the name of Revolution. I became proud, haughty, and insensitive toward anyone who did not agree with my ideas, feelings, and emotions. Today I regret having demanded from Tere that Margarita and Katia leave the house.

Another time I took Lucio to a meeting with "Oscar," a school teacher from the Federal District, if I remember correctly, and a member of the Brigada Campesina de Ajusticiamiento. Jacobo Gámiz García ("Javier"), a compañero from Chihuahua and brother to professor Arturo Gámiz García, who died in combat at the hands of the army at Ciudad Madera, was also present, along with Dionisio, a leader in the Organization. The meeting place was a humble home, located in an area near the garrison where Generalissimo Morelos was executed, in the municipality of Ecatepec in the state of Mexico during the independence era in the early nineteenth century. I was not invited to participate in this meeting, so I had to remain seated at the wheel for two very long hours. In spite of my exclusion, however, and because of a few indiscretions of the teacher who traveled back to Mexico City with Lucio, I began to suspect they were planning to carry out a bank robbery. At any rate, since I had no part in the plans, I concentrated on other problems and tasks.

Holy Week was approaching, and I relished the four free days that were coming my way at work. They offered a good opportunity for a trip with Lucio, so I asked him if there was anything he needed to do. He said he did not want to travel anywhere, since he was expecting some important news at anytime. That very day, Maundy Tuesday, I took him somewhere in Colonia Nuevo Atzacoalco to see the school teacher from the Federal District. As the teacher bid farewell to Lucio, he said that he'd see him soon "if everything turns out well tomorrow." Lucio wished him good luck and asked him to take care of himself. Listening to them, I became convinced that the "action" would take place the next day. Wednesday afternoon, on my way home from work, getting ready for a four-day break, I read the headline of the evening papers: "Oscar and Javier flee; they are the leaders of the bank-robber commando of the Partido de los Pobres." I bought the paper in a hurry. Oscar and Javier had fled to safety, but according to the description of the incident in the *Extra*, the police had apprehended another participant shortly after he'd chained and padlocked the gate of the bank branch and fled the scene. The police had also succeeded in detaining a school teacher by the name of Modesto Trujillo in his own home, along with several of his relatives. They were all charged as accomplices in the armed robbery of the Banco Comercial Mexicano branch adjacent to the Ministry of Education in downtown Mexico City. The booty: 2.2 million pesos.

Once home, I showed the newspaper to Lucio. He was very concerned about those detained during and after the action. He could do nothing other than hope that others would not be caught, and that the stolen money would serve the ends of the Brigada de Ajusticiamiento del Partido de los Pobres. The next morning, a holiday, I received a big surprise when I answered the phone and heard a man, who identified himself as Oscar, ask for Miguel. I passed the phone to Lucio. The conversation was quite short. Lucio gave me back the telephone so that Oscar could tell me where to meet him. He needed to come to talk with Lucio in person.

I went to look for Oscar in Colonia Maravillas, in front of the movie house of the same name, in Ciudad Netzahualcóyotl. I asked him to lie down on the back seat of the car and close his eyes since I was taking him to my house to see Lucio. I didn't know at the time that this was a useless precaution, since Oscar had already been there, invited by Lucio in my absence. He also knew my telephone number.

Lucio and Oscar talked by themselves in Lucio's room. Later they asked me to join them. They needed to provide a safe shelter for compañero Javier as well as transportation for Oscar, who had to travel to Guerrero with the bulk of the money. When I heard this I expressed my strong disagreement. I thought it a mistake to have Oscar in charge of transporting the money when he had probably been identified already by the police. I dared to ask him whether his current home was secure, both for him and the money. I needed to know whether any of the men now in custody knew its location. Oscar said yes, one of them was familiar with the house, but he was confident he would not reveal anything, even under duress. I replied that he was wrong. He'd have to clear out immediately and turn over the money to someone else—to Lucio, for example. Another person would have to be in charge of transporting the dough, while he and Javier hid out in the countryside, maybe in Morelos or Puebla with the compañeros of the Organization. Lucio shared my perspective. Right there we all agreed that I should take Oscar to Colonia Maravillas to vacate his house and give me the overnight case with the money, while he found a new place to stay. I asked Lucio to let me borrow his .38 automatic pistol. I felt a great responsibility to protect such a large amount of money. I returned Oscar to the spot right across the street from the Maravillas movie theater and waited for him in the car. He handed me the valuable case. I broke into a cold sweat as I drove the car back home, looking around nervously. Lucio's automatic was stuck in my waist, making me uncomfortable and paradoxically more insecure. Head first, I had just plunged into collaborating with a crime I had not committed. At that point, what I was doing seemed entirely justified and necessary, even heroic.

Later Dionisio and Isauro came to our house, invited by Lucio. Oscar was also present. The five of us counted the bills lifted from the Banco Comercial Mexicano. We knew from Oscar how much there was, but he insisted that we count it again in his presence. None of us had ever seen or touched that much money in our lives. As we finished, everyone was flushed and bright eyed. Miguel started to think aloud about the distribution of the money. Outside the room, in a brief conversation, I dared to make a suggestion to Dionisio and Isauro. What if we asked Lucio for some of the money for our corn and bean crop and our goat project? With considerable difficulty, we'd been trying to develop these initiatives as sources of financing for the Organization. I also thought that we could ask for money to buy a tractor and have our fellow members plow fields for a fee as a means to generate some revenue. Dionisio and Isauro were indecisive and not very forthcoming. When Lucio asked us of his own initiative how much money we needed for our own work, I audaciously jumped in without a blink and said: "Three hundred thousand pesos!" Lucio thought that was just fine. He counted the bills with flair and gave them to Dionisio, who in turn asked Isauro to keep them until we knew what we were doing with the money. Once we had dispensed with these delicate matters, we agreed that Oscar and Javier needed to be taken to a safe place.

I never requested nor spent one single peso of that money. Nor did I ever see it again or find out what was done with it. I don't know how it got to the Brigade in the Sierra of Atoyac or who transported it. I did observe that Lucio kept some of the money, and that he parceled it out to compañeros and relatives very close to him, like his mother, his half sister, and his cousin.

A bit before he returned to Guerrero, Lucio offered me cash for a new automobile. I rejected it, explaining that my personal struggle consisted of changing my living conditions, leaving behind as soon as I could all the comforts of the "petite bourgeoisie"; thus, I'd given my own car to the Organization. I later figured that Lucio's real purpose was to oblige me to be at the service of the Brigade any time it needed me. But I wasn't ready for this kind of commitment, especially after realizing how operations were agreed upon, planned, and executed.

Lucio was in the habit of carrying a guitar wherever he went, and he was fond of playing it, as he sang old ballads in praise of the struggle against Maximilian and the French, or old corridos from the 1910 Revolution. He especially enjoyed singing a song about Che Guevara that he had composed. It must be stated that his abilities as a musician were modest. One day he asked me to find someone who could teach him how to play better. I immediately thought of Juan Trigos, a composer and classic guitarist from the National Conservatory of Music. He was also a fiction writer and a friend from the time when we both worked for the Secretariat of Public Education located in the Cathedral Passageway, Guatemala and Donceles Streets, in the heart of Mexico City. I made an appointment with Juan, and Lucio and I went to his house in Colonia Cuauhtémoc. I had not seen Juan for several years, so he did not know what kinds of things I was involved in. Juan said he needed to hear Lucio—Miguel to him—play his guitar. Once he'd heard him, he made some technical suggestions about the way he held the instrument and pulsed the strings. Juan then proceeded to play masterfully and with much feeling a musical piece he had composed. We were in the midst of listening, when his wife Martha and his sister suddenly appeared in the studio. Lucio was visibly moved by the music. He said he wanted to express his deep gratitude for Juan's ready disposition to help him by singing for all of us the corrido he had composed as an homage to Che Guevara. It was a strange offering, because nobody had spoken in this gathering about anything having to do with social justice, socialism, Cuba, or revolution. Lucio began to play his guitar and to sing:

The world is singing an anthem with sorrow
while the machine-guns keep up their rat-tat-tat

because struggling for our freedom in the Sierra
Commander Che Guevara has died.

Our hosts looked at each other, somewhat intrigued by the man I had brought to their house. I didn't know what to say, or what kind of explanation I would have to give them later. Then, all of a sudden, Lucio broke out in loud sobs. Juan, Martha, and Juan's sister appeared astonished and frozen in place. Alternating between blushing and turning pale, I managed to ask: "What is the matter, Miguel?" A minute elapsed, and then Lucio apologized, saying he had been deeply affected by Che's demise. We departed from the Trigos household together, leaving a gratuitous mystery in our wake that I never had a chance to explain. Such was the state of mind and extreme sensibility of Lucio during those days.

A bit later, after talking to Gorgonio who had just come back from the Sierra, Lucio announced—seriously and unexpectedly—his decision to return to Guerrero. "There are many problems in the Brigade that require my presence there," he said. Lucio added that Carmelo Cortés was making many mistakes, and that it was urgent for him to go up to the Sierra to straighten out the situation. He said he also wanted to discipline several members of the armed detachments, beginning with Carmelo. I expressed strong disagreement, since Lucio was still under medical care and the doctors had not yet diagnosed the origin of his illness. Lucio had made the decision to rejoin the Brigade, however, so we had to plan the return trip via Acapulco to the Costa Grande. Compañeros Dionisio and Isauro asked me to deal with the logistics. I agreed to do that, but at that point I was no longer willing to put myself at risk so gratuitously. I suggested we could ask the couple of university professors whom I have mentioned before to deliver Lucio to the Sierra. "Nicolás" and "María" accepted the invitation. Lucio's increased carelessness about security made me reluctant to commit myself to traveling with him. For example, one day I discovered that Lucio had left my house by himself. He didn't return until the following day, leaving me in a condition of great uncertainty for over twenty-four hours. He confessed that he'd gone to Zitácuaro, for certain, to meet the female school teacher that we'd visited earlier. He drove a car lent to him by the doctor we'd consulted when the special treatment that Luis had prescribed had resulted in permanent diarrhea. Lucio told me that he'd been obliged to abandon the car on Constituyentes Avenue near the entrance to the city, convinced that a patrol car of the Federal Highway Police had been following him. Clearly he confided this to me only because he wanted my help in picking up the vehicle and returning it to its owner.

Lucio had behaved very irresponsibly. He had little experience in driving and no driver's license. He acted in other ways that compromised not only his own personal security, but also my wife's, my daughter's, and mine—such as when he gave my telephone number and address to Oscar so that he could call or visit during the planning of the bank robbery. Because of these experiences, I decided to protect myself better by doing what other compañeros did—delegating to others the very risky, difficult, or tiring assignments. The married couple of university professors transported Lucio to Acapulco and from there to a predetermined location between the Coyuca de Benítez Lagoon and Atoyac de Alvarez.

After they got back, the couple told me that Lucio asked them to stop to buy coconuts from one of the many stands at the spot known as *el crucero*, at the intersection of the Mexico–Acapulco highway with the road to Pinotepa Nacional. *El crucero* was located just a bit before the last in the chain of peaks that hid from the eyes of the anxious, hot, and impatient traveler the bay of Acapulco. This craving of compañero Cabañas was understandable; however, the couple doubted it prudent to satisfy it, given the large number of people traversing this location by car or on foot. Lucio insisted that they stop, assuring that they should not worry—nobody would recognize him. Fortunately, that was the case. None of the ladies or the *zancas* (paisanos or compañeros in Guerrero) who sold coconuts there identified him. Thus, they continued traveling up to the drop off point on the highway to Ixtapa–Zihuatanejo. There they stopped the sky-blue VW, pretending that it had broken down, while they awaited a sign from the members of the Brigade. They didn't have to sit there long. Very soon three or four of the Brigade appeared, well-armed. They hugged Lucio effusively and led him to a grove where another group of them waited. They were on their bellies, their weapons trained toward the road, just in case. In the excitement, neither Lucio nor Nicolás realized that a pair of enthusiastic, young guerrillas had led María to the spot where the rest of the group was lying in ambush. They imagined that she meant to stay with them. A great disappointment overtook all of the *zancas* when they had to return her to the car and to her husband, who was beginning to worry about his wife's whereabouts.

SUPPORTING THE ORGANIZATION

On another occasion, Dionisio asked me to travel to Guerrero's Costa Grande to visit his compadre, a sympathizer of the Organization, on his behalf. The man lived in a village near the federal highway between Acapulco and Ixtapa-Zihuatanejo near Atoyac de Alvarez. Dionisio made this request without taking into consideration that right at that time the Mexican army was carrying out one of its "social campaigns," consisting of granting free medical and dental care to the local inhabitants and mobilizing thousands of soldiers for that purpose.

I went to Acapulco in the Opel that my parents had given me as a present after I came back from Tijuana, Baja California, where I'd spent a year. I made the trip with Isaías, who remained in some unknown place in the port city in order to get in touch with a contact from the Brigade. Meanwhile, I went to the hamlet where Dionisio's compadre dwelled, driving on the federal highway towards Atoyac de Alvarez. In the height of stupidity, not being used to depending on others for the financing of these trips, I forgot to ask Isaías for money so that I could buy gas or take care of any unexpected expenses. I worried that I had only a bit more than half a tank of fuel and didn't know how much farther I had to go. No alternative existed but to keep on going. I'd agreed with Isaías to meet the next morning between ten and eleven at the same corner where we'd separated.

A growing anguish invaded me as I moved along the road that I only knew as far as Pie de la Cuesta. At the entrance to Coyuca de Benítez, an impressive line of military vehicles loaded with soldiers, physicians, and nurses occupied both sides of the road. I felt as if I were entering the city of Saigon in South Vietnam. I feared detention at any moment. The absence of any alibi and any money made me utterly furious with Dionisio and with my own foolishness for having ventured into a war zone this way. Unable to retreat, I continued advancing along the unfamiliar road, paying a great deal of attention to my instructions. Isaías had warned me not to miss his compadre's village, because immediately beyond it sat a military checkpoint. It was already nighttime when I saw the military roadblock, fortunately still at a distance up ahead. I jammed on the brakes and took a U-turn, heading back to the hamlet. I soon stopped to ask a resident by the edge of the road if that was the place I was searching for. When he said yes, I crossed over to the other side of the highway, driving toward a commercial establishment barely lighted by a bulb mottled with fly excrement. The place was a combination grocery store and bar, but the *zanca* said it was the address of the man I was looking for. I stopped the car in front and entered its rustic interior. The owner took care of me immediately. He was a brown man from the coast, of medium size, with a thick mustache and black hair. He answered to the name of Dionisio's compadre. Much relieved, I immediately gave him Dionisio's greetings. When I was about to say something far more compromising, the man interrupted me and said that I was looking for someone else with the same name and surname. The owner called a kid and asked him to take me to the correct dwelling.

I was lucky to find Dionisio's compadres living with their three sons in that humble adobe house with a thatched, slanted, two-sided roof. They immediately offered me tortillas, beans, and coffee, sharing with me their worries about the presence of so many soldiers who had recently arrived. The compadre in particular felt increasing nervousness for her children that the war could begin at any moment. I tried very hard to calm them, assuring them that the war that they feared would not develop for a few years yet. My explanations were not entirely convincing. At dawn, a constant line of military trucks passed by in the direction of Atoyac de Alvarez. The noise of the engines and the brightness of the beams of these heavy vehicles made it impossible for us, the three adults, to fall back to sleep. I was resting in a hammock hanging just a few steps from the double bed in which the couple and the three children lay. Obviously, they were slightly unsettled by having a guest on such a night. I was no less uneasy myself. Running low on gas, having to carry the old and most likely useless Lugar 9 mm. pistols that Dionisio had asked me to bring back to Morelos, the total lack of money, the presence of the army across the entire region—all that made it impossible for me to keep my eyelids shut during those long and hot hours.

Very early the next morning the compadre helped me tie a shoebox containing the two rusty weapons to the springs of the rear seat of the Opel. He also assured me that I had enough gasoline to get back to the spot where I would meet Isaías in Acapulco. There was no way of borrowing money for fuel. After drinking a cup of hot "canelita" or cinnamon tea and eating a piece of tortilla with salt for breakfast, I began my return on the federal highway. After I drove a few miles, I experienced something uncanny—all of a sudden the surface of my whole body acquired an extreme sensitivity, as if I had been skinned and lacked any physical protection. I feared the worst when I came upon two small military convoys. What I was feeling seemed like a premonition of what I was about to undergo. Luckily, I was able to complete the drive and arrive on time to my appointment with Isaías. The first thing I did with him was to fill the tank of the Opel at the nearest gas station. Afterwards, Isaías guided me to his place of shelter.

An attractive forty-year-old Acapulqueña lived with her children in a house near our place of rendezvous. She rented out two small and suffocating rooms. The son and daughter of Darío, one of the most experienced Jaramillista compañeros of the Organization, lived in one of them. It was a great surprise for me to discover that Darío was Guerrerense—I had always assumed that he was from the state of Morelos, given the relationship of deep reciprocal trust he had with Rubén Jaramillo.

Compañero Darío was also known among the people in the struggle as "El Muerto." During one of the legal, electoral stages of Jaramillismo, that of the Partido Agrario Morelense, Darío left the party headquarters in the town of Jojutla. The state judicial police arbitrarily detained him then and there. In a great show of violence, they shoved him into the back of a car, beat him up, and forced him to strip naked. (He had only one sock on when he was found later.) They threatened to kill him as they drove down the highway toward Amecameca and the Federal District. One of the policemen stabbed him repeatedly with an ice pick near his left nipple. Darío pretended to be dead. Immediately, the same man used the butt of his gun to remove Darío's gold-covered front teeth. The compañero remembers trying to keep his mouth open to save his lips from being smashed to a pulp. Once they took away his only wealth from him, the policemen dumped his naked body in a ravine in the middle of the night.

Darío remained still until he heard the car pull away. Then he sprinted through a field towards Amecameca. Shortly thereafter he spotted a house with a light inside and drew near to ask for help. Dogs barked. A man with a shotgun appeared in the doorway and pointed the weapon at him before the naked Darío could utter a word. "El Flaco," as he was also known, turned around, and disappeared in the darkness. He heard the gun fire, and buckshot whistled by him. Fortunately nothing hit him. He walked all the way to the Red Cross dispensary in Amecameca where the incredulous physician on duty examined him. The doctor was stunned that the ice pick had not reached his heart.

As incredible as it seems, this story is true. Darío showed me a photograph from the Red Cross in Amecameca revealing the wounds inflicted by the ice pick around his left nipple. He also showed me the sock the judicial police had left on him. Ever since, he's always carried it around with him as a sort of talisman against a violent death.

I remember that Dionisio appeared enthusiastic one morning upon return from an exploratory trip through a new zone located on the borders of Puebla and Guerrero, more or less near the city of Tlapa. He went on and on in a multitude of detail about his encounter with a group of armed peasants, residents of a mountain hamlet. He described a recent shootout that these mountain dwellers had fought with a group of foes from the same region who had assaulted their houses. Dionisio took a strong interest in a young man who had fought with skill and bravery against the attackers in spite of having been shot by them twice. The leader of the group also intrigued Dionisio. He was a tough, forty-five year-old man, a type of patriarch who kept two households full of children in front of one another, no more than two hundred fifty meters apart across a modest slope. This individual had a coterie of young men who obeyed him, all of whom were related to one another. They wore cartridge belts across their chests packed with 7.62 mm bullets for the bolt rifles that they always carried with them. They lived in huts relatively scattered over the principal hill of the area, raising goats, pigs, chickens, and turkeys. Dionisio's own origin was partially rural, and his temperament allowed him to gain the good will of peasants quickly and warmly. He understood these mountain shepherds, their customs, and their ways of thinking and feeling. He shared with them a love for the countryside and a fondness for arms and hunting. A natural and knowledgeable hunter, Dionisio made this the major activity through which he established ties to different rural groups as he got to know them. With prudence and patience, he linked them to the project of constructing the Organization.

At first, Dionisio's activities seemed to me veiled in mystery and tinged with romanticism. I imagined him as the ubiquitous architect of a new type of efficient, expanding organization moved forward by his decisiveness and personal integrity. His practical knowledge of the rural world was indispensable. Everyday he worked tirelessly to form connections with poor peasants in the states of Mexico, Morelos, Puebla, and Guerrero. Unlike most of the other *Espartaquista* leadership, Dionisio lived side by side most of the time with laboring and poor people, particularly peasants. For sure, Dionisio lacked the intellectual preparation of some of the members of the Political Commission of the Central Committee, people with a broad cultural formation like compañero "Pablo" (Martín Reyes Vayssade). Nevertheless, for me, the fact that he remained consistent in what he said and did was enough. This seemed a more important quality, and I aspired to emulate his virtues. With the passage of time, this first impression acquired important nuances: without failing to recognize his capacities as a natural leader—they were beyond question— it was also evident that Dionisio lacked the broad theoretical preparation required to lead a revolutionary process. Nevertheless, the compañeros of the Ho Chi Minh Peasant Section of the LCE—Dionisio, Isauro, and "Benito"— were capable of exposing and challenging the antiquated conceptions and practices of the Central Committee and of the Political Commission of the Liga Comunista Espartaco. They did this by means of a constructively critical proclamation aiming at the realization of our own "Proletarian Cultural Revolution" among the *Espartaquista* militancy. The idea was to bring to reality the Maoist exhortation of "serving the people, uniting ourselves with them."

I met the group of mountain shepherds during a hunt for white-tailed deer. They used the round-up method, climbing up and down the hills, edging along steep drop offs in a carefree and irresponsible challenge to death.

Dionisio demonstrated his vigor and strength on that occasion by going up the hill carrying the weight of a young buck over his shoulders. He'd felled the creature himself with one crack shot. As in all our rural excursions, we took advantage of the chance to practice the "Vietnamese step." This consisted of successively running a hundred meters at a medium pace, then walking fifty quickly, and again running another hundred. We hoped to be in the right physical condition to move rapidly in the case of any quick advance or withdrawal. Nevertheless, we didn't become obsessed with technical military matters. Our principal concerns were political and organizational within the narrow framework of clandestinity with which we had identified ourselves. We didn't try to impose any militarist concepts and practices upon people. We thought that if war broke out, it would not be because of our choice or our subjective will. Instead, it would result from the development of the popular struggle and of the consciousness of the movement, not to mention the obstacles placed by the bourgeoisie and Yankee imperialism to the progress of the working classes in the countryside and cities. In this we differed with Lucio Cabañas and the rest of the armed groups. We based our political and organizational work on the level of people's consciousness and real participation, even if this way of doing things many times placed us in situations that proved difficult, uncomfortable, or frankly dangerous.

I remember something that happened the first time that I accompanied Dionisio to meet the chief of the mountain shepherds in a hut located downhill a bit from the hamlet. Seated on stones and sections of a tree trunk, we chatted over a container of sugar cane alcohol. We'd bought and tasted the warm booze a few hours earlier at a steaming hot, clandestine still, located in the shade of a mango tree on one side of the sun baked, dusty road. During the conversation, the chief insistently proposed kidnapping a local rich man for ransom. I began to get worried at his degree of persistence only for the purpose of obtaining money. Moreover, after a few drinks, the patriarch began talking in excruciating detail about an incident that occurred when he was a recruit, either a corporal or sergeant, I cannot remember now. He and some other soldiers had detained a pair of alleged cattle rustlers. They forced them naked into a pond in order to threaten them with drowning. They wanted to force them to confess where they had hidden the stolen cattle and to reveal who their buyers were. But upon seeing the round and fleshy rear end of one of the rustlers, the storyteller reported that he'd become so aroused that he took off his pants and got right into the water in order to rape him, much to the delight and sexual excitement of the rest of the soldiers.

Everyone's raucous laughter sounded savage, like off-key trumpet sounds in the stillness of the night. I didn't have any choice but to join in the noisy celebration of the cacique's sexual exploits. I'm quite sure that Dionisio also celebrated this story of aggression against a poor wretch because he couldn't offend our host or trigger any distrust towards us. Besides, they were all armed, and we weren't. But the episode set me to thinking about how careful we'd have to be with these people. Through our naïveté and overconfidence, or through some misunderstanding between them and us, we might end up raped or dead.

In the fall of 1973, the political work of the Organization and the development of its structure appeared to advance despite our considerable material and personal limitations. Dionisio and Isauro proposed that we hold a big meeting of the members and sympathizers of the Organization. We could do it on a weekend, staying over Friday and Saturday nights, someplace in Morelos or Puebla where we could count on peasant support to provide relative security and the things we'd need such as water, firewood, and food. We quickly concluded that an area of Puebla near Morelos provided the best spot for the meeting. Foothills surrounded the place. We could camp without fear of chance observation. We'd have the help of some peasant compañeros from a nearby hamlet. Each member of the commission charged with arranging the event took responsibility for the diverse tasks of assuring attendance, transportation, and material support.

I had the job of inviting and transporting eight or nine compañeros or sympathizers, making use of two cars. Unless memory fails me, my group contained two sympathizers who belonged to CUEC, the University Center for Film Studies, one an editor, the other a movie director; a lovely, pleasant married woman who headed a cultural friendship society with a socialist country that then seemed ideologically and politically attractive; the young, university professor couple who had driven Lucio Cabañas back to Guerrero; Rafael, Dionisio's brother and a former political prisoner from 1969, along with his compañera Marcela—both primary school teachers; Luis, the doctor who had treated Lucio; and "Armando," a member of the MAR, the brother of Javier Gaytán Saldívar, the very same Jacobo with whom I'd be captured a few months later and share torture, disappearance, and anguish in the Campo Militar Número Uno—in my case, only for two months, ten days.

I was relatively familiar with the place chosen for the meeting. At the start of my work with Dionisio and Isauro, I'd asked them to be allowed to spend the entire month of December, 1972 sharing the life of a poor peasant family of the area, members of the Organization. This had been an important life experience for me. It allowed me to feel first hand the tough material conditions under which millions of Mexicans like them survived. The hut in which the family of compañero "Lucas" lived was tiny. Nevertheless, we all managed to sleep there on woven mats on the floor—four adults and several children, not to mention a dog, a cat, a broody turkey, and various hens. Every night I suffered through attacks from all sorts of bloodsucking insects—bedbugs, fleas, mites, and mosquitoes. They made sleep very hard and left my irritable, white skin covered with enormous, bothersome red welts. Each morning as the sun elevated the temperature rapidly, the itching all over my body became unbearable. I'd have to bathe in a nearby well, whose icy waters came from the Popocatépel volcano, in order to calm my burning torture.

Once back with the family, I shared a meager breakfast with the wife and children, consisting of a cup of canelita, a sweetbread baked in the house of a neighbor (the rich man of the hamlet, a kind person of the countryside, very hardworking and organized), a small portion of some dish (an egg, green beans with egg or simply tomato sauce), accompanied by two or three tasty homemade tortillas. A little while later, a girl of eight and her brother of six would turn up. Dionisio had assigned me the responsibility of teaching them how to read and write during my stay. He never should have entrusted this job to someone as hopeless at teaching as I. My failure was total; I didn't even teach them the vowels. The two kids spent the time laughing at me, driving me so crazy that I wanted to chase them out of the hut where we met. I soon understood that I possessed neither patience nor method; I quit.

To help out in some way and to kill boredom, I concentrated on going out into the field to "shoot at pigeons," purple and white ringdoves that seemed to abound during the harvests of corn and sorghum. The birds reduced even further what was already an anemic crop. I was armed with a sparking shot-gun—*cuaxclera* they called it. You load it by pushing a rod all the way into the gun from the mouth of the barrel, packing down the powder, straw, lead shot, and the cloth that holds and compresses them all together. The ignition and consequent explosion are produced by the force of the hammer on the fuse located at the tip of the thin conduit leading to the powder chamber to the side and above the front of the slender handle. Of course, the action of the hammer results from someone pulling the trigger.

The fallen pigeons contributed to improving the quantity and quality of the family table. At the same time, my frequent presence in the fields discour-aged the birds away from the grain. Two weeks after I had been there, Dioni-sio reappeared, bringing along a 16 caliber, one-barreled shotgun and a gen-erous supply of cartridges. He'd promised these so that I could hunt for something besides pigeons. On Christmas Eve, I went out hunting for badg-ers, invited by Rutilo, a neighbor of Lucas. He wanted to prepare the meat of this evasive and noisy mammal by wrapping it in banana leaves and cooking it in an open barbecue pit. Rutilo owned two country dogs trained to track badgers. The brave, persistent hounds demonstrated their great ability in a short time, discovering and treeing two of these animals. It was very easy to bring them down with two discharges of number 6 shot. The night was warm, free of clouds, and lit by millions of stars. It has remained in my mind for another reason, however. About the same time that I shot the two badgers, a forceful earthquake destroyed the city of Managua, the capital of Nicaragua. I only learned about this terrible event upon my return to the Federal District at the end of the month.

Rutilo was grateful that I'd given him the meat and skins of both animals. He invited Lucas and me for a Christmas barbecue whose careful preparation took him most of the day. The menu repulsed me, but once I reluctantly put a piece of meat in my mouth, I had to admit that I'd been mistaken. The taste was not at all disagreeable. In any case, other reasons still prevented me from feeling comfortable in Rutilo's house. Just a few hours earlier, Lucas had confided to me that Rutilo owned a bad reputation in the community, for years having engaged in sexual relations with his own daughter and now with his daughter-granddaughter. This seemed a case of moral vice stemming from the ignorance, misery, and promiscuity in which these people lived. Revelations like this disconcerted me. I knew relatively little about life and tended to idealize "the people." I viewed each worker or peasant solely in terms of his or her social condition. As time went on, shocks of this sort broadened my understanding of reality and consequently increased my ability to evaluate and to make judgments. After my month of residence, I visited this area several times again with Dionisio.

The meeting of the Organization that I mentioned previously took place smoothly on a Saturday without too many byzantine discussions. The nearly forty participants managed to finish the agenda by nighttime. The majority of attendees then voted to end the encounter so that everyone could return to their homes and customary occupations, avoiding one more night out in the open. Dionisio was the principal speaker at the meeting. He reconciled opposite points of view and smoothed the edges of difficult matters. It happened that some compañeras, who had been formed in normal schools or universities, presented proposals that affected domestic and conjugal issues from the perspective of peasant women. They claimed that peasant men were under the obligation to share domestic tasks equally with their wives. As examples, they said that men should take the *nixtamal* for tortillas to the local mill; carry water and firewood to the home; and help their wives in keeping the youngest children clean. Moreover, in what was most delicate, they insisted that men should allow the women to make the decision not to have any more children and to undergo a simple sterilizing surgery. A more radical compañera even remarked that should be the men who should submit to sterilization. These proposals sounded rational, egalitarian, and fair to middle-class, educated, urban ears. If the truth be told, this small group foisted them on the assembly, almost gaining their approval. The peasant compañeros appeared intimidated by the rhetorical eloquence of the women. Then Dionisio took the floor. Calmly and knowledgably, he explained to the assembly the reasons why it was not a good idea to impose behaviors on peasant people that went so radically against their customs and idiosyncrasies. With his detailed explanations and wise reasoning, he convinced the compañeras that the meeting offered neither the time nor place to produce a resolution in which one group forced its criteria upon another. The large majority of the peasant people who sustained the development of the Organization were illiterate. They lived in communities with strong religious and cultural traditions. The people naturally distrusted ideas imported from afar.

In terms of strategy and tactics, we all agreed that we were not ready to undertake any armed revolutionary actions. We understood instead that it was necessary to continue building the Organization up in close contact with the people, serving them in any fashion that we could, and trying to reach more advanced stages of struggle by their side. Eventually, we would attain the stage when the armed struggle would become necessary. That would open the way to the overthrow of the bourgeois government, the defeat of Yankee imperialism, and the establishment of a socialist state through a proletarian dictatorship. Without explicitly condemning the armed option proposed by all other revolutionary groups, in particular the Partido de los Pobres and its Brigada de Ajusticiamiento, we rejected any action that subjectively and arbitrarily claimed to represent the workers in the city and the countryside. Instead, we gave priority above all to politics, that is to say, the construction of the Organization and the design of a political line congruent with the varied and unequal evolution of the popular struggle. In the same manner, we resolved to apply ourselves even more to the creation of economic enterprises that would serve the growth and development of the Organization. We would take advantage of the tremendous experience of our peasant compañeros. They would contribute with their knowledge and labor to the cultivation of corn and beans and to the raising of goats and pigs. Naturally, all of this would also benefit them and their families when they sold their agricultural and livestock products.

INTO THE SIERRA AND BACK

Weeks later, Dionisio personally informed me that "El Pelón"—another name for Lucio—had invited me to participate in the Second Annual Assembly of the Partido de los Pobres, due to take place during the first week of June, 1973.

The meeting had not been able to take place on May 18, the anniversary of
the day in 1967 in which the coffee-growing caciques and state judicial police
from Guerrero had attacked a popular march in Atoyac de Alvarez headed by
Cabañas. By some miracle, he had escaped injury in the ensuing massacre and
fled to the Sierra, subsequently creating first the Brigada de Ajusticiamiento
and then the Partido de los Pobres.

I picked Dionisio up near his home in the Volkswagen that the couple of
university anthropologists had ultimately donated to the Organization. We
headed to the house of compañero "Guillermo" in Morelos, arriving late in
the afternoon. Guillermo's mother provided us with supper while we chatted
with her and with her son, a very prominent member of the leadership of the
Organization. Guillermo later led us to the part of the house that acted as a
granary, leaving us to sleep on woven mats on the floor. I fell deeply asleep,
only to be suddenly reawakened hours later by the arrival of compañeros
"Luciano," Isaías, and Darío.

We got ourselves comfortable as best we could in the limited space of the
granary-cave, and slept a while longer until dawn. We then set out for Acapulco where other compañeros close to the Brigade waited for us around noon.

We reached the outskirts of the port near one in the afternoon. Isaías got
out of the car, crossed the highway, and walked into the neighborhood high
on the hill. Its terraces and rooftops offered an easy view of most of the bay.
We saw him walk along a hot and dusty alleyway toward one of the houses.
Only he knew which one we were looking for. He checked to see if the owners were waiting for us and asked whether they could offer us shelter from the
midday heat. As expected, these people opened the doors of their home to us
and shared their food. I was still recovering from a recent attack of dysentery,
incurred by drinking from a pool of muddy water up in the mountains near
Tlapa along the Puebla–Guerrero border. So I was still feeling weak. I worried
about my physical condition as I faced the prospect of a difficult and tiring
climb up into the Sierra. When the question arose of whether we should go
by day under the burning sun or by night, I voted for climbing under the light
of the moon. Besides saving us from the heat, it also seemed to me to offer
better security.

Near six in the evening, we set out for our rendezvous with the other compañeros due to climb the Sierra with us. The meeting place was rather close
to the house of Dionisio's compadres whom I already knew. So I left my four
compañeros near the stop from which we planned to take a bus to Atoyac de
Alvarez and went to leave the VW at the house of Dionisio's compadre. By the
time I got back, everyone had arrived. Lucio had sent compañero Ramiro, one
of the leaders of the Brigada de Ajusticiamiento, as our contact. He said that

we should board the bus as if we didn't know one another. We shouldn't talk to each other when the conductor asked us where we were going. We were just to tell him El Ciruelo.

As often happens in delicate circumstances, including those fraught with danger, some of the young men could not refrain from horsing around. This time was no exception. Ramiro and Isaías couldn't stop joking. Ramiro accidentally dropped some 9 mm bullets on the floor of the bus. Luckily, the bus was almost empty at that point. Later, both started yelling out the open windows of the bus as we went by their respective neighborhoods. Months later, Ramiro would appear publicly in a photograph next to Lucio Cabañas, who is sitting with his head covered by a straw hat. Isaías would fall prisoner about the same time in the city of Iguala. He had shot and killed a man from his town who had taken refuge in that city. According to Isaías, this individual had squealed on him and other compañeros to the civilian and military authorities. The compañero who transported Isaías to Iguala waited for him to enable a quick getaway. Helplessly, he witnessed how the municipal police apprehended Isaías. This man told me, however, that the real motivation for Isaías to kill the guy was different—taking advantage of Isaías' absence, the dead man had attempted to seduce the wife of the *zanca*.

When we reached El Ciruelo, the bus stopped, and all of us got out. The bus was left with only three passengers, the driver, and the conductor. We quickly disappeared into the vegetation, following Isaías who guided us with a sure step in the solitary darkness. After a while I realized that we were walking through a large palm grove. All of us gripped a flashlight that we pointed to the ground and covered with our fingers, allowing only a very thin thread of light that could not be seen from afar. The night was cool, and the sky was full of stars with only a few white clouds. After only half an hour on the road, the column stopped at Isaías' command. I could see that he was directing the beam of his flashlight a few feet ahead of him. He extended his arm and trained his fourteen-round, 9 mm Smith and Wesson pistol toward some target located among the grasses ahead. The din of the shot deafened us for a moment. I saw Isaías lean forward to pick up something. Turning toward us, he proudly held up a good sized armadillo. He then encouraged us to resume our walk. He proceeded forward with the animal in his hand hanging by the tail.

The mountain climb took several hours. I began to feel the fatigue and weakness expected from a convalescing body. At the same time, I was immensely thirsty. Fortunately, the waning moon lit our steps. Close to exhaustion, we reached a waterfall. Without thinking, I stuck my mouth under it and drank abundantly. I immediately felt revived. A few moments later, after passing under a fallen tree trunk, the compañero ahead of me began to jump and slap the back of his neck and head with his hands. Right away I approached him with my flashlight to see what kind of insect was biting him. Instantly, I began to feel the same burning bites over my neck and hands. Somebody else had to come and help us rid ourselves of the white ants that had jumped all over us when we ducked under the tree trunk, trying to defend their territory from our intrusion.

A while later, our guide stopped, commanding us to leave a meter and a half distance between ourselves and to veer left facing the mountain. He then gave the signal to proceed through the thick undergrowth. The purpose of this maneuver was to avoid leaving a trail behind us. We began to slip between the bushes and shrubs. We had to avoid the bramble that threatened to attach its innumerable thorns to our clothing and flesh. We tripped over vines, roots, and fallen branches. Since I had more difficulty than anyone else, I was left behind. A surge of panic overtook me. I forced myself forward in despair in an attempt to catch up with the group. Tripping over a stone, and close to falling down, I grabbed at some plants. They turned out to be nettles that burned my hands. Fortunately, this difficult stretch didn't last too long. Soon we found ourselves following a thin, barely noticeable pathway. An hour later, I felt nauseated and dizzy.

Dionisio and Luciano decided to stop and let us sleep a while for my benefit. After all, it looked as if we were near the camp of the Brigade. I was very grateful. I lay down and soon I was asleep on the damp ground. A while later, at dawn, we woke up and continued climbing. I had no idea that we still had to climb a very steep hillock that forced me to stop and rest every two steps. Exhausted, I suddenly saw two *zancas* climbing further down, one with a sack of rice on his back, the other with a sack of beans. They greeted us with smiles as they passed, but they never stopped. Enviously, I saw them disappear uphill in a blink. They resembled mountain goats. While I lamented my considerable physical and moral limitations in the face of any kind of prolonged suffering, Dionisio announced "We're here. There's the guard." I turned my eyes in the direction of the mountain he was pointing to, but I couldn't see anything. Still, it was true. We were there.

A few meters beyond, we found ourselves in an open area of fifteen or twenty square meters covered with a large piece of thick, clear plastic camouflaged with leaves and branches to prevent detection from the air. I remember seeing Carlos Ceballos—Julián—first. He was teaching a group of peasants everything about a FAL 7.62 mm. He demonstrated how to prepare it for firing, either semiautomatically or continuously, as well as how to disassemble and reassemble it. Julián was dressed in olive green. He was young, thin, strong, and good-looking. Immediately the *zancas* in charge of the kitchen gave each one of us newcomers a steaming hot cup of corn *atole* that, needless to say, sat very well with me.

Hardly had we gotten settled in the camp, when Lucio Cabañas appeared among us, sporting a cap of gray rabbit skin and a thick jacket of green suede. I had sent him both of those items via Gorgonio as presents. My parents had given me the jacket as a gift. Lucio greeted everyone and told me that he hadn't believed that I'd accept the invitation to take part in the meeting. Later, he asked our group to meet separately with him in a corner of the encampment where he took care privately of the affairs of the Brigade and the Party. He also had a hammock there on which to rest. He described to us the agenda for the day and explained how he planned to operate the assembly. He told us about his problems with the members of the "partisan organization," the Liga Comunista 23 de Septiembre, and the methods he would use to keep control of the situation. He requested that Dionisio serve as president of the debates of the assembly. Large numbers of invited participants continued to arrive at the camp during the remainder of the day. At that time, the Brigade was comprised of about one hundred members. Adding another one hundred new arrivals put two hundred people in a very small space, numbers that offered considerable challenges in organization, security, hygiene, food and water, and other matters. If providing two meals a day to a hundred individuals was quite an exploit, it's hard to imagine what it would be to supply double that number from one meal to the next, all the while taking care not to emit any smoke that could give away the encampment.

The beginning was chaotic. The hungry compañeros of the Brigade swarmed around the cooks without any sense of order, forgetting their guests and the courtesy of allowing them to eat first. At the following meal, the distribution of food was well organized through lottery numbers from one to two hundred. Each person received a scant ration from the cooks—half of a large, thick corn tortilla, a large spoonful of beans, and a small cup of corn *atole* twice a day. As guests, we had to sleep curled up in the small space where we sat during the discussion sessions of the assembly. In contrast, the members of the Brigade dispersed themselves in the surrounding groves and slept in their hammocks. Not only was the sleeping space extremely reduced; it was also rocky and uneven, making sleep difficult that first night. The next morning at my initiative, my group undertook to excavate around the rocks, thinking that they looked small and easy to remove. In reality, the stones were quite large and required a very great effort to even out a small piece of terrain. Still, because of my hard-headedness, we improved our sleeping quarters quite a bit.

Other political groups were represented there. I remember mainly a couple—man and woman—from the Union del Pueblo; a young man from the

Movimiento de Acción Revolucionaria; and a representative of the Communist Party. Of course, there were also five from the "partisan" Liga Comunista
23 de Septiembre and the five *Espartaquista-Jaramillista* fellows—Dionisio,
Guillermo, Luciano, Darío, and I. No sooner had the assembly's work started
than the first confrontations between the "partisan" group and Lucio arose.
The "partisans" publicly criticized the presence of the PCM and any other
"reformist, populist, and petty bourgeois" tendencies in the gathering. It was
Renato who voiced their discontent, denouncing before the assembly the presence of the enemy in the bosom of the revolutionary armed movement, that
is to say, our presence, that of the PCM, and the UP. He was especially acer-
bic when he referred to the envoy of the PCM. He remarked on the "revisionist and bourgeois-reformist" character of this political group, which he defined
as a "traitor to the revolutionary proletarian interests." I, as a typical petty
bourgeois myself, thought it inappropriate and impolite that guests of the
assembly should be thus insulted. I asked Dionisio for the floor and explained
what I thought. The five members of the "partisan" organization sent threatening glances my way, while Renato mumbled what I was sure had been at least
a mention of my mother. To tell the truth, I was afraid. All of them were armed
with the scary FAL 7.62 mm. One could notice their eagerness to put them to
good use against anyone who didn't think as they did. I mentioned this to
Isaías, who immediately offered me the M 2.30 mm with the long, curving
loader that he had assigned for himself so that I would not feel totally pow-
erless in the face of those *zancas*.

The work of the meeting developed over a period of a day and a half,
although truly it consisted basically of the reports, analyses, and proposals
introduced by Lucio. I perceived clearly that in this armed collective, there was
no one who could counterbalance, let alone compete against, the undisputed
leadership of Lucio over those young people, the majority of whom were from
Guerrero. I also learned that I needed to spend a longer period with the Brigade
in order to get to know the guerrilla experience more thoroughly. I was lucky
that my wish could never be fulfilled. Later I made an appointment with Oscar
in Acapulco in order to go up to the Sierra for three months, but he failed to
show. Oscar subsequently explained to me in the Federal District that he and
two *zancas* had been trying to make contact with the Brigade at the time.
Close to losing their lives at the hands of the *guachos*, they spent a week literally crawling in the high forest, barefooted, without food and water, and
wounded by thorns over their entire bodies.

Since I'm discussing how different ideological tendencies competed against
Lucio for the leadership of the Brigada de Ajusticiamiento, I'll tell another
story. During a previous ascent of the Sierra, Dionisio witnessed the visit of

two top-notch leaders of the 23 de Septiembre, apparently Oseas and "Julio." One of the two expounded to the armed group of *cabañistas* about the bourgeois character of the Mexican state. It was absolutely necessary, he added, to fight for a socialist revolution and to install the dictatorship of the proletariat, both urban and rural. This last point ideologically and politically contradicted Lucio's revolution of the poor. One of the listeners asked his neighbor how much he'd understood of all of that about the "state." The *zanca* replied that he understood perfectly well "the pitiful state we were all in." Someone else added, with a scornful *costeño* accent, that he only knew the state of Guerrero. And they kept going on in this vein.

A short while before the end of the assembly, Lucio argued insistently that the most important task of the popular revolutionary movement was to work with the people, taking as a point of departure the conditions that they saw as most urgent and worth fighting for. He underscored that the people should not be pushed to assume causes which they did not understand and for which they were not prepared. Moments later, flagrantly contradicting himself, he delineated the upcoming actions of the Brigada de Ajusticiamiento, forgetting in significant ways to highlight the political and organizational tasks of the Partido de los Pobres, which in the end had been subsumed under military priorities. The Partido was, in effect, turned into a structure at the service of the armed group.

Here are the tasks that Lucio announced:

1. Attacks against the army and the police with the objective of capturing weaponry and enabling the revolutionary forces to punish the repressive apparatus more frequently.
2. Expropriations of money from banks in order to finance arming and sustaining the different regional armed groups into which the Brigade would be divided.
3. Kidnapping of prominent members of the bourgeoisie in order to obtain money and political concessions, for example, the release of political prisoners.

I had been allowed to witness the way money was wasted, cash that had been expropriated from banks at the risk of participants' lives and freedom. Given such extravagance, I knew that no sum would ever be enough for the Brigade. The problem was that they never invested any money in ventures that, in time, could help them finance the struggle permanently. Such ventures could help develop technical and administrative skills that could later be put to the service of the people. As it was, any currency disappeared too fast, given away at the slightest request from the myriad poor relatives that surrounded the revolutionaries in the area of Atoyac—the very same people in whom they expected to find the support base for an armed movement.

Once the work of the Second Assembly of the Partido de los Pobres had been completed, we prepared for our descent from the Sierra. Lucio called me aside and gave me 15,000 pesos to take to the man we had visited in Durango. He asked a compañero who was planning to go down to the coast—possibly his own brother—to guide us to the federal highway. Somewhat worried about my mission, I hid the money by taping it under one of the Dr. Scholl's metal and leather insoles that I wore in my sandals. Subsequently we started our descent, following the route that had been determined as the safest for our group.

The guide took us downhill quite fast. Running a great deal, we covered most of the descent in half the time it had taken us to go up. The bulk under the arch of my left foot began to bother me very much. I realized it had been a mistake to secrete the money there. The pressure of restraining my downward movement had caused the adhesive tape to bunch up. It rubbed against the thin skin of my foot, ultimately generating a huge blister. It wasn't long before the blister burst, and the wound became covered with dirt. With my foot hurting, I limped forward for a short while until we reached a stream. Dionisio, Darío and I took advantage of the water to bathe, shave, and make ourselves somewhat presentable before reaching the road.

We were in the middle these tasks of personal hygiene when we heard the unmistakable noise of a helicopter approaching the area. At our guide's signal, we ran naked out of the water and hid behind the bushes that grew along the banks of the creek. In addition to the natural fear that one experiences in any situation of danger, we had to add the sensation of helplessness at being unarmed and undressed. We were lucky, though—the copter kept on going. It was flying high. Perhaps because of that, the occupants saw neither Guillermo's case nor our clothing extended on nearby rocks. We dressed in a hurry, just in case the helicopter came back.

There was something our guide did that I did not like. It happened as we approached a dangerous road intersection. First, stopping our march, the man remarked that we were coming to a place where *guachos* used to wait in ambush. Then he sent us forward at intervals, one by one, while he remained behind, protected by the vegetation. It seemed to me that he looked out for himself instead of securing the safety of the men that Lucio had placed under his charge. He may have calculated that his own safety was more important than ours for Lucio, for the Brigade, and, of course, for himself. After all, we were not even members of the Partido de los Pobres.

We came to the edge of the federal road. Our guide had gone his own way shortly before, having hidden his holster in the undergrowth and wrapped the gun in newspaper to make it look like just any old merchandise. Halfway to our destination, Dionisio purchased a homemade saddle from an old peasant as we passed in front of his humble ranch. He thought he could explain our presence in the area by showing what we had been after. Frankly, I thought it was a childish alibi. Fortunately we did not run into *guachos* or judicial police. Imagine my situation! I—freckled, light skinned, wearing a hat from the hot country (I had purchased it in the trip to Huetamo, Michoacán, about which I spoke earlier), wearing sandals from Huichapan in Hidalgo, totally different from the footwear used in the coast, dressed in cotton clothing that resembled an industrial uniform. Even the most careless military or police inspection would've gotten me. The people we encountered near the federal highway stared at me. We decided to separate into two groups and to take different busses to Acapulco. We saw a bus approach the spot where Dionisio, Luciano and I were hiding. Waiting until it was even closer—two hundred meters from us—we ran across the road, signaling to the driver to stop. We thus got back to the intersection from where we had previously boarded the bus for El Ciruelo. From there, I walked on my own to the house of Dionisio's compadre to pick up the Volkswagen while everyone else waited nearby. Arriving all sweaty from the walk and the elevated noontime temperature, I gave myself a shower with a hose in an unused pigsty that had no animals. I cleaned the open wound under my left foot the best I could. Then I turned on the engine and went to pick up the rest of my group for our return to Morelos and the Federal District.

FURTHER EFFORTS FOR THE ORGANIZATION

I don't remember how we did it, but the compañeros from Durango received the money Lucio sent to them. I can't recall either how they established contact with the compañeros from Santa Clara, specifically with Nicolás, to let them know that they were around. They needed to agree on a place and time for the transfer of some "merchandise," a dozen used hunting weapons, that Miguel had asked them to get a hold of. I do remember going with Nicolás and Juan to meet them in a rustic hotel in the town of Zumpango de la Laguna in the state of Mexico. We talked in their room about conditions in Durango and the rest of the country. We agreed that Nicolás should stay with them and show them an appropriate place for the exchange, set for later that night. Close to midnight, we arrived at the location where we would receive the weapons. All we had was a 22 mm. caliber Mendoza submachine gun, which nobody involved in the operation knew how to use or had ever fired. Since I had a bit more experience with hunting weapons, the protection of the operation fell to me. I placed myself behind some large boulders. The night was dark, and it was difficult to see even our immediate surroundings. We left our VW hidden behind some bushes. The place we had chosen for the exchange was a depression in the terrain, a kind of bowl, separated from us by a few mounds covered with dry grass. It could not be seen from the road even though the federal highway was just around the corner. We waited nervously for forty long and tedious minutes, until we heard a vehicle reducing speed as it approached us. A minute later it headed right toward us with its headlights turned off. Nicolás identified the car immediately. With a flashlight, he guided the compañeros until they parked parallel to our car. As soon as we greeted one another, we transferred the arms from their vehicle to ours. Once this was over, we said goodbye and left the place behind. At that point, our problem became one of what to do with the weapons before we organized their transfer to Guerrero. Juan suggested leaving them in the house of an industrial worker, a compañero who lived near the garrison in Ecatepec where independence-era Generalissimo José María Morelos y Pavón was executed. It was a place I had already visited, when I brought Lucio to meet Oscar, professor Modesto Trujillo, and the other compañeros involved in planning the assault on the Banco Comercial Mexicano. We headed there, hoping to convince this man to keep Lucio's merchandise for us.

We had no problem with him. He understood the urgency of our situation very well and agreed to store the weapons in his house. I thought I noticed in his face some slight satisfaction that we had trusted him so much. He asked his wife to get up and proceeded with our help to place the weapons under the bed, undoubtedly the most valuable piece of furniture in his humble residence. All this took place close to two o'clock in the morning in an isolated barrio with empty streets, few dwellings or lights, and a plentiful supply of barking dogs whose efforts to alarm the neighbors continued as long as we were in the vicinity.

A few weeks later, I went back to pick up half of the merchandise which Gorgonio planned to take to Guerrero. I placed the rifles, shotguns, and ammunition in two old, cheap suitcases—almost pure cardboard—that Gorgonio had supplied me. Since they were both heavy and fragile, I tied them up with henequen rope to reinforce them. I didn't think that our packages were the most appropriate for the merchandise. They looked to me positively suspicious. But after I showed them to Gorgonio in don Jesús's house where he was lodging, he said that they were fine with him. He asked me to take him to the bus terminal that very night so that he could travel to Acapulco. I left him on San Antonio Abad Avenue, at the doorsteps of the Flecha Roja bus line, admiring his temerity in traveling in such a carefree manner with such luggage. I had to take the rest of the merchandise, five long rifles, to Ometepec in the Costa Chica, after picking up the contact that would guide me there in the village of El Cuarenta. Apparently, Lucio was in the process of organizing another armed group in that location. I made this trip in the company of a compañera of the Organization. Our plan was to pretend to be a couple of newlyweds. The arms, as had happened before, were tied to the inner springs of the back seat. The delivery proved successful, and the trip presented no special troubles, other than the fear and tension of passing through the customary military roadblock with its inspection by the *guachos*, fortunately a superficial one this time, and the delay of our contact and guide at El Cuarenta.

When I met compañero Mónico Rodríguez Gómez, I realized that his personality fully matched the legend about his life as a militant communist fully dedicated to the popular struggle. Our encounter took place on the occasion of a meeting of the Organization's leadership, convened by Dionisio and Isauro and scheduled at a mountain spot in the highlands of Morelos. Guillermo, Darío, and Luciano also attended. Along with Mónico, they had been politically active with Rubén Jaramillo in the Partido Agrario Obrero Morelense. From the beginning, I liked the way Mónico presented himself: his modesty and simplicity, the way he dressed, a bandana tied around his neck. His small, angular, and furrowed face reflected years of resistance, tension, and suffering. Particularly impressive was the man's persistence, in spite of the painful history of failures and disappointments in the struggles of the railroad union, sugar cane workers, industrial workers, and university personnel. He had been in Zacatepec, in Atencingo, and in Puebla, acting there along side Luis Rivera Terrazas in the Autonomous University of Puebla. He had participated in the agrarian struggles of the Llanos de Michapa and El Guarín. He had shared experiences with Francisco Ruiz, better known as "El Gorraprieta," Rubén Jaramillo, Félix Serdán, and Jesús Martínez Lizalde, the treasurer of the PCM and superintendent of transport at the Ferrocarriles Nacionales de México, and the father of Ifigenia Martínez de Navarrete.

Mónico was certainly a good man who had given all of his energy to the struggle for socialism and the international communist movement without placing his personal interests ahead of others. As happened to many other old communists, the 20th Congress of the Communist Party of the Soviet Union and comrade Khrushchev's denunciation of Stalin's personality cult and crimes had demoralized him, plunging him into political and ideological confusion. He had devoted the best years of his life to the communist cause, sacrificing himself, his dear wife and compañera Beta Galarza, and his sons and daughters, especially Javier, who suffered from serious problems in one of his legs—all so that an unknown bureaucrat and social climber in the Soviet party could declare that everything had been a sinister and bloody nightmare. To what an illusion he had wagered his life and that of his family!

The day of that meeting, Mónico reconnected with the struggle. Sitting on a rock in a glen of the forest, he'd recovered his old fighting spirit. He seemed concentrated in summoning back the well of personal wisdom acquired through life's blows and everyday experiences. With a natural style, stripped of any excess rhetoric, he addressed the assembly to describe the working conditions prevalent in the CIVAC industries on the outskirts of the city of Cuernavaca, and the precarious economic situation of his neighbors, the *ejidatarios* of Chiconcuac, Morelos. Mónico argued from the perspective of more than forty years in a variety of political and social conflicts.

He was in the midst of an explanation when all of a sudden the past was too much for him, leaving him overcome by emotion and tears. I had the impression of being the only one in the group surprised at the eruption of feelings, kept in check for so long and now explosively expressed.

After that day, I had many more opportunities to interact with Mónico, to learn more about his militant life, and to see him in action politically and personally. I was envious of the time he lived through, and of the challenges that he had faced. In those days, I thought myself capable of similar revolutionary deeds. Now I realize how wrong I was. Professionally, Mónico was a highly skilled worker with a specialization in metal mechanics. During the administration of Manuel Avila Camacho, at the peak of World War II, he designed and built a model automatic antiaircraft gun, which he delivered to the Ministry of War and the Navy, then headed by Lázaro Cárdenas del Río. The government in turn sent the model on to Washington, where it was apparently put to good use.

Around that time, Isauro presented me with the urgent need to find temporary shelter for a couple from the Frente Urbano Zapatista (FUZ) and from the Lacandón Commandos, Susana and Francisco. They both were much sought after by different groups of police. The couple had been forced to vacate their last residence, leaving all of their belongings behind. Isauro suggested that we use the home of the young couple of philosophy professors at the Universidad Autónoma Metropolitana (UAM), Nicolás and María. They would have to be consulted, naturally, but they seemed to have the kind of house where two more could fit. The couple accepted for two or three weeks, while a more suitable place was found in the countryside, maybe in Morelos, where Susana and Francisco could be safer and move about with greater freedom. Isauro transported them to their new home, where I met them two or three days later.

I showed up there because they needed someone they could trust to pick up a few belongings from their previous dwelling. They'd had to leave quickly due to an incident. Francisco, well known to the authorities, had been stopped by policemen one night while he urinated on the street. Since he could not afford to be searched, he decided to pull out his gun, shoot, and run. The unfortunate episode had taken place just around the corner from the house where he rented a room with Susana and their young daughter. They cleared out minutes later with nothing but what they were wearing. Their fame pre-ceded them: they had participated in kidnappings and assaults, and were reputed to be capable in armed operations. From my perspective, since I lacked experience in those areas, I was happy to meet them and hoped to learn from them.

Only two weeks later, the couple asked me to meet with them. They needed to go back to their old house to retrieve a television used to entertain their daughter. Susana explained her plan to get near the primary school attended by her former landlady's own daughter. Right when school was out, Susana could approach the child and ask what the situation was with the house. The couple described this woman, doña Lupe, as a smart and dis-trustful person. Yet they claimed to have gained her sympathy and confi-dence. Their only worry was a brother who the woman had said was a judi-cial policeman. Off we went in the Organization's vehicle, with the intention of having Susana speak first to doña Lupe's young daughter. The ten-year old child looked quite puzzled. She answered in monosyllables, obviously discon-certed by the questions. Glued to the wheel, observing the scene, I did not like what I saw. Susana had described her relationship to this girl as warm, close, and friendly, but the child looked reserved. I began to question my assumptions. The blind, absurd, gratuitous trust I had placed in the couple began to crumble. Susana came back to the car saying that there was no prob-lem, that everything was okay, and that we could approach the house. Uncon-vinced, I did what she asked. I drove past the building. All looked normal, so I decided to stop and park the car half a block away. At that point my nerv-ousness and that of my guide were quite evident. If there were any police watching the house, it had been a mistake to drive by and then park so near. The vehicle could be tracked so easily, even in the hypothetical event that we could flee the house and reach it. Anyway, we had no alternative, since we were after a television and other bulky items, which could not be carried any distance easily.

We walked slowly toward the house, anxiously observing all around us, making sure everything continued to look normal. What if the police were waiting inside the house? Susana and I were sweating by the time we reached doña Lupe's door. The compañera rang the bell and called out doña Lupe's name. Señora Guadalupe proved to be an extremely self-possessed, energetic woman with a round, red face and a scrutinizing pair of light colored eyes. As she opened the door, she looked as if she were thinking: "Here is what you were looking for." In a singsong voice, she said: "Happy the eyes that see you, güerita." Nervous and befuddled, Susana answered with an elaborate story intended to explain her disappearance in the middle of the night two weeks earlier. It sounded pretty unconvincing to doña Lupe and to me. The landlady's sagacity matched her greed. She thought she could become the owner of the couple's belongings, explaining that the police had been there asking about them that very morning, promising to return later. When she heard that, Susana started frenetically to collect clothing, books, school supplies, and various and sundry toiletries. Meanwhile Lupe looked on with growing suspicion, as Susana became more and more unhinged. I felt panic gripping me. I thought that at any moment we might see the arrival of police agents, ready to arrest us and subject us to torture.

I unplugged the precious TV set and placed it on the bed. I piled some of the clothes that the compañera feverishly continued to gather inside paper bags. Then I decided to bring the car closer by. I whispered this to Susana's ear, adding that we should really get out of there without delay since we were running a great risk. On the street my legs shook as I walked toward the car, thinking that this was the perfect moment for the police to stop me. I started the engine, and after taking a U-turn, I parked right in front of the house. Since the police were nowhere to be seen, I was convinced they would follow us with the intent of grabbing us all as soon as we met Francisco at the philosophers' house in Mexico City. Meanwhile I put the TV and the clothes in the backseat. Susana said goodbye to doña Lupe, asking her to take care of the belongings she could not take with her now—her bed, stove, and cooking utensils. She paid the rent and promised to go back to visit and pick up the rest of her things. Finally we left, flushed and tense. I drove around and around, trying to observe in the rearview mirror whether we had a tail.

Nobody followed us. I concluded that my first inkling was right. Doña Lupe had made us afraid so that she could keep the couple's most valuable possessions. But this episode with compañera Susana was a lesson to me. I should not trust a priori the reputation or supposed merits of anyone, whether they were legitimate, self-proclaimed, or invented by third parties with their own agenda—the political police, for example. Unfortunately, it was a lesson that I have not completely internalized. I still fall victim once in a while to this foolish behavior.

＼DISCOVERING GUERRILLA WARFARE

The first knowledge I acquired about guerrilla movements in Latin America was the interview of Fidel Castro, conducted by the famous North American journalist Herbert Matthews in the Sierra Maestra and published by the *New York Times* plus the pictures in *Life Magazine*. The second time, I was reading reports by Mario Menéndez Rodríguez for the weekly *Sucesos para Todos* about the Colombian ELN (Camilo Torres, the guerrilla priest) and the FARC (Manuel Marulanda, nicknamed "Sure Shot") as well as the Venezuelan guerrilla Douglas Bravo and the Guatemalan rebels (Yon Sosa, Luis Turcios Lima, and César Montes). At that time, 1966–1967, I was twenty-five and twenty-six years old, I had been married two years, and I was working in my first job in the public sector in the Office of Centers of Industrial Training, a minor unit within industrial and commercial higher education section of the Secretariat of Public Education, the General Office of Technological, Industrial, and Commercial Instruction. I was responsible for the public relations activities of this program. The offices were located in the Cathedral Passageway that connected the streets of Donceles and Guatemala through a commercial corridor occupied by locales that sold medicinal herbs, coffee, ground or whole, orthopedic prosthetics, and religious books and other articles. There were also cheap places to eat. All of this was behind the Metropolitan Cathedral.

This was a time when I dreamt of becoming a writer of short stories, novels, and poetry. Everyday, all morning long, I drank delicious aromatic coffee in the Café Río on Donceles. I left my office frequently and furtively. I had very little work to do. In less than three years we had four directors. So I would walk around the area over and over, exploring the Cathedral, the churches, and the chapels of the historic center. I was attempting to identify the alchemic symbols that Carl Gustav Jung described and sometimes reproduced in several of his works, especially *Psychology and Alchemy*, symbols that Fulcanelli also talks about in his *The Mystery of Cathedrals*. The ill-fated Nacho Vallarta used to quote the latter frequently in the nighttime gatherings at the home of his cousin Juan Trigos.

Those were the years when I displayed with pride and naïveté the slogan "I do not mean I am right; I mean this is the way I am," which I had read somewhere written on a sheet of paper and stuck on one of the walls of the tiny apartment that, as newlyweds, Tere and I occupied at 21 Veracruz Avenue in Colonia Condesa. At the time I was also reading *The Portrait of the Artist as a Young Man* by James Joyce, alternating it with the *Alexandria Quartet* by

Lawrence Durrell, *Letters to a Young Poet* and the *Notebook of Malte Lauids Brigge* by Rainer Maria Rilke, as well as *The Process* by Franz Kafka. Those were intense times in which I would wake up in the morning in a state of angry rebellion against my boring daily bureaucratic obligations. I dreamt of living like Carlos Fuentes in Europe—in Paris or Dublin—economically supported by the publication of my writings (as yet unwritten, of course) in the most famous dailies and weeklies of the world. Sitting at a small round table at Café Río, I would drink the first cup of the day while I perused the newspaper *El Día*, reading with special attention the international pages and the column "For Your Own Control" by J. Téllez Girón, the pseudonym that Manuel Buendía used at the time, as well as the column "It's an O Because It's Round" by China Mendoza.

I started a friendship with an electrical engineer, a graduate of the National Polytechnical Institute, who worked as an advisor in one of the industrial and technical education areas of the Secretariat of Public Education. His offices were one floor below mine. This engineer—I regret that I've forgotten his name—belonged to the secret Rosacrucian Society, and he proudly wore the emblematic ring of that mysterious group. Every day around noon, this man—between thirty-five and forty years old, of medium height and thick build with an oval face and fine features, with bright black hair combed backwards, and with thick eyeglasses in a wide black frame— appeared in front of my desk and invited me to have a cup of coffee. This was wonderful for me, because I had very little money, only enough for a daily cup drunk after checking in around 8:15 in the morning. Sometimes I would get lucky, and the engineer would invite me for a third cup. I talked with him about everything. I remember that he was alarmed at the possibility that the Partido de Acción Nacional could win the national elections and place a reactionary man in the presidency of the republic. He also spoke about his afternoon job, which consisted of overseeing the technical quality and transmission frequency ranges for the chain of radio stations where he also worked. He shared with me a devotion to arms and was one of those shooters who could place a bullet where his eye wanted it. I confirmed this the day I invited him to the pigeon shooting club in which my father was a member. We enjoyed going to the gun shops in the area to admire pistols, shotguns, and rifles for sale. I am writing about the years before 1968 when this trade flourished, mainly on the streets of Brasil, Donceles, and Argentina. We did exactly the same thing with the large number of stores that sold new and used books in the area. He headed for the technical books, while I went to the shelves holding fiction and poetry. Strangely enough, he never invited me directly or subtly to visit the secret society of which he was a member. The truth is that

I never expressed any interest in knowing about it, since I considered it lacking in seriousness.

During those walks, I often found the *Voz Obrera* and *Voz de México* on newspaper stands. These were publications of comrade Posadas of the IV Trotskyite International and of the Mexican Communist Party respectively. At first I started to pay attention to the headlines of both newspapers; a while later, I dared to buy and read them. The hallucinatory rhetoric of comrade Posadas attracted my attention, since reading that prose constituted an almost cinematographic experience. The masses in each country and continent he described paraded combatively before my eyes. In contrast, reading the press of the PCM was an experience in sheer boredom. Up to that moment, the Cuban Revolution, Fidel Castro, Camilo Cienfuegos, and Che Guevara had gone right on by me as if "at night." I really hadn't paid much attention to them at all, worried as I was about finding myself, searching obsessively in books and university classrooms for the vocation—the call—that would make my personal fulfillment possible. Certainly, the Iberoamericana University of those years was not the best place in which to become concerned with the social and political issues of Mexico, although, there were one or two professors who spoke to us about the problems of the country. To give an example of what we were living through at the Universidad Iberoamericana (UIA), it's enough to remember that during the inauguration of the new facilities on Avenida de las Torres in Colonia Churubusco, Carlos Trouyet, the president of the Patronato, quite seriously asked that the academic institution become the "pink university" of Mexico.[1]

At the end of 1966 or the beginning of 1967, when José María (Chema) Pérez Gay had just arrived from Germany to spend a few days, he told me of the great interest and fascination that European university communities had for the figure and trajectory of Ernesto Che Guevara. He read to me a fragment of some European essay writer about the Argentine guerrilla fighter. Thus, I became vividly interested in this mysterious man who joined in himself theory and practice, the idea and the sword. Immediately, I acquired and read in one sitting the mythical inaugural book by the Cuban journalist Carlos Franqui, *Cuba, the Book of Twelve*, published by Editorial ERA in its Popular Series, a volume that for quite a while had been winking at me from the shelves of bookstores. With growing desire, I hunted for *Guerrilla Warfare, a Method* by Che himself, without being able to find it anywhere.

That is where I was when Cuba organized first the Tricontinental Conference and later the Organización Latinoamericana de Solidaridad (OLAS) in Havana, events of international political importance to which Che sent—from wherever he was—two documents in the form of manifestos. I was impressed

especially by the one entitled *To Create Two, Three, Many Vietnams*, in particular his invitation to all Latin American revolutionaries to join the revolution
in other countries if the objective and subjective conditions for beginning the
revolution had not yet been reached in their own lands. The book by Régis
Debray, *Revolution within the Revolution?*, had just come out in Havana.
Debray was the French philosopher that the Bolivian army would later detain
as he attempted to leave the zone where Che's guerrilla force had begun to
operate. The work was a defense of the guerrilla *foco* as the primordial ember
that would start the social fire they were trying to provoke. It condemned the
reformist politics and the bureaucratic practices of communist parties, whom
he accused of wanting to stop the revolution rather than to fight it. Having
found out about the book in the newspapers, I made my way for the first time
to the Cuban Embassy to request a copy. They claimed all copies sent from
the island had already been given away. I had to wait until somebody—either
Sergio Gómez Montero or Héctor Aguilar Camín, I don't remember who—
could get a hold of a copy from *El Día* or from their friends at the embassy.
Once it was in my hands, I literally devoured it. I was fertile ground for the
sewing of these simplifying ideas. That was what I needed to read because that
was what I wanted to do.

The newspapers of the time stirred up a campaign of anti-Communist
outrage against Cuba, Fidel Castro, and Che, as well as the subversive projects that had been adopted in the terrorist conclaves of the Tricontinental
and the OLAS. The climate of ideological and political intolerance grew
stronger every day. During those months, I frequently saw Sergio Gómez
Montero and Héctor Aguilar Camín, friends several years younger than I
with whom I shared literary interests. I began to exchange ideas about the
national reality, the Cuban Revolution, and the need to commit ourselves in
the struggle against Yankee imperialism and the Mexican bourgeoisie. Most
of these encounters took place in the boarding house that Doña Emma
Camín, Héctor's mother, operated. I do remember one special occasion in
Sergio's house, in a rooftop studio room, where he read to Héctor and me
the chapter of a novel that he was writing that we both liked very much. It
was through the two of them that I met Arturo Cantú, who was working for
the newspaper *El Día*, and with whom we also examined the urgency and
viability of a new revolution in Mexico. They also introduced me to the
Cuban painter René Alís and his wife Elisa, an Ecuadorian political asylee.
The couple with their young daughter Krupskaia occupied a room in Doña
Emma's house. And these two friends contributed decisively to my getting a
visa at the Cuban embassy. Thus, I could travel to the island at the end of
September, 1967.

IN CUBA

René Alís kept Tere company as she said goodbye to me at the airport. He introduced me to Manuel Marcué Pardiñas, the editor of *Política* magazine, who was also there. Marcué Pardiñas asked me for some help for a young woman in his company who would also be on my flight. I saw no problem in agreeing to do the favor—carrying on board a heavy package containing copies of the latest issue of *Política* and later unloading it at José Martí airport in Cuba.

I must say that it took lots of effort to convince Tere that my trip was an advance mission to prepare the way for her and our daughter. I'm convinced that my wife let me go alone to the island only to prevent a possibly irreparable break with me, given my obstinate determination to make the trip. Che's idea of sacrificing everything, including one's life, served as my guide. I still hadn't learned to know myself, or anyone else for that matter. As far as life goes, I'd just begun living it on my own. In truth, I wasn't even sure that Tere and our daughter would follow me soon. I didn't know who or where they might send me to fight as Guevara proclaimed.

In those years of the presidency of Gustavo Díaz Ordaz, anyone traveling to or from Cuba was photographed by agents of the Secretariat of Government while going through the official migration procedures at the airport. Passports were stamped with the phrases "Left for Cuba" or "Returned from Cuba." Once through this embarrassing bureaucratic-police step, the young woman and I boarded the Cubana de Aviación Ylushin turboprop. I set next to her and set the Marcué Pardiñas' package of *Política* issues on the floor between us. In doing so, I realized that the magazine cover was a photo of Che Guevara, something that increased my interest in leafing through the magazine. I asked the girl if I might see one of the copies of the issue, and she urged me to go ahead. As I showed her with satisfaction Che's photograph, I asked her if she knew who he was. Her reply shook me from head to toe. I couldn't believe my luck. She told me with a candid, proud smile: "Yes, of course. He's my uncle!" I was beside myself with joy. It turned out that she was a niece of Hilda Gadea Acosta, Che's Peruvian first wife and mother of Hildita, his oldest child.

I felt like I was dreaming when she confessed to me that her aunt Hilda would personally be waiting for her at the airport in Cuba. I didn't think that my circumstances could get any better than that. She even offered me a ride in her aunt's car to Havana since the airport was several kilometers from the city. However, the Cuban migratory authorities asked me for my international vaccination certificate, a document that nobody had told me about. So I became separated from the young woman since I had to receive a shot in the infirmary. The golden opportunity to meet compañera Gadea had begun to evaporate, but luck hadn't abandoned me completely. The girl stuck her head into the infirmary in order to give me a piece of paper with her aunt's phone number, asking me to step forward to the door to wave her aunt a greeting. That I did. Hilda Gadea looked at me from behind a counter, giving me a wave and making hand signals indicating that I should call on the phone. The hope of traveling into Havana in the Guevara family's car had been frustrated. After a nurse had vaccinated me, the migration authorities let me enter the country. I left the airport, uncertain whether to grab a bus or a cab, ultimately deciding on the latter lest I get lost. The driver asked me if I had a reservation in some hotel. When I told him no, he suggested that I go to the Nacional. Lacking any alternative, I accepted.

The journey into town cost me eight Cuban pesos, eight U.S. dollars at the official Cuban rate of exchange at the time. My room at the Nacional cost another seven dollars per day without any meals. I began to worry, since I had only one hundred dollars in my pocket. It this rate it would be gone very soon. I'd planned to work wherever the Cubans wanted me; for example, cutting sugar cane, a solidarity activity in the romantic imagination of the time if there ever was one. Once installed at the Nacional, I set out to walk around nearby areas. The hotel was located across from the breakwater and from the monument to *Le Coubre*, a Belgian ship that Yankee imperialism had blown up with plastic explosives in March, 1960, costing the lives of 136 stevedores and sailors. The freighter had docked in Havana with a load of arms purchased by the Revolution. In the corner of the hotel, a rapid-fire antiaircraft gun was mounted, protected by piles of sandbags. The whole atmosphere of Havana was one of anticipation of war. Armed militiamen with bright and colorful uniforms—pants of olive green and sky blue shirts—were everywhere, guarding the entrances of public buildings. Spectacular billboards with the photograph of Fidel Castro and revolutionary slogans of the moment appeared all over town. At the hotel and its surrounding areas, one encountered people of all latitudes and of all races, of strange languages and physiognomies, some quite tall with chiseled features, with very white skins, robust physiques, and blond, red, or black hair—in particular women of a beauty I'd never witnessed before. There were East Germans, Czechs, Slovaks, Bulgarians, Hungarians, Poles, and Russians. I couldn't help but think that the Cubans had traded the gringos for these other *güeros*.

The first thing that I did the day after my arrival in Havana was to telephone the offices of the ICMRC, the Cuban–Mexican Institute for Cultural

Relations, in order to get in touch with compañera Mercedes, its director. René Alís had provided me a letter asking her to give me her support during my stay in Cuba. She asked me to come and see her at the Institute, and so I did. I handed her the letter. After reading it, she asked me what my plans were. In an open, naive, and awkward manner, I spoke of my willingness to receive military and political training in order to take part in revolutionary activities wherever necessary, as Che had advocated. Mercedes seemed surprised at my approach and replied that she did not believe that her country engaged in such training, but that she would check. I, in turn, making my clumsy behavior even worse, criticized the Mexican government and the growing anti-Castro campaigns in the public media that demanded that the Mexican government break diplomatic relations with Cuba. I reviewed all of the repressive moves ordered by the president of Mexico, Gustavo Díaz Ordaz, the most recent one being the massacre of copra workers in Acapulco. What I didn't know then, given my ignorance and lack of experience, was that the last thing the Cuban government wanted to do was to lose its friendship with the only country and government in the American continent with whom it maintained diplomatic relations along with contact by sea and air. So what I was saying about the Mexican government represented something they certainly didn't want to hear, especially because it was a Mexican who was saying it. They must have seen me as an agent provocateur sent by the CIA. But not everything went wrong that day. When I revealed my dramatic lack of resources, compañera Mercedes gave me a free room in a more modest hotel than the Nacional, as well as a subsidy of seven Cuban pesos for food every other day. She also offered me an excursion to different parts of the island, which I did not appreciate or accept given that my interest was not to practice "revolutionary tourism."

I did not desist in my decision to receive military and political training, as well as to work in the sugar cane harvest. Every day at mid morning I went to the Institute to see if they had any answer to my request. It was there that I met Alberto Ruz, and his beautiful and intelligent compañera. He was then a young and restless Mexican like me, only with more experience. He was visiting the island for the third time. Since he was the son of the famous archeologist Alberto Ruz Huiller, he was well known to the leaders of the Cuban Revolution. I have to recognize here that I did not pass up the opportunity and quickly attached myself to the couple and their attractive agenda. I went with them to the ICAIC, the Cuban Institute for the Arts and Film Industry to see Cuban documentaries, something that proved an important experience since it filled in some of the holes in my information about the Revolution. We also went to visit CUBANACAN, the art institute where we had the chance to attend an Afro-Cuban dance. Seeing our interest in this music and dance, our guide, a beautiful government employee from Havana, extended an invitation for us to accompany a group of dancers the next day to a *santería* ceremony (Yoruba, rule of Ochún) in a thatched roof establishment in a low-income Havana neighborhood.

It proved to be a memorable session of rhythms and counterpoints, a sensual mix of races, smells, and colors, all cooked in the fire of the dance: blond, blue-eyed Galicians integrated by conviction and rhythm in the syncretism of the Afro-Christian ritual; black people with shiny skin the color of ebony; mulatoes of Chinese-like skin and slanted eyes; peoples of very diverse African origins like the Nubian priest with delicate Egyptian features who led the ceremony. A concert of tumbadores, timbales, and bongos, of multiple movements, rhythms, and cadences entered our souls, altered the rhythm of hearts, and elevated the temperature of blood. Among the females, some of great beauty, the ones who most amazed me by their way of keeping time and its cadences were the oldest. Almost without moving from the floor, they set the beat for tumberos, bongoceros, timbaleros, and dancers. Before a great altar dedicated to Yemayá, goddess of water (the Virgin of Regla), built on a base of fruit offerings, the faithful of the santero cult danced to an increasingly greater resonance with the drums; they seemed to be at the point of emotional and physical collapse. The climax was not far off. In the midst of a frenetic trance, the Nubian priest was "touched by the holy one." Dressed in white, the slender and athletic celebrant started convulsing from head to toe at the same time as he was touching the heads of the women closest to him with his long and fine hands, transmitting to them the same epileptic agitation. In the midst of the hubbub, I became aware of two robust black participants, who had sandwiched my shoulders in between theirs, making sure I would not attempt to participate in the collective madness that was developing out of the *santería* ceremony at the time when bodies and spirits were reaching the boiling point. Soon all of the celebrants were exhausted; the show was over. I left in a state of agitation. A very strong headache tormented my temples and the back of my neck. The exciting rhythms of the tumbas, congas, and timbales refused to abandon my ears, remaining in them all night and for several days ahead.

Alberto Ruz engaged in constant and open criticism of diverse aspects of the Revolution, helping me to begin to see the social and political phenomena of the island in less naive and simple terms. I thus learned about situations that put into question the false and romantic idea that I had brought in my head about the universality of justice and popular consensus. Nevertheless, I began to feel a little bit uncomfortable with this couple that equally criticized the educational methods copied from the USSR (Makarenko); the lack of spirituality (imposed official atheism); the systematic and permanent

persecution of homosexuals (and their incorporation into Military Production Support Units in order to reeducate them through forced labor); the
annulment of the freedom of trade unions; the meddling in the personal lives
of people on the part of the Committees for the Defense of the Revolution
(one per city block), and the tragic consequences of this meddling in the so-
called Popular Trials, etc. On the one hand, I liked to hear their criticisms
because they taught me about problems, but at the same time, they produced
a certain resentment in me. I began to doubt the advisability of keeping company with them. It could make my plans with the Cuban authorities more difficult. This reaction made me feel exactly as if I were in Mexico.

With the Ruz couple, I met a young Cuban filmmaker from the ICAIC,
the day they projected documentaries for us. The young man had already
directed his first documentary. If my memory does not betray me, I think his
last name was Giral, and his documentary on the rebellion and violence of
black people in large North American cities was entitled *Now*. I don't remember his first name, but I do recall that he found me a few days later in the
vestibule of the Havana Libre as I was leaving the restaurant of the hotel,
where Mercedes had invited me to lunch along with a Mexican literati couple. These two were intent on doing revolutionary tourism at the expense of
the Cuban government. Since I didn't have any place to go that afternoon, the
Cuban filmmaker and I walked a few blocks to a bar to drink a beer. We conversed a bit about everything. When I asked about the existence of delinquents, he explained that there were some—"lumpen," he called them. These
misfits felt cornered by the Revolution, and thus their despair made them
potentially dangerous. After a while we left the bar, and he invited me to walk
home with him. We walked all the way to an old, two-story house that he
shared with four people, not far from the area called El Vedado. He lived in
one of the rooms with a compañero to whom he introduced me to right off.

Later a young woman who lived in the room next door arrived. We spoke
a bit about me and about Mexico. During our conversation, I commented on
my interest in seeing the *Battle of Algiers*, a film by Gillo Pontecorvo for which
I had seen an advertising poster in the street. I told them that I had always
wanted to see it, but that in Mexico the government had forbidden its exhibition. Caridad offered to go with me to see it and off we went.

The film surpassed all my expectations. Truly, I could not have found a
better tonic to reinforce my revolutionary commitment at that moment. I left
the exhibition hall with my spirit and senses uplifted by a wish for adventure
and personal fulfillment. During the projection, Caridad and I had held hands.
I succumbed to the sexually liberated ambiance that one could perceive during those years in Havana and the strong sensation of personal freedom that

had surged forward in that social context. The sexual drive typical of my age, and my own immaturity made me forget the fidelity I owed Tere. I ended up spending the night in the room of the young Cuban, contradicting in an obtuse and irresponsible way the speech I had made to Mercedes about my resolve and the consequent vital necessity to get the revolutionary government to allow me to bring my wife and daughter to Cuba.

I remember the date well. It was the first of October 1967. I went to the house of the former compañera of Che, the Peruvian Hilda Gadea, after phoning her niece who said that I could come by and visit. In my mind, I can vaguely picture a shelf with photos of Che, Hilda, and Hildita, and a large photograph of the Argentine–Cuban comandante hanging on the main wall of the living room. I recall a brief glance at the daughter who resembled her father very much, and who rapidly appeared and disappeared while her mother spoke with me. Compañera Gadea welcomed me and listened. She immediately scolded me for traveling to Cuba in such a naive and senseless way without the backing of a party or any known organization. She harangued me for my irresponsibility. She then apologized because she had to leave, since she was invited to the reception organized by the embassy of the People's Republic of China. (The triumph of the Chinese revolution is celebrated October 1). She asked that I return another day so that we could continue talking. I left ashamed and annoyed. Compañera Hilda was right, but she had hit me hard, so I never called her on the telephone or came by her house again.

Time went by fast, and Mercedes had no answers for me. My impatience increased. Meanwhile, I seemed to go out of my way to accumulate mistakes in the eyes of the Cubans. One day, as I returned to the hotel where I spent nights, the elevator operator invited me to participate in a stint of volunteer work that the personnel of the hotel and its neighbors planned for Saturday, the following day. Although I knew that he was throwing me a curveball, I nevertheless made an excuse, saying that I already had another commitment. I wanted to go with the Ruzes to see some other documentaries at ICAIC. Another morning, as I went to the ICMRC to visit Mercedes and inquire about my request, she proposed that I visit different parts of the island to see what the Revolution had done. As if the invitation had been an insult, I rejected it at once. I insisted that my aim was to further my ideological preparation and receive military training, as well as to help in the sugar cane harvest.

I left feeling quite bothered, and as Caridad and I were walking along the street in the area known as La Rampa, we passed in front of the labor department. When my companion pointed that out, I ran in to the reception area without even thinking. I approached one of the two young Cuban women in charge, informing her that I was a Mexican who'd come to Cuba to help the

Revolution, and that I wanted to get a job, preferably in the countryside, to fulfill my purpose. The young woman burst into laughter as if I'd said something very funny. She leaned toward me over the counter like a mischievous girl trying not to raise her voice and said with an air of amusement: "*Pero chico!* You really want to work? Now that we have three hundred thousand unemployed." I left feeling disconcerted. How was it possible that this was happening in the First Liberated Territory of America? In a socialist state? In a country that was run by its workers?

Days later, Mercedes set up an appointment for me with the coordinator of the Regional Committee of the Union of Cuban Communist Youth so that I could talk to him about my plans. I arrived in his offices on October 7, 1967, and I found a great deal of nervous activity. I had to wait impatiently for a long time for the head of the Committee. He appeared for a moment to inform me that he was in the midst of an extraordinary meeting to analyze foreign news wires that claimed that a group of Bolivian army rangers had surrounded Che Guevara and his armed group in the canyon of Oruro.

The revelation unsettled me. A bundle of nerves, I awaited his return. He finally reappeared and addressed me with calculated drama. He announced that he thought it very probable that Yankee imperialism would attack the Cuba militarily in the next hours or days as a result of the confirmation of Che Guevara's presence in Bolivia. In the face of such an announcement, I said with true emotion that if that were to happen, all I needed was a rifle because I was ready to fight for the Revolution. The compañero straightened up in his chair, opened the big drawer of the desk at which he sat, introduced his hand, and extracted a submachine gun of Czech manufacture. Proceeding to remove the fifteen bullet loader and making sure that the chamber of the weapon was empty, he put it in my hands as he said, half mocking me: "Don't worry. We'll give you one of these." After I sized-up the weapon, I returned it to him, and he replaced it back in the desk drawer. Then he inquired where I had learned to handle a rifle. I told him that my father used to take me hunting, and that I had also gone through a full year of compulsory military service. We talked for a while about my wishes, and I asked him if he would be kind enough to give me a copy of Régis Debray's *Revolution in the Revolution?* and *Guerrilla Warfare, a Method,* by Ernesto Che Guevara. I had left mine in Mexico. He invited me to go with him to the warehouse to see if there were any books left.

All sorts of things were stored in that place. I took notice of the dozens of bottles of Cuban rum for export, plus the many cartons of filtered cigarettes with blond tobacco, also an item manufactured for sale abroad and the enjoyment of foreigners. The consumption of both products remained forbidden in the island. The compañero found the copies of the books I had asked for, and he also gave me *History Will Absolve Me* by Fidel Castro and various and sundry political pamphlets. Before we left the warehouse, I saw him grab two cartons of filtered cigarettes and stuff them under his arm. Back in his office, he said goodbye, but not before placing both cartons in one of the desk drawers. I'd foolishly thought that he was going to give me one.

The news of the siege and death of Che was confirmed. Fidel would speak on television that night. Caridad wangled an invitation for both of us to the house of a friend of hers to see the broadcast. As can be expected, I was very excited at the opportunity of seeing and hearing a live direct image of Fidel Castro on an occasion of such importance. It was a very short message within the usual parameters of the Cuban leader. He admitted that the information about the capture and death of Che was true. He announced a mass rally the following evening in Che's honor along with three days of official mourning.

The next evening Caridad, the other three residents of her house, and I attended the huge concentration of people at the Plaza of the Revolution. On the facade of the Ministry of the Interior, a gigantic banner hung bearing the famous photograph of Che taken by Korda (Alberto Díaz). The newspaper *Granma* also filled its front-page with this photo, and I immediately and devotedly grabbed the issue. My emotion was sincere, and I felt fortunate to be there in those uniquely sorrowful moments. One could see rivers of Cubans of all ages and conditions flowing through the streets; it was an impressive human influx that soon crowded the enormous space of the square. The entire *nomenklatura* of the island sat on a very long dais. Everybody was silent. There was a great sense of expectation about what the Comandante would say. Hours later, as we walked among thousands of Havaneros also heading home, Caridad and the other three Cubans concluded that the people had jammed into the Plaza mainly to hear what would come next, to find out in what direction Fidel would take Cuba from then on.

A huge screen covered the facade of the building of the Ministry of Economics, the civilian trenches of Che's financial and economic battles, located to the right of the Ministry of the Interior. There *Hasta la victoria siempre* was set to be projected, a film made for the occasion by the Cuban director Santiago Alvarez. All of a sudden, without anybody anticipating it, Fidel appeared on the platform; it seemed incredible that we hadn't seen how he'd arrived. The master of ceremonies officially initiated the event, and the film began to run: images of Che in the Sierra Maestra on mule back next to the popular Camilo Cienfuegos, later in Santa Clara, and even later still unloading cargo on the docks of Havana or doing volunteer work in the underground nickel mines in spite of his asthma. Che could be seen finally at the UN denouncing Yankee imperialism and charging it with the death of Patrice

Lumumba: "One cannot trust imperialism, not even this little tiny bit" as he shows the audience his index finger and thumb about to make contact. The Havana crowd was overjoyed with this use of the Mexican idiom. Immediately thereafter, Nicolás Guillén read a poem dedicated to Che, just written in honor of the "heroic guerrillero" as Fidel characterized Guevara in a customarily long speech in which he urged young people especially to "be like Che." Comandante Fidel Castro seemed deliberately to convert the Argentine guerrilla fighter into one more star in the firmament, divesting him of his historical materiality, of his concrete and defined soul that ultimately had led him to capture and execution on the outskirts of the fateful Cañada de Oruro in Bolivia.

Castro's speech marked the end of an era. After that night, never again did the Cuban leader support or speak in public of the Latin American revolution.[2] The line of peaceful coexistence of the Communist Party of the Soviet Union thereafter set the course for Cuban communism. I was left with an inexpressible, muffled anger; I had a great desire to avenge Che. An hour and a half later back in her room, Caridad silently and ceremoniously removed one of her treasures from the wall and put it in my hand: an old Cuban peso bill signed by the then director of the National Bank of Cuba—*Che*. In exchange, she took the front-page of *Granma* with Korda's photo and stuck it on the wall. That night, as with others, I did not go back to my hotel; a distressed Caridad and I slept under the severe, stern expression of the "heroic guerrillero."

EXPULSION AND HUMILIATION

"I've got some news for you," Mercedes informed me one morning toward the end of the third week of October as I entered the Cuban–Mexican Institute for Cultural Relations. "Compañero Ribot is waiting for you in the offices of the Central Committee of the Party in order to speak with you," she added, barely emitting a smile. My heart leapt. Finally I had the chance to talk with somebody in a position to help me out! I felt like jumping with joy, but I restrained myself and thanked Mercedes. My appointment was for the following morning. I impatiently awaited Caridad's return to tell her the good news. She worked mornings driving a tractor in the Havana Agricultural Greenbelt. When Caridad got back, her blue overalls worn and a white kerchief over her hair, I told her about it. After asking me about the details, she suggested that we talk it over with Luis, the fourth resident of the house. He worked as an editor in the Prensa Latina news agency and also wrote poetry. For a stretch of time he and Caridad had lived together as a couple. We went to see him in his room. He was of the opinion that it would be wise for the two of them to go with me the next day to the Central Committee offices and wait for me. "With those guys, you never know," he warned.

Luis's observation tempered my enthusiasm for my appointment with comrade Ribot. This was not the first time that I had heard similar opinions from them. All the residents of the house including Caridad in some form or other held attitudes that were distrustful or carefully critical of many of the actions of those in power in Cuba, although, of course, they supported the Revolution. Most of them had also suffered some sort of reprisal for their opinions, attitudes, or status. Caridad, for example, was the daughter of a unionized worker, for years a militant in the Cuban Socialist Party, the communist organization that existed before the victory of the Revolution. In meetings, she and her father had spoken against the prohibition of the right to strike and the loss in practice of the right to organize. Consequently, Caridad had endured reprisals at school, her father at work.

Caridad's father—she herself told me this—was upset with the rationing of basic essentials, for example shoes, to which he had the right to only one pair per year. In fact, there were not even enough shoes on the island to meet this meager quota, not to mention their disastrously poor quality. He compared this situation negatively with conditions prior to the Revolution when he could afford two or more pairs of better shoes in the same period of time.

The Central Committee of the Cuban Communist Party was located in a large white building with a central staircase and Roman columns constructed *ex profeso* to house the communist *nomenklatura* of the island, as if they were nouveau riches. Caridad and Luis preferred to wait for me at a prudent distance from the building as I entered its ground floor. The luxurious interior featured piped-in music, air conditioning, and wall-to-wall carpets. North American melodies from the forties and fifties stunned me: "Gringo supermarket music in the formal heart of anti-Yankee Cuban antimperialism!" I approached one of the beautiful escorts that could be found everywhere, asking her for compañero Ribot with whom I had an appointment. "*Un momentico,*" she replied. She lifted the phone to her well-contoured, fleshy mouth, pushed a button, and announced my arrival. It was not long before a white Cuban with recently trimmed black hair and mustache appeared. He was about thirty-five years old and was dressed in a stripped, short-sleeve shirt, pearl gray cotton pants, and black shoes. This was compañero Ribot. He escorted me to a nearby cubicle, where he immediately requested my passport. A second later, this document in hand, he advised me that I'd have to leave Cuba. I had not been invited to visit the island. Hearing this, I felt as if the floor opened below me. I was in a state of shock. I clearly heard what he had said, but I did not want to understand its meaning. This was the last thing I'd expected to be told. I began to fear that I'd be expelled from the country that same day. I dreaded what I'd have to say then to the Mexican authorities, to my wife, to the friends that had urged me to make this trip. For a second I even thought the Cubans capable to turning me over to the Mexican political police. Compañero Ribot clarified the issue, however. I'd leave Cuba in three days time. There were no flights before that. He also informed me that I'd have to put in writing why I had visited Cuba, who had provided me with recommendations, and how I had obtained a tourist visa. I would have to turn in this document the following afternoon at the latest.

I left the Central Committee with a highly damaged sense of confidence in the Cuban government and its party, as well as in myself and my awkward behavior. I anxiously looked for Caridad and the poet, finding them seated on a bench in the adjacent park. Curious, they arose and approached me, hastened by my scared and afflicted expression. Caridad put her hand on my shoulder, as she nervously asked what had happened. What had Ribot said? Extremely disconcerted, I answered her insistent questions by telling them what had occurred several times in great detail. Caridad and the poet looked bothered. They said that was all you could expect from such bureaucrats. They knew nothing could be done about the decision that the Committee had taken.

My concern now had to be the written statement that Ribot demanded. We returned to Caridad's room, where she had an old typewriter. I was still encouraged by the hope of convincing the Cuban authorities of the sincerity and righteousness of my purposes, although at this point, I no longer knew what those purposes were. I worked for about three hours, until I felt I had written the whole story. Caridad read it and said it was okay, although she added that she didn't think that anything I'd written on paper could change a determination made by the Cuban authorities. I had tons of problems to face—I didn't have a job, I had no idea what I would do to get one, and, most importantly, what was I going to say to Tere?

As part of my "proletarian" attire, I had taken some denim shirts to Cuba of the type used by Mexican railroad line workers. I'd purchased them in Mexico City at a store on San Juan de Letrán Avenue. On the island, as all over the world, there was a great deal of interest in American jeans, so my denim shirts attracted the attention of young Havaneros, especially those who knew where that kind of clothing came from. The morning after I turned in my long statement to Ribot, I stood at a bus stop waiting for one of those British Leyland busses that the Cubans used at the time. Also at the stop was a young woman with an identical denim shirt. When she saw me, she smiled and asked if I were Mexican. I answered affirmatively, and in turn asked her the same. It so happened that she was Cuban, but her Mexican compañero had given her the shirt.

We spoke for a while, and I, true to my habit, told her what was happening to me. The young woman listened with great attention and asked me several times for the name of the official of the Central Committee who had interviewed me and taken my passport, as if she wanted to memorize it. She said that she worked nearby the office of the regional head of the Union of Cuban Communist Youth. She offered to intercede before him with the purpose of getting an appointment so that I could explain my situation. She gave me a telephone number for me to call her later. Of course, I did. When I reached her, she gave me the news that the high official of the Union of Cuban Communist Youth had accepted to see me that afternoon in his office. I went to meet him, and the man listened to my story with attention. He made a phone call, and I assumed that he was speaking with comrade Ribot of the Central Committee. After hanging up, he explained that my case was not exceptional: many other young men like me from all over the world were attracted by the Cuban Revolution. Some arrived on the island without luggage, even without the most essential utensils for their own personal care. This situation had become problematic for the Cuban authorities because of the Yankee blockade. They had no way of solving the most basic needs, such as getting these arrivals toothbrushes or socks. He inquired about my educational level and my family, adding that I would still have to abandon the island. He said that I should keep in touch with him by mail. It was possible that I could return to Cuba later on since they needed people with my level of preparation.

The only thing that was left to do was to pack my suitcases and say goodbye to my friends. When I'd punctually delivered my answers to his questions, Ribot had announced that on the next day around midmorning a car would come by my hotel to take me to the airport for a flight to Mexico. There was no way of warning Tere about my arrival. I was afraid of landing by myself at the airport in Mexico City with nobody there to meet me.

In Havana, especially during the first two weeks of my visit, I'd experienced a very intense feeling of freedom. I'd then assumed that the social and political context fit my existential aspirations in basic ways. By contrast, going back to Mexico meant returning to an intricate knot of social, political, and ethnic contradictions, to my personal and familiar tensions and frustrations. It was to go back to a world that I'd determined to abandon forever, stepping onto Cuban soil at the José Martí Airport a month earlier. That distant luminous morning everything appeared to smile; all the elements for the fulfillment of my plans seemed to fall into place. But as I interacted with reality, everything had gone wrong. Now it didn't matter any more, and since there is a time for every purpose under heaven, an old green '57 Cadillac in moderate condition arrived at the hotel right on time as announced. Only a driver was aboard. Caridad had arrived early to keep me company and had been waiting with me in the lobby. Now as I was about to enter the vehicle, she asked the driver if she could ride along. The man said yes without hesitation. Settled in the somewhat worn out back seat of this luxury car, we made the trip to the airport in oppressive silence.

Apprehension about what might await me in Mexico occupied all my attention. To make things worse, I didn't even have one Mexican peso! When I arrived in Cuba, I'd exchanged my one hundred dollars for a nominally equal amount of Cuban pesos. Caridad came to the rescue with twenty local pesos, which—not without some effort—I managed to exchange for Mexican currency at the official exchange booth. I obtained about fifty pesos, enough for taxicab from the Benito Juárez Airport to the apartment building in Colonia Navarte where we lived at the time. Once the exchange operation was over, an immigration official led me to a small, separate, and empty waiting room, allowing Caridad to remain with me. I couldn't understand what was happening, and why I wasn't permitted to get on the Cubana de Aviación four-motor Ylushin. We could see it through the window, and passengers were boarding. My nerves were tensed to the max. Nobody ever explained anything to me, but I was the last one to board. All of a sudden, two Cuban men in uniform took me to the airplane, almost without giving me time to say goodbye to Caridad. They escorted me all the way to my seat. I thought that they might stick with me until Mexico, but fortunately I was wrong. When they left me alone, as I felt the initial movement of the aircraft and the vibration of the engines, I was overtaken by a very intense emotion that almost made me weep uncontrollably. The sorrow I felt for what was happening to me contrasted with the apparent, if guarded, satisfaction of several passengers who were "finally" leaving Cuba. When the airplane turned 180 degrees, its right side where I sat now faced the main entrance of the airport. That's how I observed from a distance the animated, casual conversation between Caridad and my driver as they leaned over the railing of the observation balcony above the first floor. When I spotted them, my heart jumped in my chest: the suspicion I'd felt on several occasions, including the day I'd met Caridad, had proven true. On the very day of my departure it had been so easy for her to stay with me until the last instant. The fish had swallowed the bait. Cuban security had allowed me to roam around Havana for a month, often with Caridad. They'd given me necessary slack so that I could move about until they finally decided to reel me back. I couldn't blame them. It was natural that they'd looked out for the security of the Revolution, its leaders, and the Cuban state itself. Nevertheless, confirming that Caridad had been watching me and passing on information about me to the Cuban security apparatus further damaged my already battered self-esteem.

As is usual during trips, the return to Mexico seemed very fast. During the flight, I had a sensation of emptiness in my stomach—a fear of the Mexican political and police authorities, as well as fear of having to face my failure with Tere and the few friends who knew the reasons for my trip to Cuba. My parents didn't worry me, because they didn't know that I'd gone to the island. Trying to be consistent with my social and political ideas, I'd kept them in the dark. When we touched Mexican soil, I could not prevent a deep sob at the strong emotion that surged through me upon my failed return to my point of departure. I'd come back only a month after my chimerical exit. Immigration authorities stamped my passport with the line "Returned from Cuba." That was all. I left the restricted area of the airport, turning around, watching everything, convinced that I would be detained or followed to my home. But nothing happened.

With my heart in turmoil and a guilty conscience, I arrived at the door of the apartment where I lived with Tere and my daughter. In a state of total vulnerability, I opened the door and entered the silent dwelling, not knowing how I was going to explain to my wife the reasons for my sudden return. I walked through the empty rooms, experiencing a growing disquiet. Neither Tere nor the child was there. It looked like nobody had been in the apartment for some time. That was a situation I had not foreseen. I had no course of action other than to repair to my sister-in-law's apartment. Tere's oldest sister lived on the top floor of the building, but I didn't know what I could say to her and to her husband. I'd agreed with Tere that they shouldn't know anything about my trip to Cuba. So I pretended to them that I'd come back from a business trip and unexpectedly found nobody home. My sister-in-law, somewhat surprised, said that they had gone to Acapulco with Elisa to spend a few days. My sister-in-law had the hotel address, so I decided to go there immediately, not without shaming myself into borrowing money for bus fare. My brother-in-law offered to take me to the bus depot, and once there, I hopped on the first transport that left for the coast. It was a second-class bus, but I didn't want to wait any longer. A strong, uncontrollable force compelled me to be with Tere as soon as possible. I felt that I was about to lose her if I didn't see her before morning.

I traveled awake all night in the uncomfortable, ramshackle bus until it deposited me, sleepless and worn-out, in the port terminal just before the sun began to shine over the mountains and the sea. I took a cab immediately, indicating the address to the driver in a tone of urgency. The hotel was fairly modest and small. In the lobby, I ran into Elisa, who was most surprised to see me standing in front of her. She asked for an explanation, which I blurted out hurriedly, tripping over my own words and making no sense from the point of view of politics. The more I tried, the worse my explanation sounded. It must have seemed to her like a *gusano* rap.[3] Elisa looked at me askance, as if doubting she was quite awake. "Where was Tere?," I asked. The Ecuadorian woman answered that she was in her room with Teresita. She added that my wife was very upset with me because I hadn't contacted her during my absence. Some acquaintances, recently arrived from Cuba, had reported having seen me at the ICMRC with a Cuban woman. This last revelation only increased my anxiety, so I rushed to find Tere in her room. As I stood before her, she seemed a bit thinner but equally beautiful in my eyes. Her face registered surprise at my unexpected presence. The brilliance of her eyes harbored a spark of joy. But to my great mortification, her entire attitude also conveyed a kind of silent accusation. Looking at Tere and our daughter, fully defeated, I understood that I could not afford to lose them, that I had needed to be with them, and that I had been a fool by abandoning and betraying them so easily. I heaped kisses and guilty embraces over the two of them, wishing to wipe from their souls the distrust that my absence and disloyal behavior had caused them to feel. I understood, however, that it would not be easy. The subtle rejection of both to my endearments made this evident. From then on I would have to prove my love and constant confidence in them so that they could get over their justified resentment. I would soon realize that not being totally trusted for years to come would be part of the payment of my debt to them.

María Teresa and Alberto as a young couple. *Property of the author.*

Lucio Cabañas Barrientos. *Public domain.*

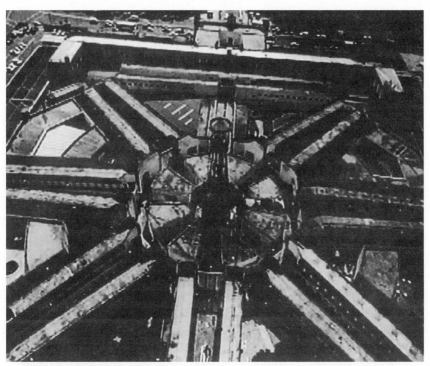

Lecumberri's panopticon design. *Courtesy of Arturo Ripstein.*

Cellblock and tower in Lecumberri. *Courtesy of Arturo Ripstein.*

La fajina in Lecumberri. *Courtesy of Arturo Ripstein.*

La fajina in Lecumberri. *Courtesy of Arturo Ripstein.*

El chocho in Lecumberri. *Courtesy of Arturo Ripstein.*

Guillermo Zúñiga in Lecumberri. *Courtesy of Arturo Ripstein.*

Alberto Ulloa Bornemann
in the Reclusorio Oriente.
Property of the author.

Under arraignment in the judicial system: Vicente Estrada Vega (*Dionisio*), Alberto
Ulloa Bornemann, Dr. Ignacio Madrazo Navarro (*Luis*), Rigoberto Lorence López,
Teresa Franco (*Olivia*), and Lourdes Quiñones. *Credit: Dirección Federal de Seguridad.*

THREE

In the Kingdom of Necessity

TORTURE AND SELF-PRESERVATION

THAT SUNDAY MORNING, time threatened to slide by even more slowly than usual. One more week of my captivity had been completed, and nothing had happened during those seven days to undo the tedium produced by my inactive confinement in my small cell. I thought I'd observed a pattern of bureaucratic behavior as I registered the coming and going of prisoners around the middle of the week, especially Wednesdays. Perhaps the apparent pattern had derived from previous agreements among high level government functionaries. Whatever the case, it had not held true this week. Still, I was lying down on the floor of the cell, wrapped in my quilt, trying to sleep as long as possible before dinner. As was usual, the radio sounded at full blast. Trying to isolate myself from the noise by using balls of bread in my ears had proven a resounding failure. Close to sixty days after my forced disappearance into the Campo Militar Número Uno, my life seemed to hang in suspense. That very morning, however, in a short while I would see that I was wrong. My life was not in suspense—I was still being tested. That Sunday morning, I'd barely begun to slide into unconsciousness when a metallic rat-a-tat shook me out of my lethargy. I suspected that someone had reached the gate of my cell and was coming for me. Even before I saw him, I knew who it was: yes, the same dark-skinned individual, the gun-bearing, irascible thug who'd appeared in the June 10, 1971 picture; the same one who'd plucked out my eyelashes and eyebrows as he removed the adhesive over my eyelids when I was interrogated the first time after my arrival at Campo Militar Número

Uno. While he addressed me, looking at me coldly and disdainfully, the man repeatedly hit one of the bars in the grill of my cell with a small metallic object held in his right hand, perhaps a key. He was trying to wake me up with that nervous, repetitive movement and get my attention. He did immediately. As I rose, a shiver traveled through my whole body, putting it in a state of alert. In fractions of a second, the lassitude that I constantly felt in those days transformed into fear and irritation. It was a situation that I absolutely hadn't expected to face that morning. It may be silly, but after weeks had gone by, I had absurdly expected that I wouldn't be removed from my cell for interrogation and torture again. That was, or so I wanted to believe, a completed stage of my detention.

The dark-skinned, somber and stern guy was accompanied by the blond, karate-practicing Halcón who opened the door of my cell and took me out gruffly. He then placed himself behind me and grabbed me by the shoulders with his small but strong and coarse hands. He took me to the fearsome room located in front of the water basin. There a short man waited for me. He had a big belly, yellow skin, and bulging big eyes; his demeanor was impatient and unfriendly; and he looked as if he were completely bored. His hair was cut to standard military fashion; his mustache was scarce and uneven; he had fetid breath, and altogether the look of a butcher. When I appeared in front of him, very thin and pale with a two-month-old beard and long and messy hair, he glanced at me from head to toe as if contemplating what he could apply to my body from his sadistic experience. The dark one ordered the other two to place me in the school chair that sat in the middle of the room. Immediately, they proceeded to tie my arms tightly behind the back of the chair with a dirty rag, while the first one supervised the maneuver very attentively. The fat one, drenched in sweat, burped acid air on my face, while without any compunction, he tightened the porous fabric around my compressed wrists. Standing before me with an air of severity, the one in charge declared that this was the last opportunity I had to give them concrete and relevant information about the principal members of the Organization to which I claimed to belong. Right after the warning, the fat man intervened. He leaned the trunk of his body and his hostile face toward me, fixing his bulging, rat-like eyes on mine, all the while exhaling his stinking breath on me. He described in abundant detail what he was going to do to me. He would start, he said, by disfiguring my face and breaking my body with blows and kicks; next, he would use a knife to remove my teeth, one by one, then the fingers of my hands, and the soles of my feet. He would crush all of these in a coffee grinder so that my dental pieces would disappear along with my finger and footprints. Then he would throw me into a ditch where my remains would be covered with lime and other chemical substances. Quickly I would turn into bare bones. My relatives would never know what had happened to me or ever have the consolation of burying me in the family plot.

The threats and savage descriptions of the fat man finished off my fragile will to resist, rather like a programmed sequence in which plastic explosives are used to demolish urban structures step by step that have been damaged by time, fire, or earthquakes. The first great blow to the structure of my morale and will had been the revelation of the old Indian man from the Huasteca of Hidalgo. A month after my arrival in the clandestine military jail, he reported that he had already "been disappeared" for two years into different prison installations within the military gulag. That story had commenced the collapse of any hope that I might be freed someday from the inhumane situation in which I found myself.

From that night on, never a moment passed by in which I ceased to imagine with ever greater anguish and despair the sorts of painful situations that my disappearance must have given rise to for my wife and daughter as well as for my parents. So the dread of being destroyed and physically disappeared in the atrocious manner announced by the fat man generated my total moral and physical breakdown. In my demoralization, I mentioned three possible locations in which some members of the Organization might be found. I cannot deny that I did this out of cowardice, of course, but I also calculated that the compañeros would surely have abandoned those locales by now, possibly even the very night of September 4th. After all, two months had gone from the day of my capture. Moreover, in the case of Dionisio and Olivia, I only knew the spot where I had picked them up or left them, not the precise place where they lived. Faced with growing physical and moral pressure, in a desperate wish to make the information seem credible, I mentioned that the couple used to travel in a current model year red Volkswagen with Jalisco plates. I assumed that they'd gotten rid of the vehicle, the only intelligent move they could make. But to their ill-fate and my sorrow, they never did. When the feds arrived at a spot near the Ayotla Textil factory, there sat a red 1974 VW with Jalisco registration, possibly right in front of the couple's abode. The federal security police only had to wait for Dionisio to appear on the street to detain him. Olivia was apprehended moments later, apparently in the house or apartment where they lived together.

A few hours later, having been taken back to the basement of the Campo Militar Número Uno, I spent the most bitter and painful moments of my life. I had to listen to Dionisio's interrogation and torture from my current cell—the first one of the back corridor, adjacent to that dreadful room. I felt horribly culpable at having facilitated his detention. Yet, at the same time, I was very angry with him for not having changed either vehicle or dwelling two months after my capture. Each time Dionisio screamed or moaned under torture, I felt his pain in my heart and in the pit of my stomach. I wanted to let him know what I had declared, so as to let him avoid unnecessary suffering. I did that very late at night, raising my voice as high as I could, almost yelling from one corridor to another. The likelihood that one of the Halcones could be listening while sitting on the stairway didn't matter to me.

To my shame, these were not the only detentions that I furthered. There were three other arrests that happened in a circumstantial way similar to the previous one as a result of my reference to a rented house in the town of Oacalco, Morelos, where months before Susana and Francisco had taken refuge. The police couldn't find them there, and they decided to pressure the landlady, who informed them that the couple had moved nearby—something that I already knew—about five hundred meters away, to an old, unused train station where they were immediately apprehended. The last person detained was Luis, the neurologist who attempted to cure Lucio. His arrest produced a mobilization and protests from members of the medical world. Together with the political influence of illustrious relatives, this may have helped make possible our departure from the Campo Militar Número Uno and a formal judicial consignment.

I know that none of the events that I am now recounting honors me. The fear of pain and of dying without my loved ones knowing became stronger than my will to resist. The time that has elapsed since then, and the experiences that I lived through in the three public prisons of Lecumberri, Reclusorio Oriente, and Santa Martha Acatitla have allowed me to understand how difficult it is for us human beings to acknowledge our mistakes and trespasses in an open and honest manner. Instead, we commonly blame others before questioning ourselves, even if we know deep inside us that we also share responsibility for the mistakes of others. If I can say something in my own defense, it is that I gave my compañeros a considerable time advantage, some sixty days, during which they could have taken pertinent security measures. I would like to say that I could have identified many more compañeros, both in the leadership and the base of the Organization, most of them peasants or urban workers. But I didn't, so none of them was apprehended. Those whose imprisonment I was responsible for also bear some responsibility—they did not take into account the fact that I was in the hands of the government, that I possessed vital information, and that they could be affected. In those days of heroic dreams, I fashioned myself invariably as a valiant social fighter, ever ready to face the pain of torture and death itself before bending to the power of imperialism and the bourgeoisie. But in my real confrontation with the ferocious political repression of the state and with myself, the basic instinct of self-preservation nullified all else. I believe that this is what happens most frequently, although I accept, of course, that there are honorable exceptions. I'm not trying to boast of cynicism, but I believe that there are not too many other explanations to the fact that so many political prisoners did not die under torture, but ended up like I did in the preventive jail of Lecumberri, in the Santa Martha penitentiary, in the Chilpancingo prison, in the municipal jail of Acapulco, in the penal facilities of Oblatos in Guadalajara and Topo Chico in Monterrey.

INTO THE CRIMINAL JUSTICE SYSTEM

Susana and Francisco were taken directly to the central offices of the Dirección Federal de Seguridad (DFS) or Federal Security Office located in a particular section of Morelia Street known as Circular de Morelia in Colonia Roma. There Miguel Nazar Haro interrogated them in person so that they did not come to the Campo Militar Número Uno. Luis was indeed taken to the clandestine jail. After around the third day following the five detentions, an agent of the Ministerio Público indicted Dionisio, Olivia, Luis, and me in processes plagued from beginning to end with juridical irregularities. It was the first time they took pictures of us, frontally and laterally. I remember the director of the operation as a distinguished-looking, polite official—fiftyish, of light complexion and finely trimmed mustache, prematurely bald, gray around the temples. He was very bothered about the way we had used the $300,000 that Lucio Cabañas had given us to advance the productive and financial activities of the Organization, such as goat and pig husbandry and the cultivation of basic foodstuffs like corn and beans. Susana and Francisco, in turn, were consigned to the Ministerio Público in the offices of the DFS in processes distinct from the rest of us.

Compañera Olivia, Dionisio's partner, used to behave in a way that created problems within the Organization. She was the daughter of a well-to-do family, educated in the conservative framework typical of that social status. The way she treated others reproduced many of the prejudices of bourgeois conduct and consciousness. She showed off her own competency. She was an authoritarian who didn't mind telling everyone else what was wrong with them. Because of all that, Olivia reminded me of my own mother. Still, she and Dionisio, in spite of their different social origins, were a tightly knit couple. One could tell they really loved one another. They were together most of the time. She would join Dionisio even when he traveled to the most distant rural areas in Morelos, Puebla, and Guerrero. They slept on a woven straw mat on the ground under the open sky or in the huts of peasants. She complained about the discomforts and insects, but it was evident she would not allow anything in the world to stand between Dionisio and herself.

Dionisio seemed amused by Olivia's ideas and expressions. He always intervened to soften her judgments or to provide nuance to her assertions. He asked for everyone's understanding when she spewed forth critical evaluations of others in the course of everyday interactions with members of the Organization. I especially remember an episode that occurred upon our return from the mountain shepherd community near Tlapa, Guerrero. We were traveling in a VW Safari. I was at the wheel. It's possible that Dionisio may have been dozing off in the front passenger seat, and that "Chano," Darío—El Flaco—and Olivia occupied the back seat. It was around four o'clock in the afternoon, and we were all very tired. The heat, the dust of the road, and thirst tormented us. Over the past two days, we'd raced up and down the hills with the shepherds of the region, using the round-up system to hunt for white-tail deer. Looking in the rearview mirror, I realized that Chano and El Flaco had fallen asleep, while to their right Olivia remained awake with an expression of real disgust on her face. I continued observing them in the rearview mirror as much as driving the Safari on such a bumpy road allowed me. I noticed that Darío, possibly because of the bouncing around of the vehicle, reclined against Olivia every now and then. She responded by forcefully pushing him away with revulsion. I began to suspect that maybe El Flaco was doing this on purpose, after feeling her rejection. It was not news to me that Darío disgusted Olivia, since frequently she censored the compañero for his love of alcohol and for his lassitude in carrying out tasks that Dionisio assigned to him. Nevertheless, I was still surprised by the vigorous emotional response with which she rejected any bodily contact with El Flaco, whether accidental or not. Since Olivia had been so intolerant and bossy with everyone, seeing her act this way with Darío made me angry, and I was about to tell Dionisio to do something. Prudence prevailed, however, and I decided to wait for a better occasion. An appropriate moment emerged very soon since I was not the only one with complaints. Dionisio listened to me and promised to talk to Olivia. I have related this long story in order to provide the context for something that happened when Dionisio, Olivia, and Luis were in the basement of the Campo Militar Número Uno with me.

Olivia was confined in the first cell at the end of the corridor near me. Given the closeness of our cells, it was possible to talk although we couldn't see each other. Olivia told me that Tere my wife had been very sick due to my disappearance. The news perturbed me profoundly, both physically and morally. I couldn't stop either my tears and sobs, or the resurgence of the heavy feeling of guilt that tormented me ever since my detention in Morelos. As I write, I now realize how much effort it takes to introduce Olivia into this narrative. Something as obvious as her condition as a helpless woman in the hands of men capable of any atrocity had escaped my consideration. Naturally, she too had to submit to interrogations, pressure, and moral and physical humiliations, aside from being forced to witness the torment inflicted on Dionisio. Seeing her go by the corridor in front of my cell, blindfolded, and ushered by an Halcón to the interrogation room hurt me more than Dionisio's afflictions. My feelings of guilt and shame were even greater, so I asked the Halcón who brought my meal in the middle of the day to give my quilt to Olivia. It was the one thing I owned, a unique and highly valuable article in that place, both bed and blanket. I had managed to hang on to it for over two months, in spite of the constant changes of cell. I thought that in some small measure, it could improve the immense discomfort of Olivia's confinement, lacking, like the rest of us in the cell, a bed or seat of any sort, equipped only with the lidless toilet.

Several months later I ran into Olivia for the first time in quite a while during visiting hours in one of the corridors of cellblock O West in Lecumberri. She and Luis had been bailed out a few hours after we were all taken to the Procuraduría General de la República (PGR), the Office of the Attorney General of the Republic, while the rest of us had remained subject to judicial process without bail. I tried to help her carry the heavy bags of food she was bringing to Dionisio. He and Francisco had recently been incorporated into the high security section of the "Black Palace." She rejected me in a manner similar to the way she had repulsed Darío. I then understood that the couple blamed me for their present situation. I accepted this and preferred to have no more contact with either one. As far as Francisco is concerned, I tried hard to look for a location where he could settle, finding a spot for him with El Puma, who already shared a cell with me. I facilitated Dionisio's placing in the next door cell with El Pocho, ineptly and unnecessarily complicating my already difficult existence in prison. It would have been sensible not to meddle and to allow these new arrivals to find their own way. I now think that it would have been lucky if they'd been situated in the other corridor of the top floor or in either one of the lower floors.

My digression is over, and I return to the Campo Militar Número Uno. The agent from the Ministerio Público was satisfied with the written depositions of all four of us. We signed them and had our individual photographs taken in front of one of the white walls of the basement, both front and side profile shots. At last the uneasy moment—I was particularly unnerved—for the formal consignation had arrived.

The emotional whirlpool in which I'd been immersed—my moral breakdown and unfortunate declarations, the capture of the compañeros, their consequent intense and harsh interrogations, physical torture, and moral pressures—stretched across the entire week. I was physically and morally broken,
depressed, and even dirty. Events made it impossible to sleep during those
days, and I wasn't allowed the weekly bath, so it had been two weeks since my
last one. I found myself reanimated by the idea of abandoning those military
installations and leaving my perverse secret confinement behind. This mere
possibility renewed my hope of seeing Tere, my daughter, and my parents once
again. During those days, as never before, I repented at not having listened a
few months earlier to the sudden impulse to leave activism and the Organization forever. I'd had an experience similar to what some call an "epiphany" or
"illumination." In an instant, the most significant events of the last three years
flashed through my mind. I suddenly understood that what we were doing as
an Organization—and what other more radical groups insisted on doing in
the marginal zones of Mexican society and countryside—would never lead the
Mexican working people to a socialist revolution. Among other things, the
PRI regime buffered the needs of the peasantry, with political perversity and
efficiency, granting credits and other means of support. Even our group had
benefited from these mechanisms in the development of its political, ideological, and organizing work. Meanwhile, the President of the Republic, Luis
Echeverría Alvarez, had considerably increased the share of the gross national
product that went to industrial workers. Moreover, their own unions controlled laborers politically and ideologically with an iron hand. Those were general considerations. There were also personal experiences, in which I lived side
by side with workers, peasants, teachers, and militants of different groups (Liga
Comunista Espartaco, Movimiento de Acción Revolucionaria, Comandos
Lacandones, Procesos, Guajiros, Liga 23 de Septiembre), and other people such
as intellectuals and students, not to mention Professor Lucio Cabañas Barrientos of the Partido de Los Pobres, the most renowned Mexican rebel of the
era. In sum, this was a set of representative experiences of the social and revolutionary movement of the late sixties and early seventies.

The epiphany came to me one morning when Dionisio, Olivia, and I were
journeying by car toward Morelos and the south of Puebla along the highway
to Cuatla that goes through Amecameca. Tired, I stopped the car to ask
Olivia—Dionisio had no license—to drive while I slept for a while lying on
the back seat. After I'd napped for some time, the movement of the vehicle
woke me up, but I remained where I was, listening to the animated conversation between Olivia and Dionisio. For half an hour I witnessed their wonderful relationship. Their communication flowed back and forth, peppered with

humor and mutual appreciation. This made me reflect on what I was doing with my own partner. Where in my life had I placed my own wife and child? Wasn't I close to destroying the most valuable, personal, dear, and intimate connection I had? Then, incredible as it seems, all the principal episodes that I'd lived through during the last three years in the Organization and the revolutionary movement suddenly came to my mind at once. I could clearly see that I'd been committing countless egregious mistakes of a political and ideological nature, not to mention the personal ones. I don't want to say that I'd never thought that I could be mistaken, but up until then a synthesis of my moments of doubt had never occurred. I decided then and there to engineer my exit from the Organization as fast as possible. I couldn't just sit up in the back seat and declare: "Listen, you know what? I've thought about it, stop the car, this is as far as I can go with you!" My commitment to Dionisio, Isauro, and the other compañeros was too strong for that. I saw myself as someone who'd won a reputation for accepting assigned tasks without reluctance or excuses, for always being ready like a boy scout, for arriving on time to my appointments, and for carrying out my entrusted tasks, whatever they might be. With great simplicity, I'd assumed that my conduct would motivate others to act with the same decision and determination that I imagined my actions revealed.

A short while after signing my deposition before the agent of the Ministerio Público in midmorning, the Halcón who used to give us toasted tortillas with salt came to my cell. With an imperative gesture, he ordered me to take off my *huaraches* and turn them over to him. Since we were about to be taken from the Campo Militar Número Uno for our consignation, I couldn't understand why this guy wanted to leave me barefooted. Nevertheless, I obeyed and gave them up. At that moment, one of the agents of the Federal de Seguridad came to lead me out of the basement. He realized that I was barefooted and asked me where my sandals had gone. I pointed to the Halcón, and the agent demanded immediately that he return my sandals. From the very first day I'd spent in the basement, this son of a bitch had coveted my *huaraches*. But the stupid fool had misinterpreted the signs, thinking that we were being removed—not for consignation before a judge—but to be killed and disappeared for good.

Before leading me up the stairway to the outside, the agent blindfolded me. Once outside the building, they placed me in a vehicle in between the driver and one other federal policeman. I had the sensation that another compañero was in the backseat, but I couldn't confirm my hunch. The vehicle left the Campo and headed downhill for a short stretch before rapidly entering the *Periférico*, which I identified from the traffic noise. Upon arrival at Paseo de la Reforma via the Fuente de Petróleos, the commander sitting on my right asked one of the agents in the back to remove my blindfold. I should see the city, he said, since my incarceration would last many, many years. Thus, I could confirm where I had been sequestered during the last two months and ten days. In a short while, the car left Paseo de la Reforma at Lieja Street near the Fountain of Diana the Hunter. Taking a left turn, it sped through the traffic along Chapultepec Avenue. The commander ordered me blindfolded again, and moments later we turned right on Morelia Street and parked in front of the building marked number eight.

In the office of the Federal de Seguridad (occupied until recently by the redundantly named General Office of Regulation and Supervision in Public Security of the Secretariat of Government), Olivia, Dionisio, Luis, Susana, Francisco, and I were reunited. One hour later, blindfolded with our hands tied, we were transported in a Chevrolet Suburban station wagon to the Procuraduría General de la República on López Street. There several veteran agents of the PGR received us in the parking lot. They immediately protested our being delivered blindfolded with our hands immobilized. They continued critical comments among themselves as they freed us from our blindfolds and restraints. They herded all of the men into one of the institution's wide, depressing, cold, and stinking holding cells. Shortly thereafter, we were called one by one to submit a new declaration before several agents of the Ministerio Público. Olivia and Susana were locked up in the female section. It was the afternoon of November 14, 1974, a time of bad weather and lots of rain. Rendering our declarations took several hours, leaving us trembling from cold and hunger. Bad faith and stupidity typified the agents of the Ministerio Público Federal. We were allowed no communication with relatives or defense attorneys, under the pretext that we were subversives, dangerous guerrilla warriors, enemies of private property and the government.

When they finally returned us to the holding cell, they let us have a sandwich with a cold and greasy egg, and a glass of sweet fruit drink. The cold pierced our bodies. None of us wore anything but shirt and pants. During the tense, long, and difficult night, I could not sleep at all. Cold and hungry, I felt very uncomfortable in front of my former compañeros and couldn't look them in the eye. But neither they nor I said anything about my responsibility for their capture. Dionisio was doubtless the most wretched among us. His face, usually almost round, looked long through pain and exhaustion. He soon fell into a deep sleep that lasted until the next morning. The savage torments that the feds had applied to him were many. They'd burned his genitals with lit cigarettes. They'd beaten his entire body severely. They'd tied him naked and blindfolded to a long, thick board in order to submerge him more easily in the water basin. Immobilized and defenseless, he reached near suffocation, while at the same time they applied electric current to his body with a cattle prod. I have to say that Dionisio is a strong and robust man. Things had gone differently for Francisco. He said that he'd received only a harsh punch to the face by Miguel Nazar Haro because it looked as if they already knew everything about Susana and him. Moreover, Francisco had the impression that it had been helpful to them that the federal agents had seen where and how they lived, separated by their own decision from the violent groups to which they'd belonged in the past. Luis only suffered pressures of a moral sort. Later in the night, the authorities of the PGR allowed him to see his wife and other family members. They brought him sweaters, blankets, and some food, enabling all of us to face the bitter cold of that rainy night much better.

Close to dawn I heard shouting back and forth between a group of detainees in one of the collective cells next to ours with a bunch of guys in another holding tank. Apparently it all had to do with narcotrafficking. They were communicating among themselves in order to make a decision about the 50,000 pesos per person already demanded by the higher-ups at the preventive jail of Mexico City, the loathsome Black Palace of Lecumberri. The money would assure that they would be well treated on their arrival and exempted from performing the *fajina* or required scut work. It would entitle them to cells for themselves alone and all other privileges only possible with lots of money. The prisoners were members of the group headed by Alberto Sicilia Falcón, a Cuban American, captured only a few days earlier by the Federal Judicial Police at a residence in the Pedregal of San Angel belonging to the *ranchera* singer Irma Serrano, "La Tigresa." From then on for over four years, the activities of Sicilia Falcón would affect in one way or another our own lives in prison, since our transfers coincided even when we never had any personal relationship with him. I will talk about this later.

The next day, close to nine in the morning, Francisco was allowed to leave the holding cell. The compañero came back an hour later looking scared. He'd been taken to Jorge Obregón Lima, who was then in charge of the Office of Investigation for Delinquency Prevention, a special body of the Preventive Police in the capital, the sinister old Secret Service under another name. In the presence of some ten additional agents, Obregón Lima had interrogated him again, this time without any physical violence, only verbal. They took several pictures of him and tape recorded his answers. Not three minutes elapsed between Francisco's return and their arrival to take me. They hauled me before a chief of police who looked at me as if he were targeting me with a gun. Unceremoniously, he asked if it was true that I'd hosted Lucio Cabañas Barrientos in my house. He wanted to know when that had occurred, if the house was rented or belonged to me, what had happened to the money taken from the bank assault, and finally whether I knew where I had been held. After repeating what I'd already declared in the Campo Militar Número Uno, I judiciously said I didn't know where I'd been detained. My answers were also recorded, and they took several pictures of me. The episode lasted half an hour.

That same morning both Olivia and Luis received provisional freedom on parole. Most likely this decision of the Procuraduría reflected the substantial family connections and political influence that both possessed, although truthfully neither of the two had really committed a crime. The authorities of the PGR decided not accuse Dionisio and me of any federal crimes, so that afternoon we were transferred to the Attorney General's Office of Justice of the Federal District to be indicted for the common crimes of criminal association and robbery. The change in location also signified a softer, more considerate treatment. For a starter, they put us in cells that remained unlocked. It seemed like nobody was really guarding us. We were free to walk about the place and to make contact with the other inmates in the processing section. The agents of the Ministerio Público were all young lawyers who treated us with respect. Those taking my declaration simply looked at each others eyes in silence when I told them that I'd been detained on September 4th, and the date was now November 16th.

Later at night, a judicial policeman came to inform me that he was going to give me the chance to see my father briefly—"we have instructions to keep you incommunicado"— through a window with an interphone. My father and I reached the window at the same moment; both of us were shaken, driven by a nervous mixture of anxiety, happiness, and pain. Just seeing each other released all our emotions, and we cried like infants. I had never seen or even imagined my father crying or ever demonstrating his love for me so strongly. His expression completely changed; his entire body shuddered with feeling at seeing the proof that I was alive. Our tears flowed on, making it impossible to converse. The agent soon returned to end our encounter. My father made sure that the policeman turned over to me some soap and a complete change of clean clothing that he'd brought including a sweater. At last I could take a cold bath and change clothes! I'd only managed to wash my shirt, pants, and underwear once in two months.

I saw my father again the next morning when they took me by elevator to the office of the director of Prior Inquiries where he informed me that I'd be able to see Tere in a few minutes. He warned me that I should not be very expressive with her since he'd lied to the authorities that she was one of my sisters. He'd been afraid that they might detain her too. My behavior upset Tere a great deal, and later she justifiably would reproach me for it.

But the dread of inflicting even more harm on her stopped me from acting any differently.

THE BLACK PALACE

As the time of my transfer to Lecumberri approached, I insisted to my father that he be very alert to my situation, and that neither he nor Tere should let me stay there any length of time without a visit. I suspected that he didn't understand very well the urgency of my concern.

When the moment arrived, a pair of suspicious, somewhat curious judicial policemen appeared. Both were chubby and short. They sported razor cut mustaches. Their tight, cheap suits had suffered too much ironing. They put Dionisio and me in an armored jail wagon. In place of windows, the vehicle had small round perforations on its thick sides that allowed entry for air and a bit of light. The trip was brief, and we barely exchanged a word. Events had slowly, increasingly, and inexorably begun to pull us apart. Fear also kept us quiet—fear of the sort that seizes hold of you in extreme situations that put you to the test and oblige you to confront other individuals better skilled and better equipped in the merciless struggle for existence. We would face these hard men, owners of alien wills, men with the balls to take charge of the coarse and ungrateful realms in which we would soon be living, individuals deeply experienced in pain, bitterness, rancor, and insensibility. These prison denizens would be convinced that only the "sharp," the "effective," the sons of bitches, and the hot shits would be in position to make it through at the expense of the rest of the jerks, the dumb fuckers that mill around in life.

Many times I'd gone by in front of Lecumberri since October 2, 1968. I always thought of the students and teachers jailed inside, never failing to tell myself that it would not be long before I too found myself locked up in this dungeon. I had visited the compañeras of El Indio and Rafael—Dionisio's brother—over matters concerning the printing of *Lucha Popular*, a publication that after the defeat of the popular student movement of 1968 took the place of *Militante*, the propaganda sheet of the Liga Comunista Espartaco. From them I knew something about the life that El Indio and Rafael led inside in cellblock M together with other political prisoners like José Revueltas, Heberto Castillo, Elí de Gortari, and Armando Castillejos. Tere, as part of my strategy to involve her in the struggle, had also accompanied Marcela various times on her visits to Rafael. The reality of the Palacio Negro of Lecumberri was always much more terrible than the worst of nightmares.

Upon our arrival, the judicial police made us descend from the jail wagon in the middle of an internal courtyard just behind the enormous gate of the principal entrance. They led us to the intake area, the end of their responsibility for us. There we had to answer the harsh questions of a chubby, dark, opaque-skinned individual in a light gray uniform. He was scarcely capable of reading the intake document that contained our name, address, marital status, religion, and occupation. The prison guards guided us to a solitary corner located to one side of the principal passageway of the prison where we had to empty our pockets. The guards could invoke prison rules to confiscate whatever they wanted. Since I knew that this was the moment in which guards were accustomed to extend their "welcome to the prison" with punches, kicks, and blows with clubs, I expected that they were about to assault the both of us. The higher ranking guard who commanded the other three spotted Dionisio's name, however. He inquired if Dionisio were the brother of Rafael, the primary school teacher who'd been jailed there in 1969 together with the students and teachers from 1968. Dionisio replied yes, thus saving us by a pure miracle from getting the shit beaten out of us. They then took us to a small room for the obligatory front and profile photos. They took prints from the fingers from both hands on numerous pieces of paper. On the way, a prisoner identified by a plastic armband as a *comando*—a member of the corps at the service of a "Mayor" or chief of a cellblock—gave me a hard blow with his open hand to the back of my neck, almost knocking me down. This was the first bad sign of what awaited me there.

With our registration finished, another two guards who smelled of old sweat, chile, and onion took us to cellblock H, also called the holding tank, turning us over to the official in charge there, known as "El Yuca" for his Yucatecan origin. A prisoner, designated as clerk of the cellblock, used an old Smith Corona to register our personal information for the third time. Right afterwards, he took us to the doctor on duty so that he could create an official—and superficial—record of our physical and mental condition upon entry into Lecumberri. A bit later, El Yuca placed Dionisio and me in separate cells located at the end of one of the upper hallways of H, advising us not leave our cells without his permission and to keep their heavy doors closed. The guard could not lock them individually, and it would not be until nighttime that a general mechanism locked up all the cells at once. So with the cell door partly open, I could sit on the floor peeking out at everything going on in the hallways and the courtyard.

The cells were wide and dark, with high ceilings and walls covered with old iron sheeting scratched with religious inscriptions, swear words, and curses along with obscene doodling and other simple drawings. An opening covered with metal grating allowed the entry of light and air at the tallest point of the rear wall. If you could get up that high to look out, you could observe a narrow passageway framed by a thick brick wall. In addition, the cells had two metal bunks built into the walls, each of which had three slats of thick metal arranged one above the other in which bedbugs and white lice nested comfortably. All I could do was to climb up to one of the beds on the second level, resigned to being bitten and sucked on by repugnant bugs rather than to sleeping on the floor and being gnawed at by one of the enormous, disgusting rats that wandered all over Lecumberri late in the afternoon and at night.

Later that first day, after roll call, El Yuca placed all the ordinary prisoners in consecutive cells and shut them in—a "lockdown"—while he ordered Dionisio, Francisco, and me to stay in the courtyard to undertake the fajina or menial labor of sweeping, wetting down, and mopping the courtyard, the defense team visiting area, the stairway, and the two upper hallways of H. Francisco's surprising appearance in our line of prisoners happened because he'd arrived the previous day at Lecumberri and had been locked up in a different cell out of our sight. The night before he'd had to carry out these tasks, so El Yuca ordered him to instruct us on how to perform them. The three of us worked at the fajina for two hours, avoiding the corners where the rats congregated, especially in the visiting area for the defense teams. We crossed the cellblock from one side to the other with the broom and mopping rag, going over what we'd already cleaned again and again. We were tired, hungry, bored, and chilled to the bone. We moved over to the entrance to the tiny chapel dedicated to the Virgin of Guadalupe, built thanks to the donations of many forgotten prisoners anxious to receive divine aid during their difficult time in jail. We kept asking ourselves how long they were going to keep us in the courtyard into the wee hours of the morning. About eleven at night El Yuca appeared again in the company of five other unfriendly looking guards. He ordered that we stop working and took us out of H, leaving behind the brooms and mopping rags. The pack of guards led us along a corridor that opened on the left to a wider one, divided in the middle by a planter that extended all the way to the so-called *Redondel* or ring, a hallway that circled around the high central watch tower that symbolized Lecumberri. At the base of the tower was the control station known as the Polygon. The central tower and the *Redondel* allowed for the surveillance and guarding of seven cellblocks: A, B, C, D, E, F, and G (I and L did not form part of this circuit; neither did M and N, the only two that reproduced at a lesser scale the functional principal of Lecumberri).

Escorted by the five guards armed with clubs, Dionisio, Francisco, and I turned the corner and entered the principal corridor. At that exact moment we spied another group of guards led by a lieutenant at the end of the passageway. Seeing us arrive, they ganged up on a young ordinary prisoner they'd surrounded, assaulting him with their fists, feet, and clubs. In the midst of this violence against him, the youth struggled to fill two large buckets with water from an enormous faucet. Blows and insults continued to rain down upon him. Amid shoves and kicks, they forced the boy to run towards us while holding the handles of both heavy buckets in a difficult balance. Once the frightened prisoner reached our side, the lieutenant ordered him to dump the water from the two plastic buckets over the cement floor. While another guard clubbed him again in the ribs, the lieutenant commanded the prisoner to demonstrate how things were done. With great speed and dexterity, the young man showed us how to wipe the wet floor while crouching, holding in his two hands old cloths that he rotated, each in the opposite direction of the other. The prisoner slid along dizzyingly on the tips of his feet with his knees bent, all the while sustaining whacks and insults from this infamous gang of guards. Upon a further order from the lieutenant, the kid urgently straightened up. Sucking in air through his mouth, he ran to wring out the soaked cloths in the nearest drain, only to respond to yet another command to come back again, crouch, and to mop once more with his improvised cleaning cloths. Perhaps at this point he believed that he wasn't going to do this again, but the new order of the lieutenant, who enjoyed his sadistic role as boss of the fajina, forced him to initiate the cycle over and over.

After a few minutes at this task, I couldn't go on anymore. My legs trembled, and I barely sustained myself upright. I began to feel dizzy and nauseated. My vision clouded over. The blows and shouts fell again and again upon Dionisio, Francisco, and me. The guards laughed at us, and pushed us so that we lost our balance and fell on our faces on the cold, wet floor. We were soaked from head to foot. The ordinary prisoner rapidly filled the buckets, spreading their contents around immediately just in front of the three of us. Hunched over and with great difficulty, we advanced forward through the puddles produced by the excess of water. Soon I reached the point where I didn't care if they beat me for ignoring the order to get up and run to the drain to wring the water out of the heavy mopping cloths. I preferred to faint and to die right then and there, leaning on the edge of the planter, rehearsing an idiotic half smile like an obsessed, nostalgic man, looking up at the sky covered with clouds. In contrast, Dionisio and Francisco toiled even harder and didn't look like they were about to weaken. The lieutenant came over and asked me if I were feeling sick. He seemed worried by the weakness of my body and my pallid face; I suppose he didn't want to run the risk of letting me die on the spot, so he relieved me from my task and sent me to spread the water that the young man was carrying. When we got to the *Redondel*, the mopping cloths were exchanged for brooms. We went all around the circular corridor, the ordinary prisoner and I throwing water right and left with our buckets; Dionisio and

Francisco sweeping liter after liter of water into the drains. The guards of the various cellblocks standing in the middle of their intake cages looked at us curiously and aggressively, constantly mocking us and threatening us.

Finally close to one in the morning, the lieutenant gave the order that we should be taken back to cellblock H. Once inside my cell, frozen stiff, I removed my soaking clothes and wrapped my body with a woolen blanket that my father had brought me. I had only begun to recover some heat and was about to sink into a deep sleep when I felt someone shaking me, forcing me to wake up. It was El Yuca. He told me to stand up and get dressed. I had no recourse. Putting on my soaking, cold clothing again jolted me and left me shivering uncontrollably. El Yuca kept quiet about what was happening, refusing to answer my question. He obliged me to go down to the yard of the cellblock. Once reunited with Dionisio and Francisco who had been brought there a few minutes before, he made the three of us from the H go back to the Polygon and the ring. There we were forced once again to slop and sweep great amounts of water around the whole circuit. Our welcome to Lecumberri proved that they could do with us whatever they wished. Fortunately, the commander of the group on duty withdrew to rest after an hour, so the guards took us back to the cells, and we got a couple of hours of sleep before dawn and the roll call at six in the morning.

That day, after chow—*atole* with milk and a roll—I found a spot by the side of the door of my cell from where I could observe any movement in the cellblock. That's what I was doing when—surprise!—I saw coming out of the cell adjacent to the bathrooms, located in one of the corners of the upper story of the cellblock, none other than Wenceslao José García, Chilo, the Oaxacan author of the shootout at the Parque Hundido. I'd assumed that he was dead after his brutal session of torture in the Campo Militar Número Uno after his release from surgery for the multiple gunshot wounds he had received in that episode. I couldn't stop wondering why in spite of what this man apparently represented, the government had chosen to respect his life and consigned him before a judge. Wenceslao would tell me months later that it was the military physicians who took care of him in the Military Hospital who'd saved his life. They had pressured his captors to grant him due process under law. From my lookout that afternoon I could confirm Wenceslao's admittance to the interior of the jail in the company of other alleged ordinary delinquents, on his way to the cellblock chosen for him by the Lecumberri authorities following his formal declaration of imprisonment. I ran into him again four or five months later when he was transferred to the O West, where half of all the political prisoners in Lecumberri at that time—close to 100—were concentrated.

On that very day a bit earlier, from my vantage point, I could also spot the arrival of my mother as a visitor to the cold and crowded yard of H. For my mother, a fine lady, extremely proud and dignified, it must have been the most humiliating and painful experience of her life to enter such a depressing and pathetic place in order to visit her only son. I discovered her as she crossed H's intake cage at the same time that I heard the sound system calling me from my cell for her visit. Everything happened at the same time, so I hurried into the corridor and then down the stairs, with eyes full of tears, a knot in my throat, and a heavy feeling of shame burdening me. Anxiously Mama came forward to meet me, with open arms to embrace me, at the same time as she imperiously asked me to control my emotions while she kept hers under check. It was all too much for her. Clearly the humiliation was greater than her capacity for tenderness, and she was compelled to repress the broad generosity of her maternal feelings. She was there, yes. I had to recognize that she had made an enormous effort, accepting personal and social degradation. But it was impossible to ask her to forgive and understand her son the jackass. Her love for me would cause her to repeat that visit once every other week during the four years that my formal imprisonment lasted, first in Lecumberri, then in the Reclusorio Oriente, and then finally in the Santa Martha Acatitla penitentiary. But, accepting my reasons, trying to understand my ideas, certainly not!

Another unexpected but logical visitor that very humid, cloudy, mid-November morning was Rafael, who came to visit his brother Dionisio. After seeing him, he requested permission to visit me. I took advantage of his presence to ask him to reveal the situation of Jacobo—Javier Gaytán Saldívar—and that of Noé, both still detained in the Campo Militar Número Uno. We three had made a commitment to inform our families and public opinion about the situation of the other two in case one of us left the camp alive. In talking to Rafael, I was fulfilling my duty to my two compañeros in misfortune. However, I never knew whether or not Rafael carried out my request, and if he did, how he did it, because I never saw him again. What is true is that my life continued its course in prison, and I never made another attempt to publicize Jacobo and Noé's situation in a more serious and efficient manner. The fear of the power of the state took a hold of me completely. I did not want to add more difficulties to the problems I was facing.

Michel Foucault has written: "He who is subjected to a field of visibility, and who knows it, assumes responsibility for the constraints of power; he makes them play spontaneously upon himself; he inscribes in himself the power relation in which he simultaneously plays both roles; he becomes the principle of his own subjection."[1] Foucault is discussing the prison architecture developed by Jeremy Bentham in which a prisoner is observed all the time by watchmen whom he himself cannot see. I believe that this principle can be applied to the attitudes and conduct of those of us who acted in clandestinity, isolated from the struggle of the masses. A despotic power like the one that fought against us uncovered, apprehended, and fully identified us, keeping us under iron-handed control in hidden detention in secret prisons. In our condition, this despotic power could do whatever it pleased with us.

LIFE IN LECUMBERRI

After the required period of seventy-two hours, Dionisio and I were taken from the H to Common Pleas Court XXV where a clerk notified us of our formal imprisonment for the crimes of theft and criminal association. Susana and Francisco had already been declared formal prisoners the day before. Once notified, all we could do was await the feared moment of full entrance into Lecumberri, each in a different cellblock, as the clock tolled six P.M., the hour of the evening roll call.

In every case, entering a jail is an unending chain of humiliations. For those born like me into an upper-middle class home, it is a very painful experience, especially lacerating for one's pride and self-respect. Imprisonment means being subject to the will of people with the power to satisfy their interests and whims at your expense. The victim lacks even the slightest possibility to oppose them or to complain. Imprisonment implies having to obey without the slightest reluctance men who have no formal instruction, not even at the elementary level, men who are resentful, opportunistic, malicious, lacking in moral scruples, and given to vice. Under this despotic exercise of the power of just a few, thousands of human beings, sunken in the catastrophe of having lost their freedom, struggle in silence and with determination to survive a reign of terror and extortion in which—fortunately—gestures of true human solidarity still persist.

After we left cellblock H, several guards took Dionisio, between eight and ten ordinary prisoners, and me single file to an interior courtyard where the clothing warehouse was located. We had to exchange our garments for navy blue uniforms made of cotton gabardine. These dirty and stinking outfits existed in either enormous or in very small sizes only. We had to choose our own rapidly from a pile of uniforms thrown in the middle of this desolate space. The clothing we were wearing was turned over to some inmates specially commissioned to receive it. They provided a ticket in exchange, informing us that our wives or other relatives could retrieve our clothing some other day by presenting the ticket, or we could do it ourselves if we were ever set free from Lecumberri.

It is difficult to describe how I felt dressed in slacks that had very short legs and a wide waist tied around my thin abdomen with a piece of rope; a visibly wide and short stinking jacket; and a soldier's cap on my head. On my feet I wore the pair of old, smelly, worn-out, grotesquely large shoes that an aggressive ordinary inmate, young and strong, had forced upon me in the solitary corridor that led to the courts. In turn, he'd walked off with the pair of new, suede shoes with rubber soles, so fashionable in the seventies, that my father had generously given me a few hours before in his ignorance of what jail life was like, eager to have me dispose of my worn-out Otomí sandals.

Uniformed like ragamuffins, with devalued dignity and with our hearts in our mouths from uncertainty and fear, we paraded like a caravan around the *Redondel*. We had to stop at each one of the cellblocks to witness the arrival and reception of one or more wretches. The comandos of each cellblock waited anxiously for the booty of their new victims following the jailhouse announcement that: "The lioness has given birth to new cubs!" Immediately, the corps of guards at the service of the cellblock chiefs confiscated all blankets, whatever their condition. The good ones ended up as rugs for the head of the violent prison gangs or his lieutenants, the lousy ones as cleaning rags for the new inmates forced to carry out the fajina. These gangs kept order in Lecumberri as well as internal control over the traffic in drugs, alcohol, and prostitution, the execution of the fajina, the operation of tiny eateries, and the renting of cells. Shoes in good shape or any other possession of value belonging to the "lioness' new cubs" naturally ended up on the feet, hands, or necks of these mafiosos. Our caravan made its round rapidly, soon stopping before the entrance to cellblock D to which I had been assigned. Cellblock D housed the *chacales* or jackals, those processed for homicide or injury to third parties. Many other wretches involved in traffic accidents that had caused injuries or death also ended up there. Naturally the worst murderers established their control over the other prisoners in D. Their boss was a former commander of the fearsome DFS who—so it was said there—had been incarcerated for having murdered a lover. This guy was the Mayor of the Mayores, *Il cappo di tutti cappi* of Lecumberri.

After crossing the threshold of the intake cage of cellblock D in the company of five more individuals, the prisoners in charge of reception ordered all of us to place ourselves in a corner near the entrance, to one side of the Mayor's office and under a stairway that led to the upper floor of the building. We were all thrown together, terrified by the aggressive comandos who gathered in front of us like fierce beasts. They ordered us to hand over our blankets and shoes. Once they'd gotten the order to do so, two of these individuals conducted us promptly to the office of the Mayor. There Alfredo, a top official and a sort of executive secretary to the Mayor, read us the rules. We'd have to carry out the fajina for at least three months unless we could pay a quota of three thousand pesos. Alfredo was impeccably dressed, a man in his Sunday best, with a fine silk shirt of brilliant colors and designs, tailored pants, and a short jacket in navy blue gabardine. He was white-skinned, with a delicate but strong build, well cared-for hands, straight and abundant black hair piled on the top of his head with a well-defined part and a well-gummed crest. His body language appeared both nervous and decisive. He smelled of expensive lavender. His round face contained large, almond-shaped eyes with thick eyebrows, long eyelashes, and a bushy mustache trimmed with a razor blade. I imagined that he must have grown up in Colonia Roma, in Santa María de la Ribera, or in Narvarte. He spoke to me in a low voice, poking my chest with the manicured nail of his index finger: "Since you come recommended, it's going to cost you fifteen thousand to get out of the fajina." When he saw my astonishment at the amount of money he'd expected, he added that it was not necessary to make one single payment, as long as I paid within a month. He added that if I didn't accept the deal, I'd have to face the consequences—during those months I'd get no truce in the fajina. Intimidated by the threat, I told him that I accepted, believing that I could ask my parents to get me the cash. I didn't want to suffer any more damage to my person.

Once they'd issued these warnings, and some prisoners had assured them of their payments, Alfredo ordered the comandos to take us out to the cellblock yard. They integrated us into one of the two long rows of inmates that faced one another, waiting with their backs to the cells for the evening roll call, an elementary and routine accounting operation carried out by three guards to the sound of drum rolls and bugle calls of Lecumberri's inmate military band. At the end of the ceremony, the military band transmitted the order to break ranks with a specific fanfare of the first bugler. A dark-skinned, young man with a bright, but absent gaze addressed us in the sing-song jail dialect. He was thin, but muscular, and wore an unbuttoned, sleeveless, uniformed jacket along with a commander's bracelet on his right arm. Both of his arms displayed multiple tattoos in all forms, sizes, and colors. He demanded that we follow him. We walked behind him as sheep to the slaughter as he marched through the yard, pushing and shoving dozens of surprised inmates. They hadn't stood in his way on purpose; they were just tripping over him because of the breaking of ranks. Terrified, we moved behind this man, bumping into other inmates of the cellblock. I could see a great, primitive mural painting on the back wall as I glanced up. A large water basin stood attached to the wall, with several metal drums full of water standing next to it. Some inmates were earning a few extra pennies by washing other people's clothes in four sinks.

In the middle of our race, a young man with light chestnut hair, white skin, and a decent appearance accosted me. I'd seen him in one of the holding cells of the Procuraduría General de la República where he stood accused of contraband operations in Persian rugs. He demanded the plastic bag of food that I was clutching, saying that he would take care of it for me. I gave it to him without thinking. In reality, it didn't matter if I lost it to him or in some other fashion. Agitated and frightened, we finally arrived at the end of the cellblock. With pushes, blows, and all manners of profanity, they introduced us into a cell they called "headquarters," placed next to the toilets and showers. We had to take off our clothing and turn over any money we had. They warned us that it could get very unpleasant if they discovered anything hidden in our clothing. I'd tucked a little bit of money given to me by my father inside my socks. Removing them carefully, I made sure that the bills would not be noticeable. In my innermost thoughts, I implored that the comandos would not find them. Our uncertainty and trepidation at what they would do to us was great—I'd heard that they raped new arrivals with a broomstick!

We were pondering all this when the corporal of fajina arrived. He was known as Yépes, a forty-something year-old man, short in stature, somewhat depraved looking with messy and grayish hair, red eyes, a broken nose, flattened, thick lips, and crooked teeth stained with nicotine. He forced us to go out naked to the yard where several inmates promenaded in twosomes or in groups. Our apprehension grew even more. We were the most wretched among the wretched, the cubs that the lioness had just birthed. It turned out, however, that this procedure had the purpose of sending a few members of our generation into the next room, where the toilets were placed in one single row, and the rest of us to the room further up where the showers and steam system were located. In both cases we were there to "do *chocho*," that is to say to take a pair of bricks, one in each hand, rub them against the floor, the walls, and the toilets. After a few hours, they would become an abrasive paste capable of removing the plaque accumulated by the constant communal use of thousands of inmates over a period of more than seventy years in the history of Lecumberri. All this was accompanied by bucketfuls of cold water thrown over the naked bodies of the fajineros every ten minutes more or less under the pretext of reanimating them in their efforts ("here it goes, slowly so that you will not think it's unpleasant, bro . . ."). The water also helped moisten the accumulated brick paste which improved the abrasion on the surfaces to be cleaned. I'd just begun to rub both bricks on the floor of the shower room after receiving the first slopping of cold water on my head and back when Alfredo appeared, escorted by "Tobi," "El Alacrán," and "El Perro." He ordered me out of there and sent me to the cell next-door where my clothes had remained. I got dressed again, relieved that the money was still inside the sock. Alfredo recommended me to the chief of fajina so that he would give me refuge during the day in what they called the "headquarters of the *paganinis*," adding that if I so wished for a weekly payment of seventy-five pesos or more I could spend the night in Yépes' cell, a proposal I immediately accepted.

The next day very early, after the six A.M. roll call, I found myself for the first time waiting in a long and slow queue formed to receive the rationed morning chow—a watered down oat-atole, hard and burned beans, and a chewy roll served in an aluminum plate divided in sections. I heard Alfredo calling me from the yard. I was in the upper story which I had reached following the queue, and I couldn't quite make out what he was trying to tell me. The inmate standing behind me told me that I should go down at once, because if I didn't obey the first officer, by the time I got to the cauldrons, he would order that the boiling atole be poured on my hands. I obeyed, and once in the yard, Alfredo advised me that I couldn't eat the regular chow. If I wanted to have breakfast, I should go to the cellblock eatery. If I had no money, they could give me credit as long as I paid the next Sunday after my family's visit.

From that moment on, it became perfectly clear that I would be the object of a permanent extortion. Mayor Campos and his people would charge me for everything: avoiding the fajina, bathing, getting a haircut, going to the store and the eatery. At the end of the first obligatory three months of fajina—which I wasn't going to undertake because I was paying to save myself from it, as someone highly "recommended" without the right to any truce—they would sell me some place in some cell at an expensive price. Even then, the cell owner would allow me access only at nights, and thus I would not be able to see my wife alone unless I paid even more for a single cell. They were selling them for several thousand pesos although they reserved the right to "recover" them any time they pleased, as a latent threat or a reprisal for having disobeyed any of the rules.

Under these circumstances, I used to spend the whole day in the headquarters of the paganinis, surrounded by peaceful people who devoted their time to crafts and to the elimination of white lice in their clothing, an occupation that I immediately learned to perform systematically. Once in a while, we were allowed to go to the cellblock yard to sun ourselves and to breathe less stale air than in the cells. Around ten in the morning, everyone had to be locked up because that was the moment when Mayor Campos took a bath. The Capo appeared in the yard in his shades with the air of a decadent Roman emperor. He walked wrapped in a thick multicolored bathing robe, while Alfredo and three or four other comandos escorted him all the way to the bath. One carried the towels, another the soap, shampoo and conditioner for his thin dyed black hair, as well as the lotion to massage and perfume the jaded, decaying body of the once powerful commander of the Dirección Federal de Seguridad.

Meanwhile, the inmates assigned to bath duty that day covered the floor with clean sheets, starting two meters before the entrance and going all the way into the showers. The Capo could set his plastic sandals on them without fear of contracting athlete's foot. The daily toilette of the Mayor of all mayores was a ceremony that could last an entire hour. While one inmate massaged his whole body, another took care of his fingers and toenails. Campos remained lying down on a stone bench sweating buckets because of the hot steam from the heater that flowed out through perforations in pipes surrounding the room along the edge of the walls.

While Mayor Campos remained in the bath, nobody could go out to the yard except for the first official and the comandos that protected him, and those inmates who received visits from the members of their defense team. That was my case. During the first stage of my imprisonment in Lecumberri, Tere arrived that early in the morning everyday as part of my defense team. Each defendant could name five people, three of whom could visit him as frequently as they needed to according to an established schedule. Visits could even take place in the inmate's cell. In our case, since that was not yet possible, we had to sit uncomfortably in the middle of the yard on the only communal cement bench and table of the cellblock. There we were at the very hour when the ridiculous, pathetic, yet sinister and dangerous Mayor Campos paraded nearby, protected by his entourage of baleful assassins, all of them armed with dreadfully huge and sharp butcher knives. Alfredo, the Mayor's main assistant, also carried an automatic Beretta 9 mm pistol, which he kept secured at his waist hidden under the back of his jacket of fine navy blue fabric.

I could never understand the advantage of paying for the right to sleep in Yépes' hovel. It was no more than a small bathroom, equipped with two toilets separated by half walls. Instead of doors, each had a dirty threadbare fabric curtain. Those toilets were used on visiting days by the mothers, sisters, daughters, friends, wives, or concubines of the *fajineros* or convicts that were not entitled to their own cells, that is, the majority of cellblock D. At ten o'clock sharp at night, the hour of curfew and lockdown, we three tenants of Yépes, tired of not having done anything during the day, would lie down on our blankets on the cold floor of the short and narrow hallway that cut across the room of the overseer of the fajineros. Our heads would face in opposite directions, alternating with the feet of another. After midnight, when the nocturnal fajina began and the three tenants were sleeping soundly, the corporal and his helpers would awaken us, going in and out of the room with the cleaning equipment in their hands, enjoying the act of stepping on us "accidentally" or dropping the foul rags used in the fajina on our heads or dragging buckets and brooms over us. These assholes repeated this deliberate act of fucking us up around 1:30 or 2:00 in the morning. It was the same thing night after night, with only a slight variation in the length and intensity of the annoyance caused by the bastards, depending on whether Yépes had obtained and consumed his nightly fix of drugs—*tecata*, a form of diluted heroin alternated with one or two marijuana cigarettes—and wasn't *peido*, on edge or angry.

Nevertheless, in spite of all this disturbance, I would surely have been worse off sleeping in the headquarters with the fajineros. They were kept in a cell three and a half meters by four, without any bunk beds or furniture that would take up space. Between twenty-five and thirty relatively new inmates were housed in that space, as was the case in the month of December of that year. The majority of the fajineros literally slept standing up, leaning on each other; only a few of them, the most aggressive, would conquer by blows and threats enough space to lie down or crouch. I know that what I am saying will seem unbelievable, but I am not exaggerating. In the morning at 5:45, the moment when the comandos on duty ordered everyone to rise, Yépes sent me out to the yard to unlock the door of the headquarters so that the fajineros could come out and stand in formation for the first roll call. Following his order, I opened the door. When I did, those poor wretches would tumble outside the cell, soaked in sweat on their backs or buttocks. They fell onto the cold, damp floor of the yard, still sleep as if they were a heap of clothing expelled by the pressure of its own weight from a closet that was too full. Immediately, once we were all in our rows, two guards—monkeys—appeared in the cellblock yard in their gray uniforms, followed by the buglers and the drummers for reveille. Two guards, who belonged to one of the three companies that worked the jail—they used to work shifts of twenty-four hours, alternating with forty-eight hours of rest—would count those of us formed in rows while a third one knocked on some cell doors to induce the reply of "present!" from the privileged few that had paid to avoid getting up so early. The mere act of having forgotten to wear one's cap or being absent from the row without permission could cause Alfredo to sock the offender in front of everyone and order the comandos to empty an oil drum full of cold water on him. That was the minimal punishment for minor violations; there were harsher forms of punishment, some of them lethal.

Most of the time, I remained in the paganinis' space in the company of inmates who were not eager to add to their afflictions. Notwithstanding, when one would least expect it, our otherwise peaceful refuge would turn raucous when a group of comandos headed by Reséndiz and Tobi barged into the cell, along with one or two unfortunate men whose bodies were being savagely beaten so as to spare their faces any telltale marks. The reasons for beatings varied, but most of the time they had to do with missed payments to the jail-house mafia. I remember in particular the first time I was forced to witness an extremely violent retribution against a man in his forties with a grown beard and messy gray hair. He'd fallen into debt after a week of asking for cig-arettes and sodas at the store, and food at the eatery, both concessions of Mayor Campos granted to him by General Arcaute, director of Lecumberri. When the family visit was over on Sunday afternoon, as each inmate was called by name through the sound system installed next to Mayor Campos' office, the man argued that he had received no visitor. He didn't have the money to pay them their debt of seventy pesos. They let him have it imme-diately—savage punches and kicks increased in number and intensity while the man, howling in fright and pain, implored them over and over to take him to his family's home so that he could pay them there. Hearing such a ludi-crous plea made Reséndiz and Tobi even more furious. They pummeled him all the more viciously, trying to inflict the greatest possible damage in their relentless demand for "our money." We other six inmates remained trapped within those four walls against our will. We intuited that we couldn't simply walk out, so we sat absolutely still and silent, frightened, eyes on the floor, almost afraid of breathing and blinking. Even so, the moment came when I was about to yell at Reséndiz and Tobi to leave the man alone, that I would pay them their seventy pesos that the poor crazy bastard owed them. Fortu-nately, fear of their reaction made me prudent, and I kept my mouth shut. To finish up, a tired and sweaty Reséndiz and Tobi pulled out two wide butcher knives and started to hit the now listless man's back and head with their flat sides. They then dragged him to the hole, the punishment cell devoid of nat-ural or electric light, toilet, or bed, located just above where we were. The pris-oner remained there for days in the dark, unable even to sit, much less lie down on the shit-covered, urinated floor, a generous haunt for mold, bacteria, insects, and rats.

Such episodes tended to happen at the end of the two days of family vis-its that we prisoners were entitled to every week at Lecumberri. In all the time I spent there, I could never get used to the daily demonstrations of sadistic violence by these mafiosos; they always appalled me.

One day it happened that Tere couldn't bring me the weekly amount of money previously agreed upon with Alfredo. Maddened, he immediately sent me to do the *chocho*, a degrading task performed in the nude in the area of the collective latrines and showers. The punished men could be observed by three or four defecators who were using the blackened stone toilets at that moment. I spent three hours crouching, trembling with cold each time they threw water at me. When another inmate came in to use the facilities, the door allowed in the cold wind of that afternoon in early December, 1974. The torment ended when I followed the advise of Yépes' assistant, sending word through him to Alfredo that the following Sunday I would unfailingly pay him twice as much.

The experience endured by the fajineros for at least a hundred days after their admission to one of the cellblocks of Lecumberri was closest to the brutal condition of slavery. The fajina boss Yépes was an efficient overseer, cold and calculating most of the time, but explosive at the slightest provocation. Yépes was full of rancor and fury, and he could turn vicious against any fajinero that he thought might have tried to play things too smart. Naturally, Yépes was also unconditionally disposed to obey anybody with power over him; he was ready to carry out immediately any explicit orders or simple hints from Campos or Alfredo. The latter was undoubtedly the main operator, the keeper of internal order through the violent means that were indispensable for maintaining control over the jailhouse regime that extorted the convicts of every cellblock. That doesn't mean that Yépes couldn't be cruel. When it was a matter of convincing the newly arrived inmates rapidly, those who the mafiosos saw as graft material, Yépes would order his helpers—the most experienced and ass-kissing of the fajineros—to place them in front the squad. At his signal, the new inmates would be held by their clothing and pulled forward while they walked in a squatting position. Naturally, in a few minutes, they were being dragged on the wet yard. In a few hours they would be asking Yépes for a truce, promising to pay the amount that Alfredo had demanded on behalf of Mayor Campos. Two or three days later the knees of these poor devils were red, swollen, and full of puss from the infections caused by the contaminated floor. It was a pity to see them walk with difficulty across the yard of the cellblock, their faces reflecting their pain.

One cold December morning, on the 8th, I learned the news of the death of Lucio Cabañas Barrientos in a bloody skirmish with members of the National Army in the sierra of Guerrero. Tobi and Reséndiz were commissioned by Campos to go to my cell and show me the newspaper photograph of a ghastly Lucio printed on the first page of *Excélsior*. Was this truly the guerrilla fighter? they asked. In a state of consternation, I admitted it was. Immediately the pair of miscreants turned around and went to talk to Campos. Later Tere arrived to visit me. She had two or three newspapers with the same news and photograph. Unfortunately the tragic event could be foreseen as coming for a long time, especially after the kidnapping and liberation of Rubén Figueroa Figueroa.

SAVED BY THE BELL

All throughout December my father-in-law, don José, and my sister-in-law Margarita had been making decisions that affected me without consulting me or thinking of the consequences that their actions might have. They spoke to some acquaintances whom they assumed to have public influence, and they visited people in positions of authority in their eager wish to see me out of prison or at least improve my situation while I was in Lecumberri. My own father had been connected for over thirty years to the most important printed communications media in the country. He represented the Association of Editors of the States in Mexico City, grouping together five of the largest dailies in the nation: *El Dictamen* from Veracruz; *El Informador* from Guadalajara; *El Diario* from Yucatán; *El Porvenir* from Monterrey; and *El Diario del Yaqui* from Hermosillo in Sonora. He would not miss any opportunity to disclose my situation before the many friends and acquaintances he had in the trade, asking them for their solidarity. In fact, very little could be done, since in those days the government exercised an almost absolute control of the mass media.

At any rate, my family's activism was soon noticed by the Secretariat of Government, especially when my father decided to meet with the main press correspondents of the United States and Europe. One afternoon around three o'clock, when the majority of the inmates in my cellblock were taking a nap, I came out of my day cell to go to the bathroom. On my way back I decided to stop at the store and buy a pack of cigarettes. The store was located in the so-called first square, right next to Mayor Campos' own office, near the entrance gates to cellblock D. As I was making my way in that direction, I saw Alfredo, flanked by one of the comandos. They walked for a stretch, and then reversed direction. I wasn't surprised, since this was a frequent way for him to keep watch. I continued walking in their direction. As I passed them, the son-of-a-bitch Alfredo deliberately crashed against me. As he did, he put his fists and forearms at the level of my abdomen and with one swift movement threw me back about three feet. I had hardly recovered my breath and balance, when—as I was trying to make sense out of what was happening—I saw Alfredo coming, ready to punch me. I instinctively raised my arms to protect myself, but did not return the blows. Everything happened so fast! While I was dodging the slugs, I heard some hurried steps behind me; a few seconds later, a tremendously sharp pain pierced my right side, leaving me breathless and turning my legs into rags. I fell to the yard floor as if stuck by lightning, fighting for air through my mouth. I was desperate to move, but could not. Two comandos arrived from behind, kicking me on the back, buttocks, and legs.

Suddenly the dry voice of Mayor Campos was heard. As if it had been the voice of God himself, he ordered them to stop the beating and take me to the *apando*, the hole. Tobi, Reséndiz, and three other comandos lifted me and ran with me through the yard, in the direction of the nearest stairway across from the eatery. Some shoved me upstairs, while others pulled me up by my uniform, my feet bouncing on every step. As soon as we arrived, Tobi opened the door of the cell, displaying the scarcely lit empty space of bare walls covered with graffiti. A pungent ammonia odor almost knocked me out, while the comandos competed with each other to be the one to push me all the way in and kick me the most. At that moment another guard arrived to let them know on behalf of Campos that they should stop the beating and just leave me there in the hole. "Saved by the bell!" I said to myself, and sighed, soaked in cold sweat and trying to breathe in spite of the heavy atmosphere that hung over the place.

I found myself in almost complete darkness, except for a slit one inch wide, between the cell door and the floor, through which light filtered in. In a spirit of solidarity, an anonymous inmate introduced an aluminum plate for me to sit on through the slit, enabling me to avoid the dry detritus of human and rat feces. But I worried that the same space permitting someone to help me could also punish me more—since rats could enter through the slit and bite my legs, arms, hands, nose, and ears as soon as I fell asleep from fatigue. But for some reason, bad luck didn't stick to me that day. After an hour and a half in the hole, I was escorted by two guards to the headquarters of the paganinis, and from there to the control center, the so-called Polygon, located at the base of the watch tower in the very center of the *Redondel*. Since one of the guards was with me in the cell as I was picking up my things, Yépez couldn't stop me from leaving without having paid him his weekly fee. He walked next to me all along the yard, gnashing his teeth, looking at me with his ratty eyes reddened by drugs and ire, demanding his cash in sign language, and threatening with a "you will see what happens to you…!" But protected by the company of the guards, I didn't even address him, treating him as a madman. That was my small revenge.

From the Polygon I was sent to cellblock O West, one of two sites in Lecumberri—the other one was cellblock M, reserved exclusively for the members of the guerrilla organizations of the seventies. It was dusk while I walked through unknown corridors. Dark corners teemed with rats. I walked as if floating, under the spell of a sense of unreality. I was guided by the two indifferent, somewhat bored guards who had been at either side of me since taking me from the hole. They smelled of something vaguely fermented, like old filth. Cellblock O was a modern building, a scaled-down prison of white

cement, with tall walls and watch towers, divided into four sections and connected to the adjacent court building through an underground passage. The
architecture and materials used in the making of cellblock O contrasted with
the old part of Lecumberri. I entered O in between my two guards as night
shadows descended over us. I remember that the silence impressed me. In
cellblock D, as in any other cellblock, the constant noise from radios and other
small sound systems was deafening, as in the housing projects of tough neighborhoods. I also took notice of the coldness and modern air of the building,
as well as the semidarkness of the stairwell in front of me. The guard in charge
of the gate to the Western section, as he opened it for me, told me to go up
that stairway and look for the other inmates on my own.

It was the first time I was walking without custody through an unknown
space in four months. The sense of freedom surprised me and made me
apprehensive. Uncertain, but also curious, I went up step by step to the first
level, where I discovered a rectangular space with metallic furniture attached
to the floor. There were tables with tin covers and benches made out of
chrome pipes. It was a dining room that doubled as a visiting area for relatives and friends. I don't remember precisely who among the political prisoners of the O West appeared before me at that point, although I think it may
have been Jerónimo Martínez Díaz, a rather strange guy that many considered an infiltrator of the left. Years later, when all of the Lecumberri inmates
of those days had been freed, I read in the paper that he'd been murdered in
one of the squatter settlements on the foothills of the Ajusco. The news report
claimed that Jerónimo had been the leader of an armed group that terrorized
the residents of the area. It said he had been killed during a shootout between
his gang and another group that was fighting for ownership of some land. He
had a long, sharp face, with a pointy and crooked nose. His small black eyes
were wide opened and inquisitive. When I first saw him he was wearing faded
blue jeans and white T-shirt. His messy black hair was held back by a white
kerchief tied behind the nape. He immediately asked: "Yo! Who are you?
What's up?"

I was about to answer when someone even stranger appeared; this person had a slight hunchback and walked with his torso leaning to the right.
His head was large; his forehead and eyebrows jutted forward; and his nose
was big. He had curly black hair, a mustache, and a goatee. He wore thick eyeglasses that made his eyes look very small. They were secured around his neck
with a plastic cord. He was Juan Francisco Ramírez Estrada, a member like
Jerónimo of the Comandos Armados del Pueblo (CAP), and was better known
in the O as "Panchoven," because he loved classical music. He was dressed in
a worn out T-shirt that had at some point been yellow, faded black shorts, and

old dirty sneakers. These two extravagant characters were joined by other younger men, militants in the MAR, who observed me with great curiosity and distrust. In spite of that, they soon invited me to a cell located in the back of the corridor. At that gathering I seem to remember meeting Fernando Pineda Ochoa ("Gallo"), Felipe Peñaloza García (Gallo's cousin), Rogeliio Raya Morales, Agustín Hernández Rosales, Jesús Torres Castrejón, and Favio Tulio Dávila Ojeda ("Tío"). Once in the cell, two other young members of MAR, whom I knew or knew of, came over. One was José Luis González Carrillo, who had been working in the countryside with peasants close to our Organization; and Juan Bosco García, who had found refuge with us after his twin brother, a member of the same group, had been captured. The young men offered me a chair and a cup of cold, burned coffee that I pretended to drink. They surrounded me and asked me many questions about the reasons for the failure of Lucio Cabañas. They also wanted to know what would happen to the Brigada de Ajusticiamiento del Partido de los Pobres after Lucio's death. Naturally, I didn't know anything about that. Among these guys was also René Arredondo Silve, who that very night, a bit later, would invite me to share his cell in the northern upper story, exactly above the cell where we were at that point.

The next morning, I was shivering, and my whole body ached when I woke up in René's cell. I had a 104° fever, so René took me to the infirmary. It was located in the corridor that faced the outside of the cellblock, the same corridor that connected to the access tunnel to the court building and acted as the link between the west and north sections. The First Aid unit was located next to a small variety store. The physician diagnosed my illness as pneumonia and gave me a shot of penicillin. I was grateful for the luck of not having gotten sick before arriving in cellblock O West. The change to better jailhouse living conditions allowed my body to relax. Perhaps the stress was flowing out of me through the illness, a stress that had accumulated since my detention in Tlaltizapán, Morelos. I supposed that while I was in the Campo Militar Número Uno and in the D cellblock, an organic self defense mechanism had protected me from the respiratory disease that would have aggravated my deplorable physical condition in those places. Fortunately the penicillin arrived just in time, and I was free of problems in three or four days.

My next problem in O cellblock happened on the first Sunday visit after my arrival. Finally, after more than four months of separation, I could embrace and kiss Tere. With great generosity, René Arredondo sacrificed his own comfort and that of his family, wife, and brothers, letting us use the cell for a bit longer than one hour. But the fact that we both had conjugal visits created a practical difficulty—what Mao called a contradiction in the bosom of the people. René solved the problem in a civil manner as soon as our families had left, asking me to find another cell to live in. His diligentconcern soon produced a solution: Norberto García, "El Guacho," from the Asociación Cívica Nacional Revolucionaria, the ACNR of Genaro Vázquez Rojas, admitted me to his cell where he lived alone. It was located at the end of one of the two corridors on the bottom floor, in the south of the cellblock where three noisy radicals lived. They called themselves the *chorizos*, and were José Luis Chagoya Remigio ("Marshal"), Javier Garibay Garibay ("Garibotas"), and Regino Castro Zavala("Sinaloa"), a member of the sadly notorious group of "sick ones" of that state. The three of them loved to be unruly and provoke everyone.

I stayed for a few months in that cell, dealing with Norberto's daily lunacy and simpleness. Shortly after my move, I also had to cope with Raúl López Ayala, "El Morro," who was very young and had the aspect and behavior of a gangster. He was a great consumer of grass and pills. Both characters honored their great social and ideological confusion every day. The two of them were considered lumpen by most of the factions housed in cellblock O. Salvador Flores Bello met Norberto and Raúl and recruited them for the "Revolution" in a jail in Michoacán, where they'd been imprisoned for ordinary crimes. Flores Bello, by the way, was the driver of the car that crashed against a bridge column in Michoacán, when Genaro Vázquez Rojas died. At any rate, during those few months when I was there, Norberto helped me keep the *chorizos* at bay, and he also allowed Tere and me to have the cell to ourselves every day for one or two hours. Those were beautiful moments that would culminate in the birth of our son Alberto, whom we had wished for so intensely. Still, I had to leave when Norberto and the Morro's shenanigans became too much. I asked Andrés González Mancilla, the "Puma," to allow me to move to his cell, located in the upper story at the beginning of the southern corridor. Andrés was also a member of MAR, and he had a brother named Eufemio somewhere else in the O, a hard working and skilled Michoacano, a good artisan and inseparable friend of "Juanotas" (José de Jesús Pérez Esqueda), also a *marinero*, of course.

The Puma also gave me permission to have Tere in the cell, since during the visit of defending teams he played front tennis in one of the yards of the O, from eleven o'clock A.M. to two o'clock P.M., and he did not receive regular visitors. Puma was a disciplined cell mate, in terms of personal hygiene and communal orderliness. He was somewhat reserved and nervous, but could express himself well. We never had a deep conversation, though, so I imagine that our different social origins created a permanent gap between us.

During the time of my arrival to the cellblock, the first members of MAR who'd been apprehended at the beginning of the Luis Echeverría Alvarez administration—close to eighteen—had now been detained for four years without a trial. They had lived locked up in four corridors, two dining rooms, and two small yards or sundecks, without ever having seen the old Black Palace, or having enjoyed the sun, air, and dust of the extensive sports fields of the prison. They had never gone before a judge for any reason except for their initial formal incarceration early in 1971. Over the next few years, the detention of MAR members continued, almost always in groups of six, all of them concentrated in Lecumberri. Because of that the *marineros* were always the dominant group in the O West, but also the least cohesive one. When the first *marineros* were confined in the new section of maximum security, they remained under lockdown for several months in the cells of one of the upper corridors. Most were very young, between seventeen and twenty-three years of age, while the leaders, Fabricio Gómez Sousa—the top one—Alejandro López Murillo, Angel Bravo Cisneros, and Salvador Castañeda Alvarez were much older and more experienced. It was the heroic stage of incarceration, when the MAR members decided to build the communist society of their dreams, right then and there by sheer force of will. Thus, they organized life in jail under communal criteria, following the strict and vigilant leadership of Fabricio Gómez Souza. Then, as time went by, contradictions and disagreements gradually began to surface. Consequently, those who were older with better judgment and deeper intellectual formation rebelled. The top leader imposed suffocating ideological, political, and moral directives with the support of an adoring young cadre.

After some time, as a result of the constant frictions and problems caused by Fabricio and his followers, the prison authorities decided to take Gómez Souza out of the O and transfer him to the M cellblock, leaving him without disciples and his followers without a teacher. This surgical measure accelerated the process of decomposition. Differences of many kinds and mutual intolerance created more and more divisions. With the passage of months and years and the wear and tear of a forced daily coexistence, organized groups dwindled. The more fortunate devoted themselves to openly personal projects. The diversity of social origins, personal backgrounds, temperaments, personalities, customs, education, and political and ideological perspectives of those from other groups who arrived in Lecumberri after the MAR members contributed to difficulties in maintaining a convergence of intentions. This situation was not exclusive to cellblock O. The same thing happened in cellblock M, and I imagine in every other prison where the Mexican government confined the "activists and terrorists" of the 1970s, when it decided to consign them before a judge instead of disappearing them forever.

The problems in the O West could be simple matters like the competition for oranges, rolls, and government-issued milk bags at the hour of chow distribution. Angel Bravo Cisneros, I remember, used to yell at the running inmates, from the second floor where he could observe them through the stairwell: "Dogs! You are like dogs! Look at them, Murillo! They behave like dogs!" And problems could be more serious. Some prisoners engaged in the manufacturing of "points" to defend like the Red Guard the proletarian revolutionary political processes from the renegades and opportunists, agents of Yankee imperialism and Soviet revisionism—for each group, everyone else who did not think like them. Fortunately all remained at the level of threats or of hostile glances. Nobody got seriously hurt. As far as I know, Alfredo de la Rosa Olguín, a member of the ACNR and an excellent draftsman and illustrator of books and cartoon stories, was the only one hurt, stabbed by a radical in the thigh. This forced the "Negrito," as Enrique Téllez Pacheco, called him, to request transfer to the northern section of cellblock O that housed ordinary prisoners from Puerto Rico and the United States, mostly small drug traffickers.

I spent about a year and a half in jail in Lecumberri, in the midst of a sad, heavy atmosphere filled with tensions, mistrust, and mutual disempowering. To all this I must add the uneasiness caused by the frequent, surprise searches of our cells practiced by the guards on any early morning they chose. Their raids in pursuit of compromising writings, forbidden books, arms, or drugs resulted in abuse, theft, mishandling, or destruction of our very scarce belongings. I also encountered more extreme attitudes, resembling those of Sendero Luminoso or Pol Pot's Khmer Rouge, when a small group of Oaxacan inmates arrived in the O West. They belonged to the Unión del Pueblo and were surnamed the *Bomberos* or Firefighters, because of their practice of using explosives in public places as a principal means of struggle and propaganda. The Oaxacans saw as their first task the physical elimination of any reformist or democrat, who for them were simply agents of the bourgeoisie and imperialism living in the midst of popular revolutionary movements. What was astonishing about their analysis is that they not only intended to eliminate us, but also our closest relatives. Years later, after they had been freed, two of these men were treacherously killed by their old comrades. In jail, not all of them acted and thought in the same manner. One of those who dissented was Romeo Valentín Maldonado, who in spite of his extreme youth was able to free himself from the radicalism of his former partners.

FOUR

The Roads of Freedom

SERGIO GARCÍA RAMÍREZ

THE PARTICIPATION IN this story of the famous Cuban American drug trafficker Alberto Sicilia Falcón started with our fortuitous encounter in the holding tank of the PGR. Although I never established contact with this character beyond a casual greeting in the court rooms of Lecumberri, our forced coexistence in the Number 4 Dormitory of the Eastern Preventive Penitentiary or Reclusorio Preventivo Oriente, and our occasional encounter in the communal spaces of the Penitentiary of Santa Martha Acatitla, some of the activities of Sicilia would eventually influence the lives of political prisoners.

In April 1976, Alberto Sicilia Falcón and some members of his band escaped from Lecumberri through a tunnel excavated from his own cell in cellblock L all the way to a house located in the Tercera Cerrada de San Antonio Tomatlán at the southern edge of the prison, on the far side of Héroes de Nacozari Avenue. As a result, the President of Mexico summarily dismissed Gral. Francisco Arcaute Franco from the directorship of the Porfirian institution and appointed in his place a reformer, Sergio García Ramírez, a criminologist, prestigious jurist, and, at that moment, Subsecretary of Government.

As soon as García Ramírez saw the general conditions of incarceration in the Black Palace, he decided to improve them. We political prisoners received some of these benefits, in spite our status as "activists and terrorists" confined to cellblocks O West and M. I remember the moment well. Saturday morning, the day after the official announcement, we rose to see that there were no guards at the access gates of the western and northern sections. We didn't know what to make of this. Nor were there any in the four watchtowers of the exterior wall of cellblock O. This was happening at the same time that the newspapers published in Mexico City were demanding a hard-line treatment for the terrorists of the Red Brigade of the Liga Comunista 23 de Septiembre. There were also those who suggested that we all be sent to the Islas Marías. I was not pleased to learn that different groups of radical compañeros had traveled from the western wing to the northern one, attempting to lead a mobilization of drug traffickers against their own Mayor. This incursion took place after one of the members of these small groups had thrown a brick through the glass section of the door of the modest store that served the inmates of both sections. As I learned afterwards, this had been done with the revolutionary purpose of expropriating cigarettes, sodas, candy, soap, cookies, and canned goods, an action said to be against Capital, with capital C. The situation was getting out of control and worried me. When I was about the only one left in the western section, I couldn't resist the temptation to see what was going on in the northern side.

The afternoon was coming to an end as I entered the gate into the territory of the *burros* from the United States, Puerto Rico, and Colombia. Up until that moment, this cellblock was unknown to me. I entered through the closest corridor and saw that most of the members of our section were there out of curiosity, like me. Only a few of them were intensely engaged in conversation with the ordinary prisoners, and even fewer could be observed in full revolutionary effervescence. It was then that I heard the familiar and fearsome noise of guard boots. Their owners were entering the dining room through the main corridor of the northern section, the areas where most of the populations of both sections were congregated at the moment. Scared, some of us tried to go back to our own territory immediately, but the way was obstructed by the men in uniform. Frankly, they looked more frightened than all of us. The monkeys, wearing neither ties nor caps, held their black clubs nervously in both hands. As if they had been mirrors, their shiny faces covered with sweat reflected the pale gray of their uniforms. With uneven breathing and bulging bellies, the members of the First Security Company occupied the dining room of that section rapidly and efficiently in a wrapping maneuver that left them surrounding the room with their backs against all four walls.

Protected in the middle of their formation was the new director of Lecumberri, Dr. Sergio García Ramírez. Memory betrays me, and I no longer recall what exactly happened then. I suppose García Ramírez spoke for a while and listened to the demands of the inmates gathered there, both ordinary and political prisoners. What I do remember clearly is that at the end of the event, García Ramírez walked next to us as we headed back to our section. Several of us asked him to pay us a visit in our section. The director agreed, and we led him to the first level of the building to a place that was always dark and dirty, the location where the chow was distributed. The spot was some kind of no-man's land, dark at night since there weren't any light bulbs in the available sockets. This gloomy detail in itself must have impressed our distinguished visitor. One of the *chorizos* went to his cell and came back with a 60 watt light bulb. Once there was light, we surrounded the young functionary and voiced our complaints, listening attentively to his answers. That day he demonstrated that he was good at mass psychology, not just a brave, intrepid man. He came to our meeting accompanied by a single guard, who looked extremely tense and worried at the start of the session, but became relaxed as he saw that the mood of those fifty dangerous subversives was one of expectation at new possibilities.

Alejandro López Murillo, known among the *marineros* as "El Giote," was a founding member of MAR. He took advantage of the occasion to denounce the assassination of political prisoner Pablo Alvarado Barrera at the hands of the Chief of Guards, Edilberto Gil Cárdenas, and the former director of the prison, Gral. Francisco Arcaute Franco. He reported many of the other anomalies that affected us all in those days. Angel Bravo Cisneros, Salvador Castañeda Alvarez, Saúl López de la Torre, and some others that my memory has blurred also spoke. I remember that one of them brought up the matter of books. It was forbidden to read certain books and publications. The criteria for exclusion were completely arbitrary. I mentioned that my father had purchased a subscription for me to *Tiempo*, a thoroughly official publication, but it too had been proscribed. He said in jest: "I am glad, because the magazine is very bad!"

The meeting with the jurist ended late, but not before García Ramírez promised that he would look into our demands and study them. Tired from so many new experiences, we withdrew to our cells, but only after taking some time to linger in the four corridors of our section to discuss the events of the day. We wondered about the personality and background of the new director, as well as about the mandate regarding Lecumberri given to him by the President. But it was time to go to sleep. The next day was Sunday and the fortunate among us were expecting family and other visitors.

The next day, about an hour before the arrival of the first visitors, I was finishing getting dressed and combing my hair after a shower when I saw Dr. Sergio García Ramírez passing in front of the cell I shared with Andrés González Mancilla, El Puma, and Rigoberto Lorence López. He was completely unescorted. I went to the front of the gate. When he saw me, he greeted me with a clear and firm voice. He walked to the cell of Alejandro López

Murillo, the last one of that corridor. They exchanged handshakes and a few words, and after that the director made his way back through the same path that had brought him in. In a short while I saw him again, walking like any inmate, back and forth, on the small sundeck on the first floor of the section. He was talking with Roberto Tello Alarcón, a member of the Frente Urbano Zapatista, sentenced to twenty-five years of prison for his participation in the kidnapping of the federal official Julio Hirschfeld Almada. When I asked López Murillo and Tello Alarcón what they had talked about with García Ramírez, they said he only wanted to view the place in the full light of day to see how we lived.

The truth is that the arrival of the criminologist and his team represented a real positive change for the majority of inmates of Lecumberri. The first benefit he granted the "activists and terrorists" was to allow us to go to the jail's extensive sports fields for an hour and a half once a week. To give an idea of what that measure meant for the veterans confined there, it's enough to say that the leaders of MAR had spent five years in the western section; they had never left it, not even to go to the courts for a legal procedure. It was fantastic for everyone to enjoy that place of air and sun, in spite of the dust; it was wonderful to move freely in a space as open as that. The most sports-oriented ones took advantage of the basketball courts or soccer fields. The ones who were not would walk all over the field or sit and speculate a while about our possible freedom in the near future, since the six-year term of President Luis Echeverría Alvarez was coming to an end. At the time, two young ex-militants from the Lacandón group had arrived at the O West, Víctor Manuel Velasco Damián and Carlos Jiménez Sarmiento. They were close to the Liga Comunista 23 de Septiembre. The latter was David's younger brother, marked as the leader of the Red Brigade and killed according to the police during the attempt to kidnap Margarita López Portillo. The two of them had been transferred from the circular cellblock M to the O after a failed attempt at escape. Along with Miguel Domínguez, a former militant of the same group, they had sealed a pact promising that in case of discovery, they would each stab themselves with a metal shiv in the heart, avoiding detention and possible torture. It was a wrong move on their part; they were discovered immediately. From the circular wall of the M they got as far as the roof of the nearest building, thinking that it was possible to reach the exterior wall and from there get to the street. This proved completely false. The guard on watch in the nearest tower saw them as soon as they went up. To make things worse, Miguel Domínguez, who it seems was in charge of the operation, stabbed himself so decisively with a metal shiv that he died instantly. Víctor Manuel and Carlos were only wounded, so they were taken to the jailhouse clinic where they were cured.

After interrogation without torture, they were first transferred to punishment cells and then a few weeks later to the O West.

One day Saúl López de la Torre, Enrique Téllez Pacheco, Romeo Valentín Maldonado, and I were having an unusual conversation with Víctor Manuel and Carlos in the sports field when a dirty, bearded inmate wearing a gray rabbit cap pulled down to his eyes and a thick chain of garlic around his neck approached us. It was Miguel Castro Bustos, an extravagant character who in the company of the painter Mario Falcón and group of *porros* from the left harassed the president of the National University of Mexico, the Universidad Nacional Autónoma de México (UNAM), Pablo González Casanova, until they forced him to resign his post. The case is that Víctor Manuel and Carlos knew Castro Bustos well, because they too had lived in cellblock M; the two of them knew how to put him on, to have fun at the expense of his madness. They asked him to repeat for us first the speech he had delivered when Carlos A. Madrazo, the frustrated PRI leader, had been sworn in, and later the one that he gave before Fidel Castro in Havana when the Cuban Revolution was new. He looked around the place where we found ourselves. He spied an old automobile tire hidden by the tall grass, and he climbed on it, using it as his soapbox. With pomp and circumstance, Castro Bustos repeated both pieces of oratory as if we were in front of each of these leaders. When he finished, Castro Bustos descended from his platform and came over to where we were. Víctor Manuel asked him how he had done with Mario Falcón, his former companion in arms at the UNAM. Miguel told us that he hadn't done well at all with Falcón, that punk, because one day that son of a bitch had been about to execute him, accusing him of being pusillanimous and traitorous, not to mention the fact that, according to Falcón, the movement needed a martyr. He added that he had only saved his life when he convinced the painter that if he shot him, his friends from the Popular Preparatory School would avenge his death by killing him in turn.

General Francisco Arcaute Franco was in the habit of personally guiding around different groups interested in knowing Lecumberri, showing them with a certain vanity the institution that he administered. As he did this, inmates greeted him with a fearful respect. One day, when Miguel Castro Bustos was killing time at the entrance to cellblock M, he saw the director and immediately called out to him "General! General!" Arcaute turned his head with a big smile, thinking that one more man was eager to greet him, but Miguel yelled at a distance of just a few yards: "General, fuck your mother!" to the astonishment of the army officer and the mortification of the visitors he guided. I don't need to say that Castro Bustos paid with a tremendous beating and was placed in the hole for several weeks in cellblock D, the one with the "jackals."

I also remember the Saturday afternoon when the director of the new administration of Lecumberri sent a folk music band to our section to delight us for a couple of hours with themes dear to political prisoners. They'd also sent a rock band to the northern section to entertain the North Americans, Puerto Ricans, and Colombians. That time a good number of the inmates in O West climbed the tall and thick wall that divided both sections so that we could see and hear the rock and roll band better. I remember that we remained sitting astride on top of the wall until the end of the concert without the guards in the tower telling us to get down. Of course, the most celebrated piece was "Jailhouse Rock."

The project to reform the prison included several talks with visitors such as Gutierre Tibón and Francisco Casanova Alvarez, with whom we exchanged ideas and perspectives two or three different times about the economic, political, and social situation in Mexico and the world. Sergio García Ramírez and the group of lawyers, psychologists, and social workers headed by Fernando García Cordero and Juan Pablo Tavira would attempt to culminate the reform with the opening of the Northern and Eastern Preventive Penitentiaries, the Reclusorios Preventivos Norte and Oriente.

A RENEWAL OF LIFE

On July 26, 1976, a month and a half before we moved to the new penitentiary, my beloved María Teresa provided me the second of the two greatest joys of my life when she gave birth to my son Alberto—the first one had been the birth of my daughter Teresita. I learned of it the next day, a Tuesday, around nine in the morning when Blanca Hernández, Roberto Tello Alarcón's wife, announced from the entrance to the cell that Tere had delivered a baby boy. I was in the shower, but I got out immediately and dressed quickly, heading to the cell that Roberto Tello shared with Dimas Castañeda Alvarez in order to ask Blanca for more news. She could only add that the birth had gone well, and that Tere and the child were in perfect health. At that moment, I heard my father's voice full of emotion. He was climbing the stairway to the second floor, calling out my name, and adding with a deep feeling that I was the father of a son. He, by the way, was now the grandfather to the only child who would eventually preserve his name.

The following Sunday, August 1, 1976, I finally met the son I had so deeply longed to bring to life during that trip to Chihuahua in the company of Jacobo and Héctor. My mother in law Margarita, aided by Milagros Huerta Coria and Fernando del Mar, took the newborn to the O West. Thanks to the three of them, I was able to contemplate my son ecstatically after Margarita placed him delicately on my cot. The child looked like a sun, so radiant and large, with a very pink face. My paternal pride overflowed the limits of the space where I was confined. Several of the inmates came to meet him.

The visit ended very soon because the baby was restless. The careful checking that he had to undergo and the ambiance of the jailhouse altered his natural tranquility, and he started to cry. I walked them all to the gate of the section, and I saw them disappearing in the distance. I fell into an anxious distress, missing the three people I loved the most: I was on the verge of a jailhouse breakdown.

The jailhouse breakdown is a state of being that threatens to take over your soul, leaving you full of nostalgic thoughts, sorrow, and anger because of your lack of liberty and the absence of your loved ones. It also takes the form of repentance for the harm you may have caused and for not having been savvy enough to evade detention. You suffer a jailhouse breakdown when you don't receive the visit of wife or partner, or because of the abandonment by parents, siblings, or friends. It can also overtake a person in the midst of a visit: after one or two hours, the unexpected, absurd, and contradictory appearance of this mood surprises the inmate. He then wishes the visit to end, and visitors to leave at once since he finds the sensation of oppression and asphyxia produced by the presence of loved ones unbearable. He needs to remain alone again to feel that he has recovered his limited freedom of decision and movement. At the same time, he eases back into the need for those loved ones that he sent away just a few moments before.

One day when I went to the store to buy some cigarettes, I discovered that there was a group of people filming in the northern section. I thought that if I were lucky, they would also head to the west side. It happened that way, and by then I knew the name of the director of the film crew—no less than the well-known director Arturo Ripstein. When he appeared in our section, I had the audacity to approach him to ask about three friends of mine: Eduardo Maldonado, Ramón Aupart, and Carlos González, movie people as well, since I was sure that he knew them. Ripstein expressed surprise to find in such place someone who knew his work and was a friend of people that he saw occasionally. Ripstein took advantage of the opportunity to find out from me who were the "activists and terrorists" that the authorities told him were the occupants of O West. I explained as well as I could how many and who we were and why we were imprisoned. With great interest, the director asked me to explore the possibility of filming some interviews with us. I spoke first with Saúl López de la Torre, Romeo Valentín Maldonado, and Rigoberto Lorence López, who accepted to participate. And then I spoke with people from the other groups, but they did not accept because of the natural distrust they felt for anything that came from the government that confined them.

My motivation in accepting the opportunity that Ripstein gave to us was the total isolation from society in which we lived. The fact was that we were completely ignored by national public opinion, let alone foreign press, so I saw the opportunity to let the world take a peek at us and call attention to our existence. As a filming set, Ripstein chose one of the two cells that originally had been destined as the hole. It was a space located on the first floor at the end of the northern corridor, vacant at that point and used as a meeting room or a place for reading. The first wave of *marineros* had painted monumental likenesses of Marx and Engels on a wall. In order to conduct the film's interview, Ripstein arranged the four of us in a semicircle facing him and the camera. He then asked questions about our identities, motivations, and the crimes we were charged with.

When it was my turn to jump into the ring, I had to be very cautious so that I would not be seen as a firebrand. Nor did I want to provoke the group of more radical compañeros who had come close to listen. After I spoke, Saúl took a turn, and then Rigoberto and Romeo. The result of that session, *Lecumberri, a.k.a. the Black Palace*, was broadcast a few months later on Channel 13, but we could not see it because by then we were in the new Reclusorio where TV sets were not allowed.

The time for the transfer arrived inexorably. The first to go were the ones whose legal processes were tied to courts located in Cuautepec el Alto in Reclusorio Norte. All the members of MAR, ACNR, and the Comandos Armados del Pueblo were sent there. Among them were Saúl López de la Torre and Enrique Téllez Pacheco, the two friends with whom I held conversations about the freedom we so desired and thought to be imminent. Also gone were Andrés González Mancilla and Rigoberto Lorence López, who had shared a cell with me. With these developments, I had a cell to myself for the first time since I arrived in Lecumberri about a year and a half before. It was quite a treat, and I enjoyed it to the hilt. For people who do not have a lot in common, the experience of sharing a reduced space obligatorily is remarkably difficult.

On August 26, 1976, in the afternoon, prison guards came to the western section of cellblock O. The few of us who had remained behind were led through the lonely and somber corridors of the Black Palace. The image of abandonment, however, began to vanish as we converged in the meeting point, where the jail wagons were waiting to transport us to the Reclusorio Oriente. We carried our scarce belongings in backpacks improvised from pillow cases. And we walked more quietly than ever, lost in thought about what awaited us in the new situation, with an absurd sense of loss as we left forever the horrors that we had lived through in this jailhouse.

We were placed in the jail wagons next to ordinary prisoners, which made us uncomfortable and apprehensive. Just before the vehicles went through the back gate of the building, I found myself somewhat bewildered and dazed in the middle of the shouting and commotion of the other inmates. Suddenly I paid attention to a small, brown-skinned man with a sparse mustache and greasy face. I thought he was the last monkey I would see; he was probably also the first one I met. The little man remained behind, reduced to the ridiculous condition of a jailer without someone to imprison and watch. He almost disappeared under the enormous concrete walls because of his natural insignificance, and because of the faded gray of the uniform that he wore without a trace of pride or grace. There he was, the little monkey, standing next to a big puddle of muddy water, precisely at the end of the curve that divided the old Lecumberri from its more modern extension. Through the iron grille of the jail wagon I observed the timid gesture of farewell that the monkey began but never completed, stunned midway through by the savage insult from the man to my left: "You're going to starve to death, fucking goddamn monkey." Like a stone thrown at his forehead, the insult crossed the air, humid with rain, exploding in the face of the miserable jailer, freezing his clumsy sign and leaving him with an expression of dumb amazement. The man who shouted, his face virtually pushed through the grille, celebrated his clever taunt with the convicts in the back of the wagon, who were also anxious to see what was going on at the gate. The two months of cumulative tension stored in all of us since we'd learned of the transfer to the new Reclusorio now found an outlet in the insolent guffawing that followed a cascade of gibes at the impotent monkeys standing along the route out of the prison and into the real world.

I felt as I was leaving Lecumberri that the harsh, unbearably painful experiences suffered by thousands of forsaken men remained inscribed in the grungy dishes; grimy, broken kitchen utensils; threadbare blankets reduced to stinking cleaning rags; the leftover, rotting food; and so many other instances of trash, rubbish, and filth.

That humiliating past seemed to remain behind throughout the sinister building, attached to its yards and empty cells. I remembered my season in hell as if that circumstance had been part of an inevitable design. My mind was occupied with those thoughts when the wagon slowed down. The ordinary prisoner sitting next to me exclaimed: "Check it out! We're here!" The new guards, uniformed in navy blue blazers, white shirts, burgundy ties, and woolen gray slacks, hurried to open the back doors of the wagons, inviting us to get out. Outside, in person, the dashing new director, Fernando García Cordero, waited in the reception area to welcome us all.

At that moment, the installations of Reclusorio Oriente resembled more a university than a prison. Everything was new, freshly painted, clean! There were wide-open spaces with trim green lawns. The modern buildings were covered by enormous windows that literally dazzled us, because we were not used to such depth of space and light. We were first led to individual cells in the area of observation and classification of the Reclusorio where we spent a short while. It was there that I participated like everyone else in the personal visit of García Cordero. I took advantage of the opportunity to speak to him about an idea that I had been pondering for a long time: the publication of a newspaper or magazine for inmates and by inmates. The director told me that he thought the project was very interesting and quite doable, and that I should discuss it with Dr. Juan Pablo de Tavira Noriega, his assistant, whom I did not yet know.

After an hour, I was assigned to dormitory four, to the first cell of one of two corridors on the first floor, in the company of the two Lacandones, Favio Julio Dávila Ojeda (El Tío) and Jesús Torres Castrejón. Our sensation of mutual discomfort was obvious. They were part of the most radical groups of the O, while I in their eyes was a mere reformist and populist. The next morning, at their invitation, I switched cells, corridor, and floor, trading with one of their group, I no longer remember whom. My new cellmates were Roberto Sánchez Ensch from the Lacandones group, who had been in the circular cellblock M in Lecumberri and somebody who had been processed for committing fraud named Raúl, whose surnames I have forgotten. We were flabbergasted because all the guards called us "Sir" and asked all their requests as if they were favors. It may be difficult to believe that the first supper we were served in Oriente consisted of thick slices of baked Virginia ham with pineapple. Naturally, such delicate treatment would not last. In the first few months, both in dormitory four and six, where the young people of Unión del Pueblo were concentrated, the authorities maintained a mixture of political and ordinary convicts, unlike in Lecumberri. In dormitory four they placed members of the Lacandones, Frente Urbano Zapatista, Liga Comunista 23 de Septiembre, Partido de los Pobres, and Espartaquistas Jaramillistas next to individuals who had been accused of white collar crimes. This situation produced a very strange and contradictory mixture of ideologies and interests. During the first few months, it was possible to see a few "activists and terrorists" playing backgammon together with wealthy Lebanese Mexicans who had devoted themselves to financial speculation or clandestine gambling.

A short while after arriving at the Reclusorio, I met the criminologist Juan Pablo de Tavira Noriega, an accessible, cultured, and sensitive government functionary. I talked with him for a long time about my past as a militant and my situation at the time, as well as about my project for the new Reclusorio. I proposed that I be in charge of editing a newspaper for the inmates to be called *Oriente*. I would have the help of Roberto Tello Alarcón, formerly of the Frente Urbano Zapatista, an architect by profession and also an expert in the techniques of design and presentation of printed texts and photos, along with some other political prisoner compañeros such as Heriberto Díaz Coutiño, from Chiapas, one of the Lacandones group, and an excellent draftsman; Jesús Arellanes Meixuerio and Javier Almaraz Olvera, both teachers from the Unión del Pueblo; Roberto Ramos Eusebio, a young poet from the 23; Roberto Sánchez Ensch and Isaías Ensch Fregoso, cousins and members of the Lacandones group; and Ricardo Rodríguez from the Partido de los Pobres. Juan Pablo de Tavira agreed with the project and wanted me to get right to work on it. To help me out, he dictated a memo in name of Fernando García Cordero to his secretary, advising the Chief of Security that I had received authorization to go in and out of dormitory four during the day. I would also have access to the other dormitories except nine and ten as well as to the workshop facilities that the reportage and printing of *Oriente* required. The only condition set by Juan Pablo was that I should also include in my team two ordinary convicts, Mario Lagos Perea, a young guy of *porro* origin, and James Norton, a North American dedicated to the arduous task of compiling and editing crossword puzzle books.

In the end, we could only print three issues of *Oriente*. For reasons beyond our control, we had to stop publishing. The chiefs of the technical commission of penitentiaries in the Federal District, who oversaw Reclusorio Oriente, viewed our project under a very different light and determined that it was their job not only to decide on the contents of the publication, but also to edit it and print it. If I remember correctly, they only published one issue, truly of lower quality than the ones we had put out. Nonetheless, that was the best period in the four years that my incarceration lasted. During the months that Juan Pablo de Tavira Noriega was technical subdirector of the Reclusorio, he gave Tello and me permission to use at will the two small theater dressing rooms located at either side of the stage of the auditorium. I took shelter in my den several hours a day, morning and afternoon, writing, reading, and listening to music. In this vein, de Tavira encouraged everyone to get involved in artistic pursuits. In particular, Juan Pablo was very interested in drama, having had personal experience both as actor and director. He gave his full support to a group organized by Isaías Ensch Fregoso that decided to put on a play based upon a poem by Efraín Huerta. He also invited his brother Luis de Tavira, the renowned theater director, to bring to the Reclusorio a troupe of university actors to perform some plays for us.

From those days I also remember gratefully the chief of social work Cecilia Méndez, who always behaved as a generous and understanding member of the staff. She was in charge of giving permission for conjugal visits to the convicts. Thanks to her kindness, I was able to spend the night frequently with my wife María Teresa.

During those days, a team of film makers arrived in Oriente. I started a conversation with a young woman who served as an assistant to the director. Both turned out to be political exiles from Uruguay. Her name was Ivonne Szasz (I am not sure I have the correct spelling of this name), and she was in charge of field research. When she heard my story, she suggested to the director that they film an interview with the three editors of *Oriente*: Roberto Tello Alarcón, Mario Lagos Perea, and me. The director and screenwriter for the documentary named Jaime Graschinaky accepted the proposal and filmed the interview, conducted by Ivonne. Since the intension of the documentary was to describe the new system of *reclusorios* in contrast with Lecumberri, it was entitled *A Different Wall*.

My friend Ramón Aupart edited the short film, which facilitated our reencounter for a few moments in one of the corridors of the *reclusorio*. The film was project of the Center for the Production of Short Films financed by the Cinematographic Bank. Dionisio also appears in this film, interviewed with a vegetable gardening group he coordinated in a section of the lawns surrounding dormitory four. Jesús Arellanes Meixuerio also appears teaching in the primary school of the Reclusorio.

DOWNHILL SLIDE

It was a good time that we lived through in those few months after arriving at Oriente, a time that was favorable for my recovery and the rebuilding of my self-confidence, as well as for improving interpersonal relationships. But everyone knows good things never last. The administration of Fernando García Cordero and Juan Pablo de Tavira Noriega was dismissed, I think, right after the escape of a convict. The opportunity was immediately seized upon by those who could benefit from control of the facilities. The gang of corrupt bureaucrats they sent to take over immediately recreated the atmosphere of Lecumberri, and problems promptly appeared. In a matter of days, the small privileges that Juan Pablo had granted to many inmates were revoked. Soon the air felt too heavy to breathe. Some of the inmates whom the general population of Oriente considered *padrinos* recovered their traditional prerogatives. It was the second time that Alberto Sicilia Falcón and his entourage transformed the conditions of our confinement, although this time they made them worse.

My memory has failed to retain all the details of the start of operation mutiny, instigated and organized by Sicilia Falcón and other ordinary criminals who shared his aim of controlling everyday life in the new Reclusorio. I do recall a general meeting in the dining room conveyed by the drug lord in which this Cuban American attempted to impose his dominion over the inmates of dormitory four. He had a plan to enact. One of his objectives was to make it impossible for guards to enter the dorm to watch us closely and to search the cells whenever they pleased. Another was the demand for better food and hot water in the showers; the cafeteria services had deteriorated in the last few weeks, and people hated to take cold showers. I remember that while Sicilia spoke to the inmates, many of us were quiet, familiar with the dangerous reputation of this man and the peril of any open confrontation with him. Dionisio, however, challenged Sicilia Falcón, expressing himself in that sensible and peaceful rural style, in opposition to the proposals, and underscoring for his audience the consequences of acting hastily and irresponsibly. The Cuban American stared at Dionisio with murderous anger in his eyes, unable to believe that someone there would dare defy him. Many other political prisoners concurred with Dionisio. I remember one of them, David Vázquez Flores, who participated in the group of vegetable growers. For that day at least, the response of these compañeros had frustrated Sicilia Falcón's maneuver, so the meeting ended.

In spite of this setback, Sicilia Falcón and his mafiosos persevered in their purposes and extended their agitation all through the population of Oriente. There were many *porros* in the Reclusorio. The next day, after convincing those more closely linked to the use of drugs and violence, they declared a general hunger strike and placed chains and padlocks on the gates of entrances to the dormitories, making it impossible for the guards to come in or for the prisoners who were studying grammar school or attending workshops to go out. The response of the authorities came in a flash. A company of riot police from the Preventive Police of the Federal District was sent immediately to dormitory number four. This showed that the officials knew exactly who the instigators of the protest were. Meanwhile, the mafiosos circulated all sorts of hairbrained directives among the convicts. Unfortunately, several of the inmates, the most revved up and surely the youngest, subscribed to these schemes or invented their own. One of the most insistent ones proposed that the moment when the riot police came in, we should all jump over the cyclone fence that separated us from dormitory five, and then along with the inmates of that dorm leap on successively to six, seven, and eight.

Without much effort, the riot police smashed the padlock and entered the yard in an attack formation, protected by their great transparent shields and brandishing their clubs in a threatening way. One of the political prisoners suggested that we sit on the floor, and the majority of us obeyed. Then the moment that the first riot police crossed the gate, Víctor Manuel Velasco Damián rose up as if impelled by a spring, shouting "Camera!" as he broke a glass bottle against the edge of trash barrel, brandishing the rest of the bottle as a weapon. Two or three seconds later, the rest of us stood up fast, although not to fight, but to enter our cells according to the order we had just been given. I also remember how Javier Almaraz Olvera straddled the cyclone fence of dorms three and four a few moments earlier, looking confused, and how Dionisio had called out to him in a stern voice: "What are you doing there, Almaraz? Come down!" Almaraz Olvera was a Oaxacan about forty years old, short and very thin with thick glasses and a finely trimmed mustache. He always wore a black beret Che Guevara style, and forever dressed in white, with a T-shirt and shorts, long socks, and sneakers. In the midst of everybody's hasty retreat, Víctor Manuel and Carlos Jiménez Sarmiento fled together, jumping over the fence between dorms five and six, followed by some ordinary inmates. The population of dorm six was as young as they were, and they had no trouble receiving hospitality.

The rest of us were locked up in our respective cells. From our windows, we saw how the riot police threw a couple of tear gas bombs at the entrance of dormitory five. The column of white smoke ascended slowly in the clear afternoon air. All of a sudden Benjamín Pérez Aragón, of the Lacandones, thinking the gas would harm us, threw a heavy object against the large window in front of us, breaking it in the midst of a great din. This senseless action did not bring any reprisal, fortunately, but the big hole on the glass was never repaired. For the next few months, the chilly night air blew into our cells.

The rallying cry to stay firm in the hunger strike traveled from corridor to corridor, cell to cell, floor to floor. Perhaps because of that, the guards rolled hot food carts around slowly, voicing the invitation to eat. The smell of the chow, so disagreeable in ordinary times, provoked an uncomfortable sensation in our stomachs as well as an abundant salivation in our mouths. As a protest for the lockdown and the evident provocation of which we were object, the convicts of dorm number five started to hit the bars of their cells with any object they could find. In a few minutes, the inmates of every dorm were doing the same, producing an infernal din that could surely be heard in the street, yet half an hour later, since no visible results came from our noisy protest, we abandoned it gradually, bored and tired. After several hours, hunger gripped us tighter, besieging and undermining our wills. When we were most irritated at the impasse of our situation, we had a very delightful surprise. From hand to hand, the occupants of the next-door cell transferred to ours a cauliflower and a cabbage, both raw. Some of the compañeros had started to distribute the fruits of the vegetable garden, cultivated and harvested by Dionisio's group, with the purpose of mitigating everyone's appetite a bit. I had never eaten these plants uncooked, with their very strong flavor. Lacking salt, I was only able to chew and swallow a few mouthfuls. They didn't sit well with me. In the midst of such vicissitudes, some of the alert compañeros surveyed anything that went on in dorm five, discovering that the inmates there had broken the hunger strike and were serving themselves food from the carts that the guards had left at the head of the corridors. What I am saying is that the same sons of bitches that had imposed on us the protest action were the first to abandon it. Immediately, the news traveled through all corridors and cells until everyone in the dorm knew. The general reaction was to end the hunger strike and to ask the guards to open our cells so that we too could serve ourselves some food. The request was accepted immediately by the watchmen. I would like to underscore that the mutiny did not have major consequences. A few moments after the entrance of the riot police within the perimeter of the dorm—they never entered the building itself—David Vázquez Flores from the Lacandones expressed a complaint to a supervisor. He was taken from his cell to the administration building of the Reclusorio, where they scolded him for his bad behavior. As for Víctor Manuel Velasco Damián and Carlos Jiménez Sarmiento, once discovered by the guards during the roll call in dorm six, they were simply sent back to number four.

It had taken much longer for the agitation in the dorms to become a collective action than for the action itself to evaporate and be replaced by the heavy atmosphere of the doldrums. The normal activities such as workshops or primary school remained in suspension for a few days. The "activists and terrorists" were regrouped in two corridors on the west side of dorm four. I was relocated to the upper story, where I shared one of the first cells with Roberto Sánchez Ensch and his cousin Isaías Ensch Fregoso. I can't remember precisely the day when I witnessed several guards taking Sicilia Falcón from dorm four and escorting him to the administration building, although it's possible that it may have happened on the same date when the other organizer of the mutiny, the Colombian Carlos Estrada, was removed from dorm five. A little time later, we all heard the rumor of the discovery of a tunnel in an advanced state of excavation. Both capos had been planning to use it to escape along with their respective minions. The whole episode had been only a distracting stratagem, cooked up by Sicilia and Estrada, to focus the attention of the guards on the massive protests of the prison population while the two mafiosos and their staff finished the tunnel and fled the Reclusorio in the middle of general confusion. However, what appeared to be the end of the episode would soon turn out to be only one more chapter.

The jailhouse routine established that before going to the dining room all inmates were locked up in their cells so that the guards charged with roll call could confirm easily if we were there or not. Once they knew nobody was missing, they opened the cells so that we could go to the dining room for our chow. The normal accounting operation never took more than twenty minutes, but that afternoon the lockup lasted too long. Since we could see no explanation, the most anxious among us began to wonder.

"What's up? What are these assholes up to?" Roberto Sánchez Ensch asked in a loud voice, bringing his face close to the bars of the cell, rubbing against them with his thick black glasses. While the myopic and inquisitive eyes of Roberto scrutinized the space between the entrance booth to dorm four and the building door, barely visible from our cell, I also began to worry. Roberto seemed to be calculating the probabilities that what was cooking could imply some risk for us, with the same spirit that as a patient silversmith enabled him to cut coins with a fine jigsaw in order to sell them to make a few pesos with which to increase his wife's income. Irked by this situation, I approached the cell bars and looked in the same direction. And that very moment, a group of plainclothes individuals, with evident police affiliation, entered the dorm running one after the other.

"Now it'll be the devil to pay," said Roberto turning toward me, his face full of dread. I felt how fear accentuated the sense of emptiness that hunger had created in my stomach. I don't know why I thought about it. Perhaps because the thought had hovered in my mind after reading an editorial in a rightist Mexico City newspaper, I assumed in despair and panic that the feds were coming for us in order to transfer us to the Islas Marías. Those moments were for me the equivalent of driving a car at high speed without brakes on a route with steep drop-offs and sharp curves full of danger. In order to stop the crazy race, I saw myself opening the front left door of the vehicle with the absurd purpose of dragging my left foot on the pavement and avoiding the fall into the abyss. Of course, I was conscious of how perfectly useless such an attempt would be. I thought of Tere, my children, and my parents. I anticipated the profound sorrow that this separation, perhaps permanent, would cause us all. In the midst of my anxiety, I realized that a compañero whose name I've forgotten, who had come to our cell just before roll call, was pacing the floor desperately, trying to hide a twenty-five centimeter shiv that he had produced from his clothes before the imminent arrival of the police. All of a sudden, he leaned over a broom, stuck the shiv among the bristles, and put it back in the corner where he'd found it. Frankly, I was furious at his lack of sense, since he was putting us all at risk of being interrogated during a good beating about where the shiv had come from.

The incident did not last more than a minute. The agents, members of the White Brigade, arrived in our corridor. The first ones glided rapidly along the corridor in front of the cells at the same time that they yelled, ordering us to come to the bars facing them. Behind them came other agents. In a display of professional prowess, these identified us one by one. Without having so much as to glance at a document or photograph, they stated our names, surnames, and the organization we belonged to. In truth, this demonstration had a powerful impact on us and intimidated us even more, since in most of the cases many years had elapsed since we had been in the Brigade's hands. The agents opened the cells at the back first, forcing their occupants to come out, placing them face down on the ground, and extending their arms beyond their heads while looking forward. All these orders came amid shouts and insults. The moment that the compañeros left their cells, they received a shower of kicks and blows. I realized that it was worse for the slower or reluctant ones, so that when my turn came, as soon as the door was opened, I avoided the beating by diving on the floor as fast as I could. Meanwhile, other feds were searching the cells, trashing everything. During those tense minutes I expected the worst—I hadn't forgotten about the broom. Fortunately, they did not check it carefully, in spite of the fact that one of the policeman did pick it up off the floor.

The scrutiny lasted between forty and forty-five minutes. During that time, the agents kept us all on the floor. At the end of the search, they took Víctor Manuel Velasco Damián and Carlos Jiménez Sarmiento with them. The rest of the inmates remained locked up in our cells, tiding up the mess that the White Brigade had made, while we commented on the event and wondered why they had taken Víctor and Carlos, even though we all had a slight suspicion why.

TERE'S KIDNAPPING

The evening progressed and shadows grew. The passage of time increased my anxiety because I expected a conjugal visit that night. The impossibility of calling Tere on the phone to ask her not to venture out put me on edge. In those anxious moments, the only reasonable supposition was that any conjugal visit would be suspended. In any case, I would have given anything to save Tere from the long and risky night trip to San Lorenzo Tezonco in Iztapalapa, only to find that she could not enter the Reclusorio Oriente to spend the night with me. Only her love and loyalty could compel her to remain by my side all these years, withstanding the welter of problems and so much daily suffering. To my surprise, one of the guards called me for my conjugal visit. As I heard my name, I got ready very fast and went with the guard to the installations that the Reclusorio had for that purpose, a kind of small hotel halfway between the dorms and the main administration building. Once there, the woman in charge of assigning rooms told me which one was Tere's. My wife was waiting impatiently, anxious to tell me that as she'd gone through the inspection booth, she'd witnessed the detention of Dr. Blanca Hernández at the hands of plainclothes individuals. Blanca was the wife of Roberto Tello Alarcón, and also Tere's carpool companion in their evening trips to Oriente to see their husbands. The news astonished and worried me: at any point the agents could come to detain and interrogate us both.

Tere and I remained awake and in a state of alert all night, conjecturing in a thousand ways what the motives of the White Brigade agents might be. I was intrigued by the connection between Blanca's detention and the seizure of Víctor Manuel and Carlos, with whom I doubted that Roberto Tello Alarcón had any working relationship. Roberto and I had only worked together in the publication of *Oriente*, a task that we had shared. Other than that, we had no ties to one another. But the night was coming to an end. I embraced Tere forcefully, telling her how afraid I was that she might be picked up as she left. I told her that if that happened she should inform the agents that the two of us were not aware of any plans or activities of anyone; that the only interest that we had was in my ability to be freed from jail so that we could rebuild our family life in a legal context; and that since I had been detained three years earlier, I'd ceased all contact with the compañeros of my organization.

With that agreed, we departed, Tere in the direction of the entrance, and I in the direction of dorm number four. Once there, I went to Tello's cell to inform him of what had happened to Blanca. The news took him aback, upsetting him to the point of leaving the dorm building, ranting and raving, causing the guards to take him to the infirmary.

Not an hour had passed by since Tere's departure when one of the Lacandones came to my cell to let me know that his family visitors had witnessed Tere's kidnapping while they waited to enter the *reclusorio*. His visitors had seen a white old model Taunus cut her off as she started her way back home. They added that several men in T-shirts and sweaters or wearing jackets left the Taunus and surrounded the VW, opening the driver's side door, lifting María Teresa from her seat and throwing her onto the back floor. They saw how immediately one of the agents had covered her with a cloth, and had sat in the back with his feet on my wife with the evident purpose of keeping her still and unseen. Meanwhile, the other two agents had occupied the two front seats. The youngest one was at the wheel, and he peeled out quickly, followed by two other agents in the Taunus.

The news hit me like a blow in the middle of my face. I again suffered the realization that our lives were a fragile toy in the hands of anonymous powers, capricious and unpredictable. I don't know how I recovered, but without wasting any time I walked decisively to the control booth with the purpose of leaving the dorm and reaching the administration building. The guard on duty allowed me to go through after he asked where I was going. Maybe he had gotten used to seeing me coming and going during the publication of *Oriente*. I'm sure that he didn't know what was happening to me at that moment. Walking fast, I reached the administration building, convinced that I needed to call Teresita, who was home in charge of her young brother. I greeted the guard in charge of telephone calls. Unflustered, I asked him for a line, and gave him the number I wanted to call and the name of the person I wanted to talk to. He dialed the number and indicated that I could lift the phone and talk. I calculated that I barely had time to explain to Teresita what had happened. I was afraid that the guard could interrupt the communication as he heard what I was going to say. I made a great effort to explain in a few words that her mother had been detained as she left the Reclusorio, that she needed to call her grandfather Salvador—my father—to appraise him of the situation, and to tell him on my behalf that he should promptly denounce Tere's disappearance at the Secretariat of Government by talking to Ernesto Alvarez Nolasco, director of the office of information in that ministry. My father had developed a friendship with this man, whom he knew because of his work with the Association of Editors of the States, and had already spoken to him about my situation. I also asked my daughter to call her aunt Margarita to inform her about the events and ask her to take her and the child to her house. As the conversation with my daughter progressed, the guard paid more and more attention to what I was saying. I realized that he was hesitating whether or not to interrupt the call. Maybe his curiosity got the better of him, and I finished what I needed to say.

I asked the guard to allow me to go in and request an interview with the director. The man took the telephone to consult with someone, who evidently said yes, and I was able to walk into the offices of the top administrators. I asked a secretary for an appointment with the functionary. The young woman asked me to take a seat and wait. I heard a telephone ringing insistently and almost at the same time I saw the new technical subdirector of the facilities approaching me to ask what I needed. A solicitous assistant that walked next to him offered to pick up the phone, which had continued to ring without anyone else worrying about it. I was starting to tell the subdirector about what happened to my wife when the assistant interrupted to say that someone named Salvador Ulloa Robles from the Association of Editors of the States wanted to confirm the kidnapping of a lady at the gates of the Reclusorio. Mr. Ulloa argued that the kidnapping had occurred right after the woman left the building where she had been for an intimate night visit with her husband who was confined in Oriente. The journalist also added that he had been told that the detention had taken place a short while ago. I realized that the subdirector was truly disconcerted, so I informed him that the caller was my father. His unexpected reaction was to tell me to pick up the phone. I did. Naturally, I emphasized to my father the urgency that he talk to Ernesto Alvarez Nolasco at the Secretariat of Government and denounce Tere's disappearance, asking him to communicate what had happened to his boss, Secretary Jesús Reyes Heroles.

After I finished talking with Papa, the subdirector took me into the director's office. Lic. Trujillo Guarneros pretended very hard not to know what had happened to my wife. The reason I wanted to talk to him was to ask him to let Tere's kidnappers know that she had nothing to do with my actions. They should talk to me if they still needed to know anything. When Trujillo Guarneros heard me, the involuntary gleam in his eyes revealed the pleasure he took in becoming the liaison for an interview between the political police and me.

I returned to the dorm plunged in uncertainty and worried to death about what could be happening to Tere. Since I didn't find solace in anything, I wandered by myself from one side of the perimeter of the dorm to the other, trying to quiet my feelings of despair and impotence. All I could do was to wait for news. It finally came on the third day. I was called to the director's office where I found that Lic. Trujillo Guarneros had company. The visitor was a dark-skinned man, of regular stature and strong appearance, between thirty-eight and forty years old. He wore a gray windbreaker with an open hood hanging on his back. As I approached them, he extended his hand, which I shook firmly. At the invitation of the director, we sat at a round table where I faced them both. Without any preamble, I told them I couldn't understand the reasons for my wife's abduction. I explained that shortly before my detention I'd decided to leave the clandestine struggle of armed groups, in fact any struggle based on violent means. Since I had been in jail, all my actions had been above board. I was not involved in politics, and I deliberately kept away from old my old compañeros and all other groups. My wife was dedicated to caring for my children, to working for their upbringing, to visiting me, and to nothing else. The connection she had with Blanca Hernández was not political. It had developed out of solidarity, since both had to travel at night to the Reclusorio to visit their husbands. They had also been involved in some efforts related to our situation in jail, in particular to push for our eventual freedom.

The man with the windbreaker listened to what I had said. When I finished, he spoke to me about the investigation he was conducting of the alleged introduction of weapons and drugs into Oriente in preparation for a collective escape from the Reclusorio organized by drug traffickers and guerrilla fighters. He added that Dr. Blanca Hernández and her husband Roberto Tello Alarcón had a lot to do with it. The story struck me as ridiculously contrived, and I told him so. I added that I was convinced that the majority of political prisoners had waged their future on a possible amnesty law at the end of President Echeverría's administration or the beginning of the next one. Evaluating my explanations, the federal policeman indicated that it was not necessary to continue with the conversation. He stared at me coldly and harshly for a few seconds, and then announced that my wife was already in her apartment, reunited with the children. He added that Tere would not have any more problems. He said that if I wanted to see for myself, I could call her on the phone at that very moment. In one step, I put myself anxiously in front of the phone that Lic. Trujillo Guarneros was pointing to with the index finger of his right hand. I dialed in a hurry. I could feel every full beat of my heart. An unknown Tere, distant and frightened, answered the phone. Her replies to my questions were monosyllabic. I told her not to be afraid, that next to me was an officer of the Federal de Seguridad who had just assured me that nothing would ever happen to her again. Since it was Saturday, and the next day was a general family visiting day, I asked to please come see me.

Her answer froze my blood.

She said that she didn't think that she could ever come back to see me. She said that she was not sure at that moment if she ever would some day, but she couldn't visit me the next day at the Reclusorio.

Heartbroken, I said good-bye to Tere. I exchanged some courtesy words with the commander and Trujillo Guarneros, and returned to dormitory four, feeling wounded. I could hardly sleep that long night. Sunday would be the bitterest and longest day since I left the Campo Militar Número Uno. I tasted again what it means to be alone, and felt sorry for myself and for all the inmates who never had a visitor.

The following week, Tere did come to see me at the Reclusorio. The real danger of being separated from her children, parents, and siblings, plus the daily tensions she had lived through in the last three years, added to the many troubles I caused in the previous years of our marriage had all come to a head.

Still, her love for me made it impossible for her to abandon me to my own fate. The anguishing incident of her abduction, however, helped my father, through the efficient assistance of don Ernesto Alvarez Nolasco, to secure a personal meeting with the Secretary of Government, Jesús Reyes Heroles. This important federal functionary heard my father describe what had happened to Tere. In a commanding voice, hard and dry, he used the internal phone system to call in Subsecretary Fernando Gutiérrez Barrios. Before my father, Reyes Heroles upbraided his subdirector for Tere's disappearance, insisting that they had agreed that no such means would be used ever again in the course of investigations. He then instructed him to look for the best way to deal with all those incarcerated young people being punished for their misunderstood political idealism. He said it was time to open new spaces for those activists in national politics. The Secretary confided in my father, saying he was in favor of a political opening toward the left, one which could well begin with the promulgation of an amnesty law and the legalization of the Communist Party.

SANTA MARTHA

Tere's abduction, her liberation, and my father's conference with Reyes Heroles all filled me with both pessimistic omens and crazy hopes. Consequently I became impatient and irritable. I badgered Tere with questions—some of them necessary, but the majority foolish—about my legal process. On August 17, 1976, the Judge in Common Pleas Court XXV had condemned me to 13 years and 9 months, plus reparations. I had appealed and was waiting for the resolution of the Court of Appeals. I also pestered Tere with questions about what was happening with the Secretariat of Government. Before long, Dionisio and I were taken by jail wagon to the Superior Court of Justice, where we were notified of the resolution of Court IX about our appeal. The magistrates had taken two years off our sentence, but the two of us still had to pay reparations for two million and three hundred thousand pesos.

Once I had been notified, it was urgent for my lawyer Guillermo Andrade Gressler to file a writ of habeas corpus in the Supreme Court of Justice, the third and last level of appeal. Without this protection, I could easily be sent to the Santa Martha Acatitla prison, where inmates who do not have any legal decision pending are sent to complete their sentences. Over the following days, Tere had to put up with my nerves, as I asked her again and again to make sure Andrade Gressler would not miss the five day legal period a defendant has to request this type of protection. Finally Tere told me that my lawyer had submitted the writ, and this gave me a false sense of victory. One should never trust the fulfillment of the law in a country where what is normal is the violation of law at every turn.

In the summer of 1977, in mid-morning, while I was working in a new commission in the administrative area of the Reclusorio, a guard came to escort me back to the dorm to pick up my belongings without telling me why. Roberto Sánchez Ensch, Carlos Salcedo, and Ricardo Rodríguez González, who were in the cell or nearby, asked me questions with their eyes: "What's up?" to which I replied by shrugging my shoulders and telling them that I didn't know. Meanwhile the guard was pushing me to be quick. I decided to leave almost everything and send for it later. Then the guard took me to the control area of the Reclusorio. He asked me to sit on a bench, still refusing to answer my questions. I saw one of the coordinators of guards who had always been nice to me, and asked him what was up, but he also denied knowing anything. I later thought he was saying the truth.

Sitting on the hard bench and observing the coming and going of the inmates, I felt nervous, not knowing whether I was going to be set free or what this was about. Although I wanted with all my heart to be sent home, I was merely being transferred to the Santa Martha Acatitla Penitentiary, in spite of being still subject to judicial proceedings and not a condemned prisoner.

As a curious fact that day and in those very moments, I saw Félix Barra García, President Luis Echeverría Alvarez's former Secretary of Agrarian Reform. He was at the point of completing the seventy-two hour legal requirement in the area of Observation and Classification. Soon he would be declared formally imprisoned and sent to one of the dorms. Like any influential personage fallen in disgrace, he was going from one place to the other in the prison administration, presumably trying to negotiate the best possible deal for his time in the Reclusorio.

The transfer to Santa Martha was quick, but the ambiguity of my situation and sheer anguish turned it into a slow and heavy trip. Fortunately, as I arrived in the Penitentiary, I ran into Cecilia Méndez, the Chief of Social Work at Oriente, whom I asked to please call Tere and inform her of my transfer. Then I went through the intake process, which included the humiliation of undressing and giving up my Topeka beige uniform, which I liked, exchanging it for a threadbare navy blue uniform in the wrong size, with the obligatory cap. I was assigned to dorm three and was taken to a collective cell on the first floor of the building, which I would occupy with other recently admitted prisoners while I fulfilled the initial time of *fajina*—three months, just as in Lecumberri. I remember now that as I left the office building I ran into several compañeros from the O West. It gave me great relief—in those moments of dejection and fright—to run into friendly, known people. A few minutes later, after seeing the cell, I met with them to chat in the inner courtyard of dorm number three. There, I encountered for the second time Andrés González Mancilla, El Puma, who had shared his cell with me in the last few months we spent in Lecumberri. Also there were the most veteran prisoners from the MAR, ACNR, and the three Castañeda brothers, Eufemio González Mancilla (Andrés' brother), José de Jesús Pérez Esqueda (Juanotas), Enrique Téllez Pacheco, Alfredo de la Rosa Olguín (El Negrito), and David Jesús Mendoza Gaytán (El Pocho), among others. Some of them told me they were about to go free, after completing five years or more in prison. Hearing this news built up my hope that perhaps I would not have to be here for many years. Meanwhile, I sill had to do the fajina.

My first tasks consisted of unloading large sacks of flour from pickup trucks, destined for the prison bakery. As anyone can imagine, at the end of such a task we were like grotesque clowns, whitened from head to toe. Another fajina, to which I was sent, consisted of sanding and repainting the ironwork in gates, stairway railings, window guards, and fences. The fajineros worked all day without interruption, unless a visitor requested our presence in the visiting room. That was my case on the second day of my arrival in Santa Martha Acatitla, when Tere came to visit me for the first time in the company of our little son Alberto.

The place where one spoke with members of one's defense team was a room of good size. In its center, occupying three quarters of the total surface, was a rectangular metallic structure mounted on a wall about a meter and a half tall. All was covered by a thick metallic net, creating a cage-like space. Its purpose, of course, was to keep the visitor completely separated from the inmate. Tere awaited on the other side of the fence. Her strong, beautiful hands were holding our son by the waist, and he was standing on the wall, holding on to the thick wire with his hands. He was staring right at his father! I drew closer to him, feeling hurt in my pride and dignity as I faced my family in such an abject appearance. I was surprised at myself when I sobbed with shame. All of a sudden we had blinked, and everything had gone back to the days of Lecumberri, those gray days of November, 1974, when I had no hope in cellblock D.

One morning Dimas, the youngest of the Castañeda brothers, suggested that if I wanted he could recommend me to be in charge of the fajina he'd been doing, which consisted of picking up, twice a day, the trash from the bins located in the corridors and the large yard of the penitentiary and taking it to the incinerator, just outside the back of the compound. The reason for his offer was that he was going to be freed in a few days, and the commission would be vacant. He explained that the convenience of this fajina was that it took a bit over an hour each time, while other commissions took four and five hours. It was an opportunity to buy some free time. Dimas recommended me and the guard in charge of supervising the area accepted.

A few weeks later, Negrito De la Rosa, a fabulous artist, made an excellent cartoon in which I am pushing the traditional trash cart while many flies are hovering around my head. My nose is raised up in an aristocratic but useless gesture, trying not to breathe the putrid air that rises from the waste.

In Santa Martha, as in Lecumberri, self-government ruled. Convicts were distributed in four dorms within the penitentiary, each one of which was ruled by one inmate, the Mayor, designated by the director of the institution. That director, Eduardo Antolín Lozano, was a fearsome political policeman, who said that he had been head of the bodyguards for María Ester Zuno, the wife of President of the Republic Luis Echeverría Alvarez. The Mayor of dorm three, David Noriega, was a thirty-six year-old man, thin, of regular build, nervous and irritable, who had accumulated several sentences for homicide that added up to over fifty years of prison.

As in my previous jails, Santa Martha had three companies of guards to watch over the inmates. However, in the Penitentiary of the Federal District there was one more informal company known as the fourth, made up of the most dangerous criminals in residence. The fourth company was the product of the sinister imagination of the director, who used it to exercise a regime of terror and complete internal control of the big house, especially its main business: the introduction, distribution, and sale of drugs and other addictive substances—pills, marijuana, cocaine, heroin, alcohol, thinner, and shoe-makers glue. David Noriega, by designation of Eduardo Antolín Lozano, commanded the fourth company. His competence was beyond doubt: in dorm three, theft had been forbidden, as was violence among inmates—assaults and rape, for example. He, in fact, had eradicated larceny. All of us residents of the dorm walked on the right side, so I did not find an atmosphere as oppressive and suffocating as in cellblock D of Lecumberri. But like other inmates in Santa Martha, I suffered the daily harassment of numerous pressures. On the first floor of each dorm, there were some fenced-in spaces that were used for the businesses that the director of the penitentiary allowed as concessions to the villainous inmates that associated with him. One of the most important ones was the eatery, where inmates with a little bit of money could drink a soda, have some coffee, a milkshake, or eat something a little better than unspeakable prison chow. The other stands included a cleaners, barbershop, ice cream parlor, and craft shops.

One morning, as I used to do everyday, I was in the eatery of the dorm waiting for a milkshake with two eggs and fruit that I used to drink as breakfast when unexpectedly David Noriega came in. The eatery was serviced by a couple of young gay men from Puerto Rico. They and I saw that behind David a younger inmate was coming along. The mere presence of Noriega intimidated and made anyone nervous, but at that moment the brusque and determined way in which David came in and dropped some objects on a table announced that trouble was brewing. Then, in a series of darting movements that couldn't have lasted more than two minutes, David Noriega pivoted rapidly around, and hit the pale, resigned face of the young criminal with a hard left hook. At the same time his right hand produced from behind his waist something that flashed in the air like lightening: a wide and horrific butcher knife which he used to abuse his victim further by hitting him on his head and face with its flat side. As a consequence of the ferocious assault, the young man fell to the ground. The chief of the fourth company kicked the convict savagely in the ribs, stomach, and back. Presently, he grabbed him by the hair, set him in a standing position, and threw him face down outside the eatery. Then David Noriega, with hardly a show of emotion, proceeded to correct the disarray of his hair and clothes, pick up the objects scattered on the table, and without glancing even once at the three petrified witnesses of his implacable punishment, he left the place just as he had come in.

Only then were the islanders and I able to breathe again. As we looked at each other in silence, we recognized in each other's faces as if in a mirror the livid imprint of horror. During several minutes, we tried to control the shivering of our bodies. This incident made me conscious of the fact that the year and a few months that I'd lived in the relative calm of Reclusorio Oriente had made me forget the daily violence of which I had been an object and witness during my incarceration in Lecumberri.

As soon as I came to Santa Martha, I came to discover the degree of violence that the director of the Federal District Penitentiary could exert against inmates, most of the times using the members of the fourth company as his instrument. Convict deaths were frequent events. When I was newly arrived there, I remember hearing about the tragic end of a member of dorm one who was killed in a horrifying way, with his head inside a bucket full of thinner. One afternoon comes to mind, when a group of us political prisoners took our customary walk side-by-side from one end of the yard to the other. We passed in front of dorm one when an inmate threw a small ball of cloth reeking of solvent at us, asking Adalberto Loperena, the closest to him, to throw it in the nearest trash bin. Loperena did as he was told while the rest of us continued walking and talking in subdued tones about what had just happened. Very soon a group of guards rushed into the same dorm with a stretcher. They emerged again carrying a body covered completely by a white sheet. Our group knew someone had been killed. Before long, we found out that the man who had been stabbed to death by the fourth company was from a well to do family of Greek origin from Tijuana surnamed Kiriakides, a distinguished member of Alberto Sicilia Falcón's gang. A few weeks later, we learned that Kiriakides had indeed survived the knifing he suffered for having tried to outsmart the director of the prison.

One week after the violent episode in the eatery, I was ambling along with David Mendoza Gaitán and Enrique Téllez Pacheco on the first floor of dorm three when we decided to get something to drink. We were surprised to find David Noriega eating by himself at a back table. Of all the political prisoners of the dorm, Enrique Téllez Pacheco was the one who treated Noriega with greatest familiarity, due to his sociable, warm personality. He greeted Noriega and asked whether we could keep him company. Noriega accepted immediately, so the three of us sat at the table with him. Frankly, I didn't like the situation, since it was difficult to ignore the fact that Noriega was the Mayor of our dorm and chief of the fourth company. Enrique introduced me to him. Noriega continued eating quietly, while the three of us ordered coffee and sodas from one of the Puerto Ricans. While we waited, Téllez commented the details of the American football game that he had seen on TV the night before. After he listed to Téllez, Noriega addressed me unexpectedly and referred to the beating I had witnessed. Pushing away his custard desert, David explained his behavior of that day. Neither Enrique, nor El Pocho, nor I had asked any questions. He said that the kid was a petty thief who didn't listen when warned to stop stealing in the dorm. He'd earned his punishment. Noriega argued that he had to act that way. If he didn't instill fear in such a criminal, he'd be ambushed any day in one of the many dark corners of the dorm by a hood ready to stick a shiv in his throat or stomach. Noriega then became interested in my watch, a relatively new but fairly ordinary one that my father had given me a few months before. He began by praising it and ended by suggesting that I give it to him. I surprised myself by saying that I would get him a better brand. I never fulfilled that promise.

In Santa Martha, Alberto Sicilia Falcón set himself up as a big *padrino*. I remember him dressed in fine clothing in obligatory navy blue, unhurriedly crossing the main yard of the penitentiary with the help of a cane, limping slightly as he went to the cafeteria he operated in the vestibule of the area of the conjugal visit rooms. Almost invariably a fine huge German shepherd walked next to him on a leash. Those rooms were known by inmates as the Metro, since they were located under the main lobby of the penitentiary administration. Many people walked through that lobby at all hours, causing couples to have to withstand the noise of the fast comings and goings above

their embraced bodies. Sicilia Falcón spent his time in the cafeteria talking to
visitors and taking care of business.

Another character of jailhouse life, who accompanied my confinement in
all its stages, starting with cellblock H in Lecumberri, was a criminal with a
long background named Guillermo Zúñiga. I remember having seen him for
the first time at the last roll call on the first day of my arrival at H. Yuca had
sent Dionisio, Francisco, and me to join the row of ordinary prisoners in the
back of the yard in front of the stairway that led to the first and only story of
the building. The inmate commissioned as scribe or secretary read the name
and first surname of each man, waiting for the person named to produce the
second surname as the correct answer that certified each man's identity, after
which he would place a checkmark. One could see from afar that Zúñiga was
an expert in the ways and customs of Lecumberri. Yuca himself treated him
as an old comrade with a certain deference. For instance, he allowed him to
choose the cell and cellmates with whom he would spend the night locked up.
Seventy-two hours later, once we were declared formally imprisoned by our
respective judges, Zúñiga, Dionisio, and I entered the interior of Lecumberri
together, first to be given a uniform and later to be led to the cellblock to
which the authorities had assigned each one of us.

In the row of inmates, Zúñiga and I were next to each other as we walked
around the *Redondel* in the middle of which stood the watchtower. Only a few
steps separated us from the guard that led the group of inmates. Unsettled,
we awaited our turn to be released into our cellblocks: Zúñiga to F, Dionisio
to B, and I to D. Francisco had spent the day before in cellblock G. Zúñiga,
who had expressed curiosity about the cause that had led the three of us to
prison, asked me suddenly which cellblock would be mine. When I answered,
he suggested that I should tell the comandos that I came from Colonia Morelos, where I used to hang out with the boys of Paileros Street. I was truly grateful, but of course, I didn't follow this advice. I imagined myself with my helpless middle-class look saying something so moronic to a bunch of hoodlums
from Colonia Morelos.

In my first outing from cellblock D, when I had to fulfill my obligations
to the vampire—donation of a third of a liter of blood in the infirmary, something that each newly arrived convict was required to do—I ran into Zúñiga
again. He appeared transformed, dressed in a dashing navy blue Topeka uniform and reeking of Jockey Club cologne from afar. One could see that the
king had returned to his kingdom and was entirely devoted to the recovery of
all his privileges. I learned then that he had been sent back from the Santa
Martha Acatitla Penitentiary because he had won a new judicial process while
he was there. I also learned that this was not the first time that had happened.

Among Zúñiga's many abilities, besides a sharp natural intelligence, was playing the bugle, which granted him the privilege of leading the military band
by special designation of the Chief of Security, Edilberto Gil Cárdenas. In the
documentary *Lecumberri a.k.a. Black Palace* by Arturo Ripstein, Zúñiga
appears playing "La cárcel de Cananea" on the harmonica. In Reclusorio Oriente and Santa Martha, Zúñiga acted as a strict, professional, and much feared
soccer referee.

The last contact I remember having had with Zúñiga happened in the late
afternoon one day of October 1977 in a dark passageway of dorm three in
Santa Martha Acatitla. I was on my way to the cell I shared with Alfredo de
la Rosa Olguín, when I saw Zúñiga leaning on the wall next to a window. I
don't remember whether I greeted him, but as soon as I had gone beyond
him, Zúñiga yelled at me: "Ese . . . !" I stopped and turned toward him, assuming that he was *peido*, meaning that he urgently needed heroin or *tecata* and
was going to hold me up. As if I were not afraid, I approached him saying
"Hi Zúñiga, what's up?" When he saw me closely, Zúñiga seemed to recognize me and instantly changed his attitude from that of a feline about to
jump his prey. I spent a while with him sharing a couple of cigarettes. He then
told me the story of a judge who denied him permission to attend his
mother's burial. He did it with hatred and rancor, with a harshness in his eyes
and tight fists, which caused me to shudder with fear. He told me that the
only thing he wanted to do before leaving this world was to get out of prison
and take his revenge on this judge, killing him like a dog. He was not just
boasting. I knew very well that Zúñiga had murdered Pato in cellblock O
West: El Pato and Zúñiga were both jailhouse scum. Their criminal biogra-
phies teemed with violence and blood. In the year 1971, both were confined
as punishment in the maximum security area of Lecumberri, the western section of cellblock O. Everyday, El Pato would steal something from Zúñiga,
maybe toothpaste or soap or shaving blades or weed. Zúñiga pretended not
to notice. He didn't say anything, waiting to see how far this fucking dude
would go. There were those who told Zúñiga what El Pato was doing, but he
would only answer "Wait until this asshole gets to me." He got to him one
night when Zúñiga discovered that El Pato had taken all of his meager possessions, even a shiv that was hidden under the mattress of his bunk bed.
Rabid, Zúñiga rushed to El Pato's cell and found him asleep. Searching carefully under the mattress without waking him up, he recovered his steel. He
then awoke El Pato and announced that he was going to kill him, holding him
tightly by his hair and cutting the skin of his neck with the shiv. He forced
him to stand up and took him to the bathroom. He made him weave a rope
two meters long with the nylon fiber they both used to knit belts and lady's

handbags, which they sold to visitors. All this time, Zúñiga was holding El Pato by the hair while he made him bleed at the neck with his sharp steel. When the rope was ready, Zúñiga forced El Pato to make a loop and put it around his neck. He then made him climb on a wooden stool and tied the other end of the rope to the shower pipe. All this time El Pato obeyed Zúñiga with resignation, thinking that Zúñiga was going through the motions of teaching him a lesson. But when he least expected it, Zúñiga kicked the stool. As he fell, the rope broke El Pato's neck. He died staring at Zúñiga with eyes wide open in astonishment.

That same year, the first eighteen captured members of the Movimiento de Acción Revolucionaria who had been trained in the Popular Republic of Korea (North Korea) were locked up in the western section of cellblock O. Zúñiga learned to respect and appreciate the young guerrilla fighters of the MAR. Not only had they treated him well—they had also instructed him on important aspects of the revolutionary theory they professed. They shared with him many things like food, cigarettes, and books. I believe this is the reason why I was spared that afternoon in Santa Martha.

The first few hours of the night were the most dangerous time in the penitentiary. As taps drew near at 22:00 hours, addicts would have exhausted their best stratagems for getting drugs. They would have begun to envision their prolonged torment through an arid, sleepless night without the relief of a fix. During their last moments of relative freedom of movement, the frenetic impulse of their desperate search for a fix seemed to reverberate among the rest of the inmates. Those of us who were not addicts needed to expend our sudden surplus of energy, even if we could only pace the limited spaces of our dorm over and over—the vestibule, the stairs, and the corridors. All of us were immersed, users or not, in a frenetic flight of wasps swarming at the entrance of their nest before the imminent sunset.

CONDITIONAL FREEDOM

The two months before Christmas in 1977 were full of rumors, contradictory news, and proposals that at that time appeared nonsensical. The functionaries at the Secretariat of Government told my father that I should give up the writ of habeas corpus that I had requested from the Supreme Court of Justice so that they could proceed to apply whatever protection I may have coming under the new Ley de Normas Mínimas, and thus grant me some form of pre-liberation. In other words, I should assume to be processed by accepting the sentence given to me by the second court of appeals. I would thus resign my last possible juridical protection. I resisted for a time, thinking that if all my father was hearing proved false, the results could be fatal. Still, at the insistence of my family and based on my own desire for freedom, I gave up the writ.

The evening walks we used to take in those autumn days in the yards of dormitory three released some of the tension we experienced at the mere possibility of being discharged in a short time. During those compulsive promenades, Enrique Téllez Pacheco, David Mendoza Gaitán, Alfredo de la Rosa Olguín, and I could not talk about anything but our impending liberation. (The Negrito participated less than the others in these walks, because he was always busy with some publicity work or other.) At the beginning of the month of November we were lost in a reverie about being home for the holidays. Thinking about it, we would talk about the traditions each of our families kept on those days, and the dishes our mothers prepared for the celebration. Then we would talk about what we most wanted to do on our first day out on the streets again, where we would go, what we would eat and drink. Of course, we never talked about how petrified we were about the need to try to make a living again, that is if someone would give us a job. We were also afraid of the political police and the army, not knowing how they would react to our new freedom. Nobody ever talked about politics; nobody made plans to join this or that political party or leftist group. Instead, we dreamt of seeing the ocean, being out in the countryside among trees and flowers, or going to the movies or the theater, or entering a bar to down a beer or a shot of tequila. We wanted to walk freely on the streets and avenues of Mexico City in search of other adventures, and to find out what had happened during the four or five years of our absence.

In mid-December, thanks to my father's persevering efforts and the political good will of don Jesús Reyes Heroles—Lord of the Great Power, as Saúl, Enrique and I used to refer to him—I finally got a break. The Secretariat of Government's subdirector Ernesto Alvarez Nolasco informed my father on behalf of his boss that I would be allowed to leave the penitentiary on Saturdays and Sundays while remaining confined during the rest of the week. My new routine would start on the 23rd—I could spend Christmas with my family.

When Friday, December 23 finally arrived, a new trek filled with impatience and tension was about to begin. Tere came to visit me in the morning to tell me that on the previous afternoon a mature man accompanied by two young men, all dressed informally, had gone to our apartment to check on the veracity of the information I had submitted about my family's domicile. He wanted to know who else lived there, what relationship each dweller had with me, and other such information. María Teresa confirmed for me that I was still expected to leave that afternoon, but she didn't know the time. I decided it was better if she did not wait for me. I told her I would take a taxi home. The last few hours of that afternoon were spent trying to shake off my nervousness, walking around the dormitory yard in the company of David Mendoza Gaytán, Enrique Téllez Pacheco, Adalberto Loperena Martínez, and Alfredo de la Rosa Olguín. The compañeros were very excited about my imminent departure. After innumerable turns around the yard, I began to think that the authorities had postponed everything, but just when I was about to give up hope, a guard came to escort me to the central offices. I embraced each of my compañeros, promising to drink to their health and to return on Sunday afternoons to tell them how it felt to be free again, even if only for such a short time.

I had to wait for over two hours in the administrative offices before I could set one foot out the door. It happened that the technical subdirector of the penitentiary, an attorney named Alfonso Corona, insisted that one of his officers drive me home. Since he was busy finishing some work, I had to wait until he was done. Meanwhile, I was allowed to call Tere and explain to her the reason for my delay. I asked her to trust that she would see me later that evening.

The experience of entering or leaving prison is a long and complicated bureaucratic journey in which there is always one more piece of paper to stamp, one more step, one more formality as one gets closer to or farther from freedom. I had imagined the moment of setting foot on the street as a rebirth steeped in happy sensations. That was not what happened. It was something far more natural that I enjoyed quietly, nothing as dramatic as being reborn. That would take work, and a lot of time.

The trip home in the car of the officer was fast, despite the distance between Santa Martha and the apartment where Tere and the children lived in Colonia del Valle. My driver traveled at normal speed along the Ermita–Iztapalapa Causeway. He took a right turn at the intersection of División del Norte and continued on that avenue until Eugenia, where he took a left. Traversing that part of the city at night made it difficult for me to identify the route we were taking confidently. It seemed to me we were going on streets quite different from the expected ones saved in my memory. As an attorney, the man at the wheel seemed intrigued by my case. Perhaps he was, especially because it must have been very unusual to leave the penitentiary as the sole escort of a dangerous guerrilla fighter of dubious legal status. The granting of my temporary release had ignored the juridical requirements for the provisional freedom of a sentenced man like me. I wish I could have told the lawyer that the process of my imprisonment had been even less legally correct.

At the end of half an hour, we arrived at the entrance of the apartment building where Tere and my two children lived at that time in the company of my in-laws don José and doña Margarita. I left the lawyer's car expressing gratitude for the lift. Once inside the building I felt uncomfortable at the possibility of running into one of the neighbors I might have met years before. I really did not feel like explaining my long absence, nor my navy blue wardrobe dictated by Santa Martha's regulations.

When I rang the bell, Tere opened the door, welcoming me with an embrace and a kiss full of tenderness. Then don José and doña Margarita greeted me warmly. Next, I hugged my daughter Teresita and my little Alberto, who seemed very surprised to see me there. He looked at me with a certain curiosity and distrust. It would take him a while to get used to my presence at home and to be ready to share with me his mother and sister. Since I was out of cigarettes and there were none in the apartment, I went out in the street again to buy a package at the variety store on the corner. It was a strange experience to walk on the street again and to enter *La Florecita* to purchase a pack of *Del Prado*. The owner was the same as ever, but although he was trying to remember who I was, I didn't say anything to help him. I paid and left. I couldn't believe it was I who was walking carefree on a street in Mexico City. Once back at home, Tere offered me a cold Corona beer which I enjoyed very much while smoking slowly. Presently I called my parents to let them know I was home. Mamá answered the phone and politely responded: "I am so glad, son! Here is your father!" Papá sounded extraordinarily happy and told me he would come by the next morning to go buy some clothes. That night, for the first time in more than three years, I slept on our double bed at Tere's side. Beto slept in his crib, close to us. When I woke up early in the morning, he was standing, holding on to his crib's railing, looking at me. I greeted him touching one of his small hands with mine. He smiled at me for the first time, and babbled something I did not understand.

Papá arrived early, as he had announced. He took me first to the barber shop where he was a customer, a few steps beyond the main entrance of the building belonging to the newspaper *Excélsior* on Paseo de la Reforma. Next, we went to Zapico, a clothing store on Avenida Juárez across the street from the statue of Carlos IV, called "El Caballito," near the corner of Bucareli. Once inside I tried on several suits. My father bought me two, plus shirts, ties, and socks. We also bought shoes. He could not hide his satisfaction in seeing me free, next to him. He was eager to see me reinserted in society, doing the kind of work that would allow me to make a living for my family and create a patrimony for myself. I understood this, and without telling him, I felt enormously grateful toward him for taking care of me and supporting my family while I was imprisoned. All the same, in those days I still thought of myself as some sort of social hero, so I chose not to understand the deep disillusionment my failure had caused my father and mother.

The two days I spent in freedom were shorter than a sigh. Tere took me in her VW to Santa Martha in the first hours of Sunday afternoon. My return was in some way eased by the pleasure of talking to the compañeros who'd remained in prison over the weekend. I thought they were in a position to appreciate all the nuances of the narrative that I would soon offer them on the experience of being out on conditional freedom. I said good-bye to Tere at the door of the penitentiary, agreeing that she did not need to visit me, since I would be home again by Friday.

My reinsertion in prison would present me with a nasty surprise. As we arrived and entered the penitentiary, the twenty or so beneficiaries of weekend conditional freedom had to undergo a minute inspection of our clothes, hair, and mouths in the admissions office. Once inside, the guards took us to a large empty room where we were asked to stand in rows. After the roll call, those of us in the front row were ordered to pivot for half a turn, lower our pants and underpants all the way to the ankles, and squat several times. Then we were commanded to bend over, while a guard with a flashlight examined our naked bottoms. This shameful humiliation was designed to make it impossible for the pre-liberated inmates to introduce drugs.

As I had anticipated, several compañeros were waiting for my arrival a few meters away from the main yard of Santa Martha. David Mendoza Gaytán, Alfredo de la Rosa, Adalberto Loperena, and Enrique Téllez Pacheco greeted me there, all impatient to know how it felt to be out in the street again. We started our customary stroll back and forth while I related my first extramural experience. The prison authorities made me a member of the painting crew from then on, along with other inmates involved in the same process of pre-liberation. This work acted as a prerequisite that allowed us to leave on Friday afternoon rather than Saturday morning. Monday through Friday from eight o'clock to two o'clock, we painted gates, fences, pipes, drains, door and window frames, and interior and exterior walls.

One of those first weekends, my father, with the help of Ernesto Alvarez Nolasco, made an appointment to see the Secretary of Government, Jesús Reyes Heroles. The minister received us in his large and imposing office on Bucareli Street. He was very cordial toward us. After thanking him for my conditional freedom, I told him that the path he had decided to follow—amnesty and legalization for the PCM—was undoubtedly the best, and it would open new political spaces for the country. We also visited Subsecretary Fernando Gutiérrez Barrios, who said it had been a difficult matter to convince the top brass of the army that I should be set free. He advised me to forget about my experience in the Campo Militar Número Uno, adding: "Concentrate on the present, and most of all, on the future." When he extended his hand to me, I understood the signals he was sending to me and determined to take them very seriously.

I spent a bit more than six months under this pre-liberation regime, bored to death by the painting job. As for the visits, every Sunday it was harder to go back to the penitentiary than before. Time between Monday and Friday moved like molten lava, while the days with Tere and my two children vanished like a sigh. Impatient to reach full freedom, I kept pressing my father to lobby the Secretariat of Government to flip my pre-liberation arrangement: freedom from Monday through Friday and confinement from Saturday at twelve o'clock to Monday at 6 o'clock in the morning. I could be locked up weekends in the Casa Oficial located within the perimeter of the penitentiary rather than in a prison cellblock. That way I could get a job and earn a salary. Experience had demonstrated to me that nobody can be content with the recovery of freedom in stages. The need for full freedom is an irrevocable hunger of all human beings.

A happy circumstance came to my aid one of those weekends. I'd phoned Héctor Aguilar Camín to tell him I wanted to talk with him. Héctor proposed that Tere and I meet him at the house of Luis Linares Zapata and María Angélica Luna Parra, since he and Angeles Mastretta were invited, along with other friends such as José María Pérez Gay, José Antonio Alvarez Lima, and Verónica Rascón. When I said I had not been invited to the dinner, Héctor assured me that we would be welcome. He would call the hosts immediately to let them know of our presence. It was wonderful to be reunited with all those friends in the home of Luis and Manqué. Most of them had visited me several times in Lecumberri and Oriente, in spite of the risks to their jobs and persons during those years. At some point during the meeting, Héctor Aguilar Camín, José María Pérez Gay, and José Antonio Alvarez Lima suggested to Luis Linares that he should give me a job in the General Office of Information and Distribution, which he directed in the newly-created Secretariat for Planning and Budget. Luis accepted the suggestion immediately, although he made it clear that he needed to consult with his boss, Secretary Ricardo García Sáinz. It was my luck that he had no problem with the plan, and only requested that Luis ask the permission of the Secretariat of Government by talking to Subsecretary Fernando Gutiérrez Barrios. My friend Linares did, and learned that there was no objection to my participation in the work of such an important office in the government of José López Portillo. This circumstance paved the way for my change of status—finally!—so by the next week, I was working Monday to Friday, and I only had to be confined Saturdays and Sundays in the Casa Oficial. As for the job, Luis Linares Zapata was extremely generous, offering me a beginning salary that my wildest prison dreams could not have imagined I'd obtain right after being discharged. The central offices of the Secretariat for Planning and Budget were located on the second floor of the National Palace, just above the offices of the President of the Republic. The General Office of Information and Distribution occupied an ample space on the same floor of that building, next to the Honor Yard. Thus, from Monday to Friday I was at the National Palace, and on weekends I lived in the Casa Oficial, in the external perimeter of Santa Martha Acatitla.

A NEW LIFE

The Mexican government's policy of offering opportunities for social and political reincorporation to the previously repressed opposition is a difficult one to imagine in other countries. In Cuba, for example, the dictatorial regime of Fidel Castro keeps its detractors under lock and key until the very last day of their thirty-year sentences, if they evade execution. In the Soviet Union, in the People's Republic of China, in the countries of Eastern Europe, and in North Korea, governments have behaved in a way similar to Cuba or continue to do so. Of course, I am not trying to exculpate the illegal and criminal behavior of the PRI administrations for all those years, nor am I implying that we should forget the hundreds of Mexicans whom government officials detained because of their social, political or revolutionary activities, disappearing them for months or years in military installations, assassinating them, and throwing their corpses out of an airplane over the Pacific Ocean. I am saying that some of us who went through a similar predicament were lucky enough to be liberated or indicted formally before a judge. After a few years in prison, we had the good fortune to receive an amnesty from the very same political system. It finally yielded to the imperative of opening legal ways in politics, creating the possibility for the left to participate in elections.

I have no doubt that there are some who will think that my personal behavior was merely opportunistic. Such a view is likely to interpret the López Portillo administration's granting of conditional liberty and eventual amnesty to more than two hundred political prisoners as a simple cooptation or seduction. Personally, I would answer that more than the state or PRI government of the moment, reality itself had convinced me. I am also sure that for the first time in my life I was seeing reality. In my previous life what prevailed in my motivations was a chain of emotional reactions to the lack of public freedoms in Mexico, the narrowness and hypocrisy of the dominant social morality, the absolute misery of millions of Mexicans, and the corporativism and authoritarianism of the PRI governments. Acts of massive repression in 1957, 1958, 1968, and 1971 dramatically unveiled these negative features of Mexican life.

My behavior was also based on a pathetic ignorance of the history of Mexico and the rest of the world, and a total absence of knowledge about the social fabric in the country. Most of all, I was guided and compelled by a simple, persistent, and regrettable political naïveté. Only the gradual knowledge of several historical facts that occurred in my youth helped me to overcome the ideological prejudices on which my previous actions had been based, and to develop a more mature relationship with the social and political events that I witnessed. I think now of many testimonies of the post-Stalinist era, of the Hungarian rebellion, of Khrushchev and the XX Congress of the Communist Party of the Soviet Union, in the Gulag, in Castrismo, Guevarismo, and the Cuban Revolution. I think of the atrocities committed during Mao Tse-tung's Cultural Revolution, in the Brezhnev Doctrine, in Dubcek's "socialism in liberty" and the invasion of Czechoslovakia by the troops of the Warsaw Pact to terminate a reformist experiment. I think of the wars of liberation in Algeria, the Congo, Angola, Vietnam and the Indochina peninsula, especially the messianic insanity of Pol Pot's Khmer Rouge in Cambodia, in Gorbachev's *Perestroika* and the subsequent disintegration of the USSR, in the fall of the Berlin Wall, in the arrival of the era of Boris Yeltsin and the rapid political, economic, and social decomposition of Russia and its old satellites. I also think, inevitably, about the economic, political, and military supremacy of the United States over the whole world. All these hard facts have widened, clarified, corrected, enriched, or destroyed my ideas—vague, simplistic, or false as they were, but held with such conviction for more than twelve years.

The period I spent in the Casa Oficial lasted around three months. Every weekend I arrived there on Saturday at noon. The only thing we could do while living there was to kill time and avoid boredom. If the pool had water, we could swim when we arrived; otherwise, we'd have to fill it up all afternoon and night in order to be able to swim on Sunday. Occupants of the house were almost entirely political prisoners. We prepared our own simple meals in the kitchen and slept in one of the three bedrooms. In general everything looked abandoned and dirty, but none of us felt the impulse to clean up. There was not much to do. I remember one occasion when the guards in charge of our watch placed a horse and a large female donkey in the garden, with the purpose of letting them mate and obtaining a mule. The event caused much laughter among the inmates, since the donkey was strong and protected herself by kicking the horse on the jaw and neck.

This was the time when President López Portillo declared that Mexicans needed to learn how to administer their new abundance well, and that he really did not know what to do with the thousands of millions of dollars worth of petroleum and natural gas that Mexico had under its ground. The future looked promising. Having caught the enthusiasm and optimism from Luis Linares, I tried to convince the compañeros I lived with of the impossibility of developing a social and revolutionary movement under these circumstances. I was falling back into my old habit of taking a momentary event as if it were a permanent truth, something that I'd soon have a chance to realize.

Months went by slowly, and it was increasingly difficult to go back to the penitentiary, even for two days. Fortunately the political grapevine—the columns of national newspapers—began to talk about how the Secretary of Government, Jesús Reyes Heroles, had convinced President López Portillo to send a bill to Congress, an Amnesty Law, that would include all political prisoners. Meanwhile the constellation of political prisoners that spent time in the Casa Oficial was kept changing. Those who had completed their sentences were completely and permanently released, and others entered the pre-liberation system.

One of those boring Sunday afternoons, as I was looking for shelter from the cold rain that was suddenly falling, I entered the bedroom where the majority of us slept. There a group of compañeros—at least one of them a member of the Partido de los Pobres—sat around a member of Asociación Cívica Nacional Revolucionaria. He was an elementary school teacher from Guerrero who had spent five years in prison, all this time studying Marxism and Leninism with rigid discipline and reading the periodicals of the time. When I walked in the teacher was in the middle of an explanation, as if he were giving a class at a university. He was talking about the writer José Revueltas and why he had to be considered a revisionist, a traitor to the proletariat, to socialism, and to Communism. Uncomfortable because of my presence, he lowered his voice and added in a soft but energetic tone: "For all those reasons, if Revueltas were still alive, he would have to be executed." Such an unbelievable and absurd posthumous death sentence to the author of *The Headless Proletariat, To Sleep on the Earth, The Walls of Water, The Days on Earth,* and *The Apando* caused me to quiver with disgust, although I chose not to say anything. What I had just heard made it very clear that it was a waste of time to argue with such a person and with others similar to him. The best thing to do was to watch out for the actions that could stem from their dogmatic and ignorant primitivism. I was fed up with so much stupidity, arrogance, presumption, and falsehood, and the assumption that having political ideas—of the left or the right—entitled someone to act as an owner of the truth superior to the rest of mankind. And—what was worse—that these people should think that their ideas could be imposed on others by persecuting, incarcerating, and killing those who did not share their thoughts. Humanity's sad history reveals little more than intolerance, savagery, and massacres on all sides. Stalin and Hitler were but two sides of the same false, bloody coin.

Finally, Congress passed the Amnesty Law on September 28, 1978. The afternoon dailies published the list of beneficiaries, which I anxiously read until I found my name. I felt immense joy. Immediately I asked myself whether I had to return to Santa Martha. I was inclined not to go back ever again, but I decided to play it safe. I looked for the telephone number which Subsecretary Fernando Gutiérrez Barrios had given me during the visit with my father in case I had a problem.

When he gave me the telephone number on a personal card, Gutiérrez Barrios had asked me to call him in case of an emergency. Since I had never called him before, I didn't expect that he would answer the phone himself. But that's what happened. The Subsecretary listened to me, telling me to be sure to return to the penitentiary, where I had to be processed before I could consider myself legally and completely free. I thanked him for the clarification and made the decision to go the next day to Santa Martha. After that, I never called Fernando Gutiérrez Barrios again nor did I ever see him in person.

The processing in Santa Martha Acatitla took more than three hours. The longest part of that time I was simply waiting for the legal documents to be ready. In the end, the listed reason for my discharge was in error. Instead of saying that I had benefited from the Amnesty Law approved by Congress, they declared I had "purged my sentence." In reality, the new law legally obliterated all juridical processes against the political prisoners of the seventies, as if the deeds that originated them had never happened. Anyway, I suppose that the jailhouse bureaucracy couldn't find a better way of putting me out on the street legally and getting my file out of the juridical and penal apparatus. What mattered most to me is that the long nightmare that began on the September 4, 1974 had come to an end that day.

After the 28th of September, 1978, I was obliged to begin a new life. I needed to learn anew how to walk in the real world, under the sun, without the burden of my old ideological blindness. That year appeared as the beginning of great economic, political, and social opportunities for Mexicans. At least that was the way it looked, since the country's economy and politics gained a boost from the high price of petroleum and the fabulous reserves of crude oil that the administration of José López Portillo affirmed were lying under our seas.

Personally, during those years I would live new experiences at work, with my family, and with my friends. With a great deal of effort and many frequent and painful setbacks, I tried to move toward greater personal maturity. I would learn more about my country and its economic, political, and social structure. Later, in the mid-eighties and nineties, some moments of enthusiasm and even euphoria would arrive, only to change into disenchantment and pessimism about Mexico's destiny. The Mexican political class showed itself to be selfish, mediocre, myopic, irresponsible.

In my modest assessment, Mexicans of all stripes need to learn how to exercise tolerance, appreciate differences, and abandon narrow personal, partisan, or class-bound pathways. We need to act and think rationally about what this country truly needs in order to develop its economy, and in that way to begin solving in a serious fashion the ancient social problems we have been dragging with us throughout our history. Revolutionary shortcuts and reactionary backlashes—as recent world history shows—do not solve the economic, social, and political problems of the people. They complicate and worsen them. I think it is necessary to abandon any ideologically prefabricated idea in order to interpret the social changes of our country and the rest of the world correctly. I believe that we need to give up both facile demonizations and delirious messianisms. We must energetically and decisively reject the temptations of any form of authoritarian populism, along with its demagogic instigators. The bloody legacy of dictators of the right or the left should not be revered, let alone revindicated. They have only left behind sorrow and injustice for their people and for all of humanity. The dictatorships of the left have socialized poverty, while their leaders amassed power and its privileges, suppressing—often brutally—the civil and human rights of millions of people. The dictators of the right have done the same, but they have also brought death and destruction to other nations, or defeat, humiliation, and shame to their own people.

When my mind goes back to my journey in the Volkswagen up the slope of the freeway between Cuernavaca and Mexico City as the military took me to the Campo Militar Número Uno, I remember thinking that if I were not disappeared forever, I would face at least ten years in prison. Today I am very conscious of the good fortune I had, since I was saved from permanent disappearance, and I spent only for four years in jail.

BRIEF BIOGRAPHICAL NOTE

Alberto Ulloa Bornemann

A S ALBERTO ULLOA BORNEMANN described in his memoir, even while he was on a provisional part-time release from the Santa Martha Acatitla penitentiary, he had begun work in information gathering, analysis, and diffusion within the newly-created Secretariat for Programming and Budget. His university training in communication sciences along with his organizational and analytical talents enabled Ulloa Bornemann to establish a career dealing with information management for various branches of the Mexican federal government. For a quarter century after his release from prison, he remained responsible for coordinating news synthesis in the Secretariat for Programming and Budget, the office of the Presidency, the cultural section of the Secretariat of Public Education, Fertimex, and the international department of the Mexican Institute of Social Security.

Since his retirement from the public sector, Ulloa Bornemann works for CIAM, S.C., a private company engaged in the analysis of Mexican media coverage of public events. Its daily reports survey how Mexican radio, television, and print media have reported and interpreted the principal national and international events affecting Mexico. Ulloa Bornemann has also become a writer, first with the publication of *Sendero en tinieblas* (*Dark Pathway*, the title of *Surviving Mexico's Dirty War: A Political Prisoner's Memoir* in its original Spanish-language edition) in 2004, and subsequently with a novel currently in progress. Its plot centers upon three young people from Mexico City whose lives intertwine in their country's momentous events between 1950 and 2000.

Ulloa Bornemann and his wife María Teresa have continued to live in Mexico City. She is active in the fields of physical therapy and family counseling. Their two children, María Teresa and Alberto, are now grown and engaged in their own careers on the stage and in the world of fashion design.

NOTES

{ornament}

INTRODUCTION: TRANSLATING FEAR

1. Albert Camus, "Banquet Speech," (Stockholm: December 10, 1957), http://nobelprize.org/literature/laureates/1957/camus-speech-e.html/.

2. Alison Brysk, "Recovering from State Terror: The Morning After in Latin America," *Latin American Research Review* 38.1 (2003): 239.

3. "Guerra sucia: memoria y justicia," *Nexos* 27 (julio 2004): 15.

4. See for example, Gustavo Hirales Morán's account of *La Liga Comunista 23: orígenes y naufragio* (México: Ediciones de Cultura Popular, 1977) and his work of fiction, *Memoria de la guerra de los justos* (México: Cal y Arena, 1996). Both *Nexos* and the weekly magazine of political analysis *Proceso* have published short accounts of personal and family experiences by former guerrillas. In 1989, a group of ex-guerrillas formed the Centro de Investigaciones Históricas de los Movimientos Armados, A.C. Located in Mexico City, the Center acts as a repository of material on armed movements in Mexico, particularly between the years 1960–1996, and promotes their study.

5. Ulloa Bornemann underwent, in fact, an ideological rebirth of the sort that Hungarian-British author Arthur Koestler, who was imprisoned by the Spanish fascists, expressed in *Darkness at Noon* (1940).

6. For critical treatment of this subgenre, see John Beverley, *Testimonio. On the Politics of Truth* (Minneapolis: University of Minnesota Press, 2004).

7. Between 1961 and 1964, Alberto Ulloa Bornemann was a student in the School of Communication Sciences at Universidad Iberoamericana (UIA), a private Jesuit school in Mexico City. At the UIA, he, his wife María Teresa Alvarez Malo, and Aurora Camacho de Schmidt were part of a circle of friends who gathered around Rumanian philosophy professor Horia Tanasescu Carjan, a disciple of Croce and Gentile. In January, 1968, Aurora Camacho de Schmidt left Mexico permanently. While living in Philadelphia, she visited Alberto Ulloa Bornemann in Lecumberri in 1975.

8. Martín Luis Guzmán, *La sombra del caudillo*, prólogo Antonio Castro Leal (México: Editorial Porrúa, 1996), 120–121.

9. The literature on the "Madres" is abundant. See for example Diana Taylor, *Disappearing Acts: Spectacles of Gender and Nationalism in Argentina's "Dirty War"* (Durham: Duke University Press, 1997); and Marguerite Guzman Bouvard, *Revolutionizing Motherhood: The Mothers of the Plaza de Mayo* (Wilmington, Del.: Scholarly Resources, 1994). On Chile, see Ariel Dorfman, *Exorcising Terror: The Incredible Unending Trial of General Augusto Pinochet* (New York: Seven Stories Press, 2002). Greg Grandin analyzes the historical limitations of truth commission reports in "The Instruction of Great Catastrophe: Truth Commissions, National History, and State Formation in Argentina, Chile, and Guatemala," *American Historical Review* 110.1 (February 2005): 46–67.

10. Jacobo Timerman, *Prisoner without a Name, Cell without a Number* (New York: Alfred A. Knopf, 1981), 17.

11. Héctor Aguilar Camín and Lorenzo Meyer, *In the Shadow of the Mexican Revolution. Contemporary Mexican History, 1910–1989*, trans. Luis Alberto Fierro (Austin: University of Texas Press, 1993), 161.

12. For the workings of the one-party system, see Aguilar Camín and Meyer, chapter five and Alan Riding, *Distant Neighbors. A Portrait of the Mexicans* (New York: Alfred A. Knopf, 1984), chapter four.

13. See Sergio Aguayo Quezada, *La charola. Una historia de los servicios de inteligencia en México* (México: Editorial Grijalbo, 2001) which employs the newly available records of the Centro de Investigación y Seguridad Nacional at the Archivo General de la Nación. For a critical view of the constraints put upon use of these records, see Kate Doyle, "'Forgetting Is Not Justice.' Mexico Bares Its Secret Past," *World Policy Journal* 20.2 (Summer 2003): 61–72.

14. See Luis Unikel, *El desarrollo urbano de México* (México: Colegio de México, 1976).

15. Enrique Krauze, *Mexico. Biography of Power. A History of Modern Mexico, 1810–1996*, trans. Hank Heifetz (New York: HarperCollins, 1997), 671.

16. Sources provide a wide variation in numbers of deaths and detained. Foreign correspondents estimated those killed between 300 and 400; see Jesús Vargas Valdez, "Student Movement of 1968," in *Encyclopedia of Mexico. History, Society, and Culture*, ed. Michael S. Warner, 2 vols. (Chicago: Fitzroy Dearborn Publishers, 1997), 2: 1381. Recently the question of how many died at Tlatelolco has resurfaced with some arguing that the extensive documentation compiled by the Special Prosecutor for Social and Political Movements of the Past demonstrates that only sixty-eight students and one soldier perished. See Jorge G. Castañeda, "Los 68 del 68," *Reforma* (30 agosto 2006), http://www.reforma.com/. Sergio Aguayo Quezada in *1968. Los archivos de la violencia* (México: Editorial Grijalbo, 1998) numbers those detained at 2,360. Elena Poniatowska offers a moving testimonial account of the student movement and the Tlatelolco massacre in *Massacre in Mexico*, trans. Helen R. Lane (Columbia: University of Missouri Press, 1975). Recent studies in Mexico have begun to take advantage of new documentation that has become available, for example Aguayo, *1968. Los archivos de la violencia* and Julio Scherer García and Carlos Monsiváis, *Parte de guerra. Tlatelolco 1968. Documentos del General Marcelino García Barragán. Los hechos y la historia* (México: Aguilar, 1999). See also the documents on Tlatelolco made available by the National Security Archive's Mexico Project, http://www.gwu.edu/~nsarchiv/NSAEBB/NSAEBB99/.

17. Susanne Bilello, "The Massacre in Mexico—Twenty Years Later," *APF Reporter* 11.3 (1988), http://www.aliciapatterson.org/APF1103/Bilello/Bilello.html/.

18. See chapter three of Julia Preston and Samuel Dillon, *Opening Mexico. The Making of a Democracy* (New York: Farrar, Straus and Giroux, 2004).

19. Vivienne Bennett, "Orígenes del movimiento urbano popular mexicano: pensamiento político y organizaciones políticas clandestinas, 1960–1980," *Revista Mexicana de Sociología* 55.4 (julio–septiembre 1993): 89–102.

20. Barry Carr, "The Many Meanings of 1968," *Enfoque* (Fall–Winter 1998), republished as "The Many Meanings of 1968 in Mexico: The Student-Popular Movement Thirty Years After," http://www.latrobe.edu.au/history/news/digital/carr1.htm/.

21. Jorge G. Castañeda, *Compañero. The Life and Death of Che Guevara*, trans. Marina Castañeda (New York: Alfred A. Knopf, 1997), xv.

22. Alan Knight, "Historical Continuities in Social Movements," in *Popular Movements and Political Change in Mexico*, eds. Joe Foweraker and Ann L. Craig (Boulder: Lynne Rienner, 1990), 78–102.

23. See Barry Carr, *Marxism and Communism in Twentieth-Century Mexico* (Lincoln: University of Nebraska Press, 1992), chapters six and seven.

24. For a summary of Jaramillo's life, see Donald Hodges and Ross Gandy, *Mexico Under Seige. Popular Resistance to Presidential Despotism* (New York and London: Zed Books, 2002), chapter three.

25. For a short account of this background, see Armando Bartra, *Guerrero bronco: Campesinos, ciudadanos y guerrilleros en la Costa Grande* (México: Ediciones Sinfiltro, 1996).

26. On teacher activism in Mexico, see Maria Lorena Cook, *Organizing Dissent. Unions, the State, and the Democratic Teachers' Movement in Mexico* (University Park: Pennsylvania State University Press, 1996). Pages 66–70 discuss the MRM.

27. The most complete recent source in English on civic struggles and revolutionary actions in Guerrero is the Ph.D. dissertation of O'Neill Blacker-Hanson, "*La Lucha Sigue!* ('The Struggle Continues!') Teacher Activism in Guerrero and the Continuum of Democratic Struggle in Mexico" (University of Washington, 2004). We wish to thank Dr. Blacker-Hanson for generously sharing her work with us.

28. See Blacker-Hanson, chapter five, and Barry Carr, "Lucio Cabañas," in *Encyclopedia of Mexico*, 1: 175.

29. Cited in Kate Doyle, "The Corpus Christi Massacre. Mexico's Attack on its Student Movement, June 10, 1971," National Security Archive Mexico Project, http://www.gwu.edu/~nsarchiv/NSAEBB/NSAEBB99/.

30. National Human Rights Commission cited in Kate Doyle, "Human Rights and the Dirty War in Mexico," National Security Archive Mexico Project, http://www.gwu.edu/~nsarchiv/NSAEBB/NSAEBB99/. The figure on bodies dumped into the sea comes from Preston and Dillon, *Opening Mexico*, 88.

31. Human Rights Watch offers a critical account of government enforcement of human rights in Mexico in *Lost in Translation. Bold Ambitions, Limited Results for Human Rights Under Fox* (New York, 2006). The National Security Archive in Washington has placed the leaked draft report on the dirty war on the internet at http://www.gwu.edu/~nsarchiv/NSAEBB/NSAEBB180/index.htm/. For the comments of *La Jornada*, see "Editorial: Impunidad," *La Jornada*, 27 julio 2005, http://www.lajormada.unam.mx/.

32. Amnesty International, *Report 2005*, http://web.amnesty.org/report2005/mex-summary-eng/. Police abuses, including sexual mistreatment of female detainees, in the case of the community of San Salvador Atenco in May, 2006, indicated the continuing validity of Amnesty's assertions.

33. Lessie Jo Frazier and Deborah Cohen, "Defining the Space of Mexico '68: Heroic Masculinity in the Prison and 'Women' in the Streets," *Hispanic American Historical Review* 83:4 (2003): 629.

34. Ulloa Bornemann in the TV documentary *Cárceles: Lecumberri*, prod. Enrique Quintero Mármol, Salamandra Producciones, Canal Once, México, D. F., julio de 2005.

35. Ioan Davies, *Writers in Prison* (Oxford, England and Cambridge, U.S.A.: Basil Blackwell, 1990), 16.

36. Alberto Ulloa Bornemann, interview by Aurora Camacho de Schmidt and Arthur Schmidt, Mexico City, 11 July 2005.

37. Julia Kristeva, *Powers of Horror: An Essay on Abjection*, trans. Leon S. Roudiez (New York: Columbia University Press, 1982), cited at http://social.chass.ncsu.edu/wyrick/debclass/krist.htm.

38. Elaine Scarry, *The Body in Pain. The Making and the Unmaking of the World* (New York: Oxford University Press, 1985); Juan E. Corradi, "Towards Societies Without Fear," in *Fear at the Edge: State Terror and Resistance in Latin America*, eds. Juan E. Corradi, Patricia Weiss Fagen, and Manuel Antonio Garretón (Berkeley: University of California Press, 1992), 267–292. The book does not discuss Central America or Mexico.

39. José Joaquín Blanco, Vicente Leñero, and Juan Villoro, "Questioning the Chronicle," in *The Contemporary Mexican Chronicle: Theoretical Perspectives on the Liminal Genre*, eds. Ignacio Corona and Beth E. Jörgensen (Albany: State University of New York, 2002), 65.

40. We are aware of the tensions between history and literature, narrated facts and verifiable facts. For an excellent discussion of these tensions in the context of the Mexican chronicle, see the work of critic Beth E. Jörgensen, "Literatures of Fact: Theoretical Approaches" in *The Contemporary Mexican Chronicle*, 72–78.

41. Testimonies of life in prison in Mexico continue to grow in number. Of particular interest are those assembled by journalist Julio Scherer García: *Cárceles* (México: Alfaguara, 1998); and *Máxima seguridad. Almoloya y Puente Grande* (México: Aguilar, 2001).

42. See also Julio Scherer García and Carlos Monsiváis, *Los patriotas. De Tlatelolco a la guerra sucia* (México: Aguilar, 2004).

43. See Jean Franco, "Gender, Death, and Resistance: Facing the Ethical Vacuum" in *Fear at the Edge*, 104–118, most of which refers to Argentina.

44. Frazier and Cohen, "Defining the Space of Mexico '68," 618. See also the special edition of the *Bulletin of Latin American Research* 24.4 (2005) devoted to "Tlatelolco 1968 in Contemporary Mexican Literature."

45. See Ariel E. Dulitzky, "A Region in Denial: Racial Discrimination and Racism in Latin America" in *Neither Enemies nor Friends: Latinos, Blacks, Afro-Latinos*, eds. Anani Dzidzienyo and Suzanne Oboler (New York: Palgrave Macmillan, 2005), 39–60.

46. On the left in Mexican political life today, see Enrique Semo's two volume work *La búsqueda* (México: Editorial Océano, 2003–2004).

47. See Chappell H. Lawson, *Building the Fourth Estate. Democratization and the Rise of a Free Press in Mexico* (Berkeley: University of California Press, 2002).

48. According to press reports, the Mexican government has identified eight or nine armed political groups that currently operate, all but one in the states of Chiapas, Guerrero, Morelos, and Puebla. None are considered serious threats to the existing order. See, for example, "Registra Sedena 8 grupos armados," *Reforma*, 11 julio 2005, and Benito Jiménez, "Niegan especialistas riesgo por guerrilla," *Reforma*, 12 julio 2005, http://www.reforma.com/. Nevertheless some journalists remain worried about guerrilla infiltration in regions of political discontent such as Oaxaca. See Jorge Fernández Méndez, "El EPR y su estrategia oaxaqueña." *Excélsior* 29 (agosto 2006), http://wwwnuevoexcelsior.com.mx/.

49. Alberto Ulloa Bornemann, interview by Aurora Camacho de Schmidt and Arthur Schmidt, Mexico City, July, 12, 2005.

TWO: THE LONG MARCH

1. The phrase "pink university" means that the university should be for the sons and daughters of the upper-class, not that it should be "pink" in the sense of sympathetic to Communism.

2. Cuba withdrew from supporting armed revolution elsewhere in Latin America after Che's death as Ulloa Bornemann notes. Cuban-backed insurgencies in the region had failed. The Soviet Union, embarked upon policies of peaceful coexistence with the United States, earlier in

1967 had given "due warning that Soviet economic assistance, notably the oil lifeline, might dry up if Cuba were to continue exporting revolution to Latin America." Richard Gott, *Cuba, a New History* (New Haven: Yale University Press, 2004), 233.

   3. The term gusano or "worm" is used by pro-Castro Cubans to refer to anti-Castro Cubans.

THREE: IN THE KINGDOM OF NECESSITY

   1. Michel Foucault, *Discipline and Punish. The Birth of the Prison,* trans. Alan Sheridan (New York: Vintage Books, 1995), 202.

GLOSSARY OF NAMES AND TERMS

AGUILAR CAMÍN, HÉCTOR. Noted Mexican historian, journalist, novelist, and publisher. Born in 1946, Aguilar Camín was graduated from the Universidad Iberoamericana where he was a friend of Ulloa Bornemann and later received a Ph.D. in history from the Colegio de México. His novels, essays, newspaper columns, and historical works have focused upon Mexico's social, cultural, and political issues. He has directed the journal *Nexos* and Cal y Arena, the Mexican publishing house that issued *Sendero en tinieblas*, the original Spanish-language edition of *Surviving Mexico's Dirty War: A Political Prisoner's Memoir*. Aguilar Camín received a Guggenheim fellowship in 1989. He is married to the novelist Angeles Mastretta.

APANDO. The "hole" or punishment cell to which prison officials could consign a prisoner. Besides reducing the prisoner to total isolation, the cell lacked light, air, and sanitary facilties. The Mexican writer and political prisoner José Revueltas published a novel entitled *El apando* in 1969.

ASOCIACIÓN CÍVICA NACIONAL REVOLUCIONARIA (ACNR). The organization headed by Genaro Vázquez Rojas in the state of Guerrero. Vázquez Rojas was a school teacher and dissident civic organizer whose foundation of the Asociación Cívica Guerrense in 1962 and his leadership of major protests resulted in his jailing in 1966 . After escaping from prison two years later, Vázquez Rojas created the ACNR and headed a guerrilla uprising independent of that of Lucio Cabañas until his death in an automobile accident in 1972.

BRAVO, DOUGLAS. Venezuelan guerrilla leader. Bravo's leadership of the Fuerzas Armadas de Liberación Nacional (FALN) in support of Che Guevara's *foco* theory of guerrilla insurrection caused his expulsion from the Venezuelan Communist Party. Bravo rejected one amnesty in 1969 that many other Venezuelan rebels accepted, persisting in the armed struggle until he accepted another amnesty offer a decade later. A strong anti-imperialist, Bravo has remained active in Venezuelan politics, heading a movement known as Tercer Camino, and maintaining a posture critical of both President Hugo Chávez and the opposition.

BRIDGADA DE AJUSTICIAMIENTO DEL PARTIDO DE LOS POBRES. The execution brigade of Lucio Cabañas' movement whose function was to punish powerful local figures and office holders in Guerrero considered notorious in their mistreatment of ordinary citizens.

CABAÑAS BARRIENTOS, LUCIO. Head of the Partido de los Pobres and leader of the largest armed insurrection in Mexico since the generation before World War II. Born in 1938, Cabañas, like Genaro Vázquez Rojas, was a school teacher concerned with the social issues of Guerrero and a leader of protest actions against abusive local officials. After the repression of a local demonstration in Atoyac de Alvarez, Cabañas began the guerrilla campaign in Guerrero that he headed until killed in action in December, 1974.

CACIQUE. Local or regional political boss.

CAMPO MILITAR NÚMERO UNO. Major military base in Mexico City. Also the clandestine site of illegal detensions, torture, and disappearance of prisoners during Mexico's "dirty war."

CAUDILLAJE. Political leadership that relies upon an excessive personal dominance that concentrates authority, hampers diversity of opinion, and discourages the consolidation of institutions and formal procedures.

CHARRERÍA. An elaborate Mexican social and cultural tradition of horsemanship that combines folkways, national patriotism, and public entertainment. Its origins can be traced back to Spain, especially to Moorish influence. *Charreadas* or charrería events are organized by family and community *charro* associations.

COMANDOS ARMADOS DEL PUEBLO (CAP). One of the armed groups formed by radicalized students. Often associated with a group of similar composition, the Frente Urbano Zapatista (FUZ).

DÍAZ ORDAZ, GUSTAVO. President of Mexico at the time of the 1968 student movement and the Tlatelolco massacre. Born in 1911, Díaz Ordaz advanced through the ranks of the official party, becoming Secretary of Government, 1958-1964, and President, 1964–1970. Rigid in his attitude toward society and political dissidence, Díaz Ordaz became a personal symbol of government brutality. He died in 1979.

ECHEVERRÍA ALVAREZ, LUIS. President of Mexico, 1970–1976. Born in 1922, Echeverría advanced in politics through posts in the official party. He married María Ester Zuno, the daughter of José Guadalupe Zuno, a former governor of the state of Jalisco. Echeverría served as Secretary of Government during the regime of Gustavo Díaz Ordaz, 1964–1970. Like Díaz Ordaz, he bore significant responsibility for the October, 1968 Tlatelolco massacre. His own term as President, 1970–1976, combined populist economic and political policies with the repression of the "dirty war," including the June, 1971 Corpus Christi attack. In recent years, a special prosecutor has been unsuccessful in his attempts to bring Echeverría to trial on charges of genocide.

EJIDATARIO. Member of a collective landholding village community with rights to use of some parcel of that land.

ELN. The Ejército de Liberación Nacional or Army of National Liberation. A Marxist guerrilla army in Colombia that young radicals formed in the early 1960s to pursue Che Guevara's rural *foco* methodology of guerrilla warfare. The ELN still operates and is second in size only to the FARC. Camilo Torres was one of its most famous combatants.

ESPARTAQUISTAS JARAMILLISTAS. Ulloa Bornemann and his "Organization" identified themselves with this revolutionary political orientation that linked the memory of Rubén Jaramillo with the Liga Comunista Espartaco.

FARC. Fuerzas Armadas Revolucionarias de Colombia or the Revolutionary Armed Forces of Colombia. The largest of the guerrilla armies still operating in Colombia, the FARC emerged in 1966 to unite Communist elements and peasant self-defense forces.

FIGUEROA FIGUEROA, RUBÉN. Powerful *cacique* in Guerrero. Born in 1908 to a politically influential family in Guerrero, Figueroa Figueroa became a significant figure himself in local and national politics, serving as a federal senator from Guerrero, 1970–1974, and as governor of the state, 1975 to 1981. As Ulloa Bornemann relates in his narrative, the forces of Lucio Cabañas kidnapped Figueroa Figueroa in May, 1974, for whom they obtained a large ransom. The Mexican army rescued him in September. Figueroa Figueroa died in 1991. His son, Rubén Figueroa Alcocer, was governor of the state in October, 1995 when police forces massacred unarmed farmers at Aguas Blancas.

FOCO. A theory popular among many Latin American insurgent groups in the 1960s. It held that a *foco* or small band of revolutionary fighters could generate the conditions for a successful radical national revolution by igniting a rural uprising. Identified with Che Guevara, *foquismo* received elaboration from Régis Debray's 1967 book *Revolution in the Revolution*, which Ulloa Bornemann mentions as having influenced him.

FRENTE POPULAR INDEPENDIENTE (FPI). Social movement involved in urban land and housing issues in northern and central Mexico.

FRENTE REVOLUCIONARIO ARMADO DEL PUEBLO (FRAP). Formed by former members of the Communist Youth Movement, the People's Revolutionary Armed Forces evolved from the Revolutionary Student Front, formed in 1970 in Guadalajara, Mexico's second largest city. The FRAP was involved in the kidnappings of U.S. Consul Terrance G. Leonhardy, José Guadalupe Zuno, a veteran Jalisco politician and President Luis Echeverría Alvarez's father-in-law, and the wealthy Margarita Saad. Ulloa Bornemann mentions all three of these cases in his narrative.

FRENTE URBANO ZAPATISTA (FUZ). Armed revolutionary group formed from radicalized students, the FUZ organized the 1971 kidnapping of Julio Hershfeld Almada, the General Director of Airports and Auxiliary Services.

FUERZAS ARMADAS REVOLUCIONARIAS (FAR). Small armed group established by Carmelo Cortés when he broke away from the Partido de los Pobres of Lucio Cabañas.

GÁMIZ GARCÍA, ARTURO. Local dissident in Chihuahua who struggled against the power of large landowners. Influenced by Fidel Castro's famous 1953 attack on the Moncada barracks in Cuba, Gámiz led a group of about twenty in an unsuccessful armed assault on the Ciudad Madera Barracks on September 23, 1965 in which they all died. The Liga Comunista 23 de Septiembre took its name in memory of this event.

GARCÍA RAMÍREZ, SERGIO. Mexican jurist responsable for closing Lecumberri and opening the more modern Reclusorio Oriente while Ulloa Bornemann was a prisoner. Born in 1938, García Ramírez studied law at the Universidad Nacional Autónoma de México and established a career as a legal scholar, jurist, and politician. As Subsecretary of Government, 1973–1976, he engaged in penal reform. Later he served as Secretary of Labor, 1981–1982, and Attorney General of Mexico, 1982–1988. He was one of a handful of public figures considered by the PRI as a possible presidential candidate in 1988. He is currently President of the Inter-American Court of Human Rights.

GUACHOS. Government soldiers.

GUAJIROS. Armed guerrilla group formed in Chihuahua by students and others influenced by radical Christianity and by the 1965 Madera barracks attack.

GUTIÉRREZ BARRIOS, FERNANDO. Subsecretary of Government at the time of Ulloa Bornemann's release from prison. Born in 1927, the son of an army colonel and businessman, Gutiérrez Barrios entered the army himself, rising to the rank of Captain before resigning in 1950 and beginning an influential career in security matters. As a civilian employee of the Federal Security Police he cleared Fidel Castro of pending charges and released him to return to Cuba in 1956. Gutiérrez Barrios occupied key positions during the "dirty war" and its aftermath, first as Director of the Dirección Federal de Seguridad, 1965–1970, and then Subsecretary of Government, 1970–1982. After a short period as governor of the state of Veracruz, 1986–1988, he became Secretary of Government, 1988–1993 under President Carlos Salinas de Gortari. Gutiérrez Barrios died in 2000.

GÜERO. Term used for a blond person in Mexico.

HALCONES. Hawks, the paramilitary forces at the service of the Mexican government responsible for the Corpus Christi massacre of June 10, 1971. Officially dissolved in 1971. Many former Halcones continued to work in the service of the government. Ulloa Bornemann considered many of his jailers in the Campo Military Número Uno as ex-Halcones.

ISLAS MARÍAS. An archipelago of four islands in the Pacific Ocean about seventy miles off the coast of the western Mexican state of Nayarit. María Madre, the largest island, was designated the site for a federal government penitentiary in 1905. In recent years, its prison population has undergone expansion due to overcrowding of penal facilities elsewhere in Mexico. President Ernesto Zedillo declared the Islas Marías an ecological preserve in 2000.

JARAMILLO, RUBÉN. Veteran political dissident. Born in 1900, Jaramillo dedicated himself to improving the lives of workers and peasants in his home state of Morelos. Government forces assassinated him and his family in 1962. He exercised an impact upon national affairs and served as an inspiration to Ulloa Bornemann and others in his generation. Jaramillo organized the Partido Agrario Obrero Morelense from which some members of Ulloa Bornemann's "Organization" came.

LACANDONES. Armed group formed from student and former PCM elements that conducted numerous assaults on urban businesses and banks in

Chihuahua, Mexico City, and Monterrey. Members joined the Liga Comunista 23 de Septiembre in 1974–1975.

LECUMBERRI. Notorious prison in Mexico City opened in 1900 by Mexican President Porfirio Díaz as a modern penitenciary employing the panopticon model. Over time it became known as the "Black Palace." It housed both political and ordinary prisoners. Closed in 1976, as Ulloa Bornemann describes, and subsequently converted into the Archivo General de la Nación, Mexico's most important public historical archive.

LIGA COMUNISTA 23 DE SEPTIEMBRE (23). Formed in the spring of 1973 in an effort to unite various urban guerrilla movements. One of its major leaders was Ignacio Salas Obregón, mentioned by Ulloa Bornemann as a prisoner in a nearby cell in the Campo Militar Número Uno. Engaged in some of the most famous kidnappings of this period, including those that ended in the deaths of the businessmen Eugenio Garza Sada and Fernando Aranguren. Disintegrated in 1975–1976 after the capture or deaths of important elements of its leadership.

LIGA COMUNISTA ESPARTACO (LCE). Spinoff from the Liga Leninista Espartaco. Ulloa Bornemann joined the LCE upon his return from Cuba in 1967. Former militants in the LCE were leaders of the "Organization" that figures so prominently in Ulloa Bornemann's narrative.

LÓPEZ PORTILLO, JOSÉ. President of Mexico when Ulloa Bornemann emerged from jail. Born in 1920, López Portillo pursued a career as an author, lawyer, and politician, becoming Secretary of the Treasury in the government of his friend Luis Echeverría Alvarez, 1973–1975, and President, 1976–1982. His term was noted for the expansion of Mexico's oil production and government spending. It ended with a major debt crisis and López Portillo's defiant expropriation of the country's banking system in September, 1982. He died in 2004.

MASTRETTA, ANGELES. Mexican journalist and novelist. Born in 1949, Mastretta studied journalism at the Universidad Autónoma Nacional de México. She wrote for several newspapers and magazines and served on the editorial board of the feminist magazine *Fem* before winning the Premio Mazatlán in 1985 for her first novel *Arráncame la vida*. In 1997, she won the prestigious Rómulo Gallegos prize for the novel *Mal de amores*. She is married to another writer, Héctor Aguilar Camín.

MATTHEWS, HERBERT. Famous *New York Times* journalist. Born in 1900, Matthews worked for the *New York Times* for forty-five years. As a reporter, he covered Italian dictator Benito Mussolini's invasion of Ethiopia, the Spanish Civil War, and World War II. He joined the *Times* editorial board in 1949 where he wrote most of the newspaper's editorials on Latin America for nearly twenty years. His February, 1957 interview with Fidel Castro in the Sierra Maestra became a landmark event in the Cuban Revolution, proving that Castro was still alive, contrary to what the Cuban government claimed, and offering the world an encouraging image of the guerrilla leader and his followers. Matthews died in 1977.

MINISTERIO PÚBLICO. Public prosecutor or district attorney's office that, besides prosecution, exercises a wide variety of other legal functions.

MONTES, CÉSAR. Guatemalan guerrilla insurgent. In November, 1960, a group of young, nationalist Guatemalan military officers unsuccessfully attempted to overthrow President Miguel Ydigoras Fuentes. The coup plotters opposed the presence of a CIA training camp in their country and sought social, economic, and political reforms. Marco Antonio Yon Sosa, Luis Turcios Lima, and some of the other rebellious officers determined to carry on the struggle. Young Communists from the Partido Guatemalteco del Trabajo like César Montes joined their guerrilla insurgency, forming the Fuerzas Armadas Rebeldes (FAR). Before the decade was over, the government had crushed the guerrillas and the Guatemalan left. Turcios Lima died in an automobile accident in 1966, and Mexican soldiers killed Yon Sosa in exile four years later. With assistance from the United States, the Guatemalan army had become one of the preeminent counter-insurgency forces in the Americas. It repressed Guatemalan society for another generation and outlasted a subsequent set of guerrilla movements. Montes has lived on, first as a guerrilla fighter in Nicaragua, El Salvador, and his native country, and subsequently as an opposition political figure in Guatemalan politics after the end of the Central American guerrilla insurgencies. He has published an autobiographical account of his experiences as an armed rebel.

MORELOS, JOSÉ MARÍA. Catholic priest and major national hero of the Mexican independence wars. Born of humble parentage in 1765, Morelos contested Spanish forces for control of southern Mexico from 1811 until his capture and subsequent execution at San Cristóbal de Ecatepec outside Mexico City in 1815. The state of Morelos bears his name.

MOVIMIENTO DE ACCIÓN REVOLUCIONARIA (MAR). Radical armed movement formed by former participants in Communist Party youth organizations, many of whom received subsequent training from the government of North Korea. The government captured large numbers of *Marineros* (also

Marinos or members of the MAR) in the early 1970s, and they figure heavily among the population of political prisioners in Ulloa Bornemann's narrative. MAR survivors joined in the foundation of the Liga Comunista 23 de Septiembre in 1973.

MOVIMIENTO REVOLUCIONARIO DEL MAGISTERIO (MRM). Movement of dissident members of the teachers union that emerged in Mexico City and played an important role in popular radical politics from the late 1950s onward.

NAZAR HARO, MIGUEL. One of the more notorious officials of the Dirección Federal de Seguridad during the "dirty war." Nazar Haro served the security services for twenty-two years, attaining the position of Director of the DFS, 1978–1982, before being dismissed by President José López Portillo. During the 1970s and early 1980s, he acted as an important contact for the Central Intelligence Agency of the United States. According to the *New York Times*, the CIA blocked his indictment by a San Diego grand jury in 1982. In 2004, special prosecutor Ignacio Carrillo secured the arrest of Nazar Haro for the torture and disappearance of Jesús Piedra Ibarra, a student activist and alleged member of the Liga Comunista 23 de Septiembre. A Mexican federal judge subsequently brought similiar charges against Nazar Haro in the case of Ignacio Salas Obregón.

PARTIDO COMUNISTA MEXICANO (PCM). Founded in 1919, the PCM acted as a political force within the Mexican left for generations until it dissolved itself in 1981 to become part of the Partido Socialista Unificado de México (PSUM). For many years, a narrow orthodoxy dominated the PCM, resulting in the expulsion of members such as the painter Diego Rivera, the writer José Revueltas, and railroad labor leaders Valentín Campa and Demetrio Vallejo. In the 1960s and 1970s, many young dissidents left the PCM for more radical organizations.

PARTIDO DE ACCIÓN NACIONAL (PAN). Founded in 1939 by conservative and Catholic interests, the National Action Party constituted the major opposition party over the decades of PRI dominance. Although not a traditional *panista*, Vicente Fox Quesada gained its nomination and won the election for the presidency in 2000.

PARTIDO DE LOS POBRES. The Party of the Poor, led by Lucio Cabañas Barrientos, constituted the political expression of Mexico's largest guerrilla movement in the 1960s–1970s. Many of Ulloa Bornemann's activities had to do with the relationship between the "Organization" and the Partido de los Pobres.

PARTIDO REVOLUCIONARIO INSTITUCIONAL (PRI). The Institutional Revolutionary Party, the name given in 1946 to the Mexican government's official political party. The party was originally born in 1929 as the Partido Revolucionario Nacional and took the name Partido de la Revolución Mexicana in 1938. Under these three names, the official party monopolized Mexican politics and government until its absolute grip weakened in the last third of the twentieth century. The PRI ultimately lost the presidency in 2000, but it still remains a powerful force in Mexican politics.

PORROS. Gangs of political thugs and provocateurs maintained by powerful politicians in Mexican government during the heyday of the PRI.

REVUELTAS, JOSÉ. Mexican writer and political dissident. Born in 1914, Revueltas was a member of a famous artistic family and the author of several major novels, among them *El apando*, published in 1969. Revueltas was imprisoned in the wake of the Tlatelolco massacre, one of several times that his political views landed him in jail. He joined the Communist Party in 1928, but was expelled in 1943. After rejoining the PCM in 1956, he left the Party in 1959, convinced of the uselessness of its views and practices. He then founded the Liga Leninista Espartaco, an antecedent of the Liga Comunista Esparataco that Ulloa Bornemann joined. Revueltas died in 1976.

REYES HEROLES, JESÚS. Secretary of Government at the time of Ulloa Bornemann's release from prison. Born in 1921, Reyes Heroles was a lawyer, intellectual, and politician who occupied several high posts of importance, serving as Director General of PEMEX, the national oil company, 1964–1970, Secretary of Government, 1976–1979, and Secretary of Education, 1982–1985. As Ulloa Bornemann describes, Reyes Heroles achieved a modest liberalization of the Mexican political system while he was Secretary of Government and secured an amnesty for political prisoners in 1978. He died in 1985.

SALAS OBREGÓN, IGNACIO. A principal founder and leader of the Liga Comunista 23 de Septiembre. Born in 1948, Salas Obregón studied at the Instituto Tecnológico y de Estudios Superiores de Monterrey where he became a Catholic social activist. His work with urban poor brought him into contact with other young radicals, some of them from the Communist Youth. He played a major role in efforts to unite Mexican urban guerrilla groups that culminated in the March, 1973 meeting in Guadalajara that created the Liga Comunista 23 de Septiembre. The government captured Salas Obregón a year later. Ulloa Bornemann and others have provided evidence of his being in government hands. A Mexican federal judge has formally charged Miguel Nazar

Haro, former head of the Dirección Federal de Seguridad, with Salas Obregon's disappearance.

SICK ONES. Ultra-radical armed group with a heavy composition of university students from Sinaloa. They considered the university a potential "factory" of revolutionaries that would overthrow the existing order.

TORRES, CAMILO. Colombian priest and revolutionary. Born in Bogotá in 1929, Torres expressed interest in the priesthood at a very early age. Following his ordination, he studied sociology at the University of Louvain in Belgium. After his return to Colombia, his committment to the poor propelled him into the guerrilla struggle with the ELN in 1965. He died in combat the following year.

TROUYET, CARLOS. Prominent Mexican financier and public figure. Trouyet began his business career at a French bank in 1917 and ultimately accumulated a large fortune as an executive and board member of numerous companies in telephones, textiles, hotels, steel, banking, cement, and beer, among them Teléfonos de México, Multi-banco Comermex, and Cervecería Moctezuma. He died in 1970.

TURCIOS LIMA, LUIS. See César Montes.

UNION DEL PUEBLO (UP). Radical armed leftist group some of whose members later merged with survivors of Lucio Cabañas' Partido de los Pobres after Cabañas' death. Subsequently involved in armed activities in Guerrero and in kidnappings.

VÁZQUEZ ROJAS, GENARO. See Asociación Cívica Nacional Revolucionaria.

YON SOSA, MARCO ANTONIO. See César Montes.

ZABLUDOVSKY, JACOBO. Longtime Mexican radio and television journalist. Born in 1928, Zabludovsky became a pioneer in Mexican television broacasting in the early 1950s. He is most widely known for the program "24 Horas" that Ulloa Bornemann mentions in his text. Zabludovsky's journalism embodied the powerful TV network Televisa's close collaboration with the Mexican government. Since leaving Televisa in 2000, Zabludovsky has continued his career on the radio.

ZANCA. Inhabitant of the state of Guerrero.

ZAPATA, EMILIANO. Insurgent rural leader from Morelos who led one of the three principal armed movements of the Mexican Revolution. Zapata and his followers fought for "Land and Liberty" under the banner of the Plan of Ayala of November, 1911, the principal articulation of agrarian issues during the Revolution. Rivals from other segments of the Revolution assassinated Zapata in 1919. The present-day indigenous insurgency in Chiapas, Mexico, the Ejército Zapatista de Liberación Nacional, named itself after him.

ZUNO, JOSÉ GUADALUPE. Prominent politician in the state of Jalisco. Born in 1891, Zuno gained fame as a writer, painter, politician, and promoter of cultural institutions. While governor of Jalisco, he founded the University of Guadalajara in 1925. His daughter, María Ester, married Luis Echeverría Alvarez, President of Mexico, 1970–1976. He survived kidnapping at the hands of the FRAP in 1974 and died in 1980.

INDEX

ALBERTO ULLOA BORNEMANN lives with his wife in Mexico City, where he works as a private media analyst. For over twenty-five years, he has been responsible for news analysis and public communications in various branches of the federal government in Mexico. He is currently writing a novel about three young people from Mexico City whose lives intertwine over the events of the years between 1950 and 2000.

AURORA CAMACHO DE SCHMIDT is an Associate Professor of Latin American literature and Spanish at Swarthmore College where she has also directed Latin American Studies.

ARTHUR SCHMIDT is a Professor of History at Temple University.